Contemporary German Legal Philosophy

Contemporary German Legal Philosophy

James E. Herget

PENN
University of Pennsylvania Press
Philadelphia

Printed in the United States of America

Library of Congress Cataloging-in-Publication Data to come

Herget, James E.
Contemporary German legal philosophy / James E. Herget.
p. cm.
Includes bibliographical references and index.
ISBN 0-8122-3360-3 (cloth: alk. paper). —ISBN 0-8122-1591-5 (pbk.: alk. paper)
1. Law—Philosophy. 2. Jurisprudence. 3. Law—Germany—Philosophy. 4. Jurisprudence—Germany., I. Title.
K231.H47 1996
340′.1—dc20 96-28509
CIP

Contents

Preface vii

1. Historical Introduction 1
2. A Summary Catalog of Contemporary Scholarship 13
3. Critical Rationalism 30
4. Discourse Theory 44
5. Rhetorical Theory 62
6. Systems Theory 73
7. Institutional Legal Positivism 93
8. An Assessment of German Legal Philosophy 104

Appendix: Biographical Information 123

Bibliography 131

Index 153

Preface

This book describes the current varieties of German jurisprudential thought for an audience of scholars in law and related disciplines. Jurisprudential writing in the United States has been on the upswing for the past dozen years or so, and articles on legal philosophy have again achieved respectability with the law reviews. However, American legal scholars are traditionally somewhat provincial. For historical reasons we tend to read only what is written in the Anglo-American tradition and to write in that tradition as well, ignoring ideas from foreign traditions—French, German, Italian, Japanese, or other—that only occasionally filter into our framework of thinking. These overlooked ideas are often fertile and productive; so, a better look is due: hence this book.

My impressionistic estimate is that substantially more legal philosophy is being written in German-speaking countries than in the United States. This phenomenon is not surprising when one considers the two philosophical and legal traditions. The abundance of scholarship published in Germany, Austria, and Switzerland requires some sorting out among various "schools" of thought. Consequently, in view of the purpose of this book, I have concentrated on those philosophies that meet three criteria: (1) they are not widely publicized among legal scholars in the United States (although some are familiar to philosophers and sociologists); (2) they have intellectual connections with contemporary developments in other disciplines; and (3) they are characteristically German. Applying these criteria turned out to be difficult. Therefore, in chapter two I give thumbnail sketches of views which do not as clearly meet the criteria as do those discussed in chapters three through seven. The bibliographical essay guides readers who wish to pursue the thinking of particular authors.

What the Germans usually call *Staatstheorie* or *Staatslehre* and what we usually denominate political theory have been purposely excluded. Obviously political theory often blends imperceptably into legal philosophy, but the limitations of time and space require that a review of this scholarship be deferred to another day.

I have included a substantial critique of those philosophies that I took to be of most interest to the book's audience (chapters 3–7). This critique is largely drawn from the general literature and is not original, although I occasionally add particular criticisms where appropriate.

The book therefore proceeds as follows: (1) some introductory explanation from an historical viewpoint, (2) a catalog of "schools" that do not fully qualify as of special interest under the criteria mentioned above; (3) discussions and critiques of Critical Rationalism, (4) Discourse Theory, (5) Rhetorical Theory, (6) Systems Theory, (7) Institutional Legal Positivism, and (8) some general observations and conclusions about contemporary German legal philosophy.

The book could not accommodate the work of individual scholars whose contributions to the general discourse of the discipline were substantial but who did not espouse a "school" or unique perspective. Some of the more prominent of these are Klaus Adomeit, Ralf Dreier, Winfried Hassemer, Eric Hilgendorf, Walter Ott, Hans-Martin Pawlowski, and Gerd Roellecke. Special note should be made of the work of Hilgendorf, who regularly reviews new literature in this field in various periodicals. His reviews are penetrating and critical, agreeably short, and reflect good judgment based on a mastery of the field. They were a valuable source of guidance to me.

I want to thank the German Fulbright Commission for funding my year's research at the University of Heidelberg. I also want to thank Professor Winfried Brugger of that university for being my host and mentor. He provided valuable help in every way, and the book could not have been done without it. The views expressed, however, are my own, not his; indeed, we disagreed on many points. I also wish to acknowledge helpful suggestions from Heiner Bielefeldt, who read the entire manuscript, and from David Dow, John Mixon, Joseph Sanders, and David Dyzenhaus, who read selected chapters.

Chapter 1
Historical Introduction

> The long-range problems of a social order in competition with rival ideas can certainly not be solved by those who fail to understand the force of ideas. It is ancient wisdom that in the long run nothing is so powerful as an idea when its time has come.
>
> —Felix S. Cohen[1]

Sometimes ideas pop into our heads seemingly from nowhere. But theories are different; they are developed within a tradition or pattern of thinking. A theory does not emerge full-blown from the brow of a great thinker; rather, it is a product of an intellectual heritage, often matured through considerable debate. It is therefore helpful, if not necessary, for understanding a particular legal philosophy to know something about how it came about and what intellectual concerns prompted its development. For this reason developments in German legal philosophy from 1945 to the present will be briefly sketched in this chapter.

The Revival of Natural Law: 1945–60

The great concern that permeated the scholarly world after the Nazi experience was to provide an answer to the questions: How could it have happened? How could the perverted and unjust Nazi legal system be explained? How could such mistakes be avoided in the future? For the first decade or so after the war the conventional wisdom expressed in the scholarly literature held that legal positivism, dominant as a legal philosophy at the time of the Nazi takeover, was responsible for the ease with which the courts and the law were corrupted. Positivism, in most ver-

1. Preface to Felix S. Cohen and Morris R. Cohen, eds., *Readings in Jurisprudence and Legal Philosophy* (Boston: Little Brown, 1951), v.

sions, insists on the separation of law and morality; law has validity independent of its moral content. In this view it is not the province of the legal scholar to be concerned with right and wrong or good and bad; the scholar's work is to clarify, conceptualize, and explain the authoritative legal precepts. Therefore, it was argued, this unwillingness to inquire into the morality of law by judges, lawyers, and legal scholars led to an easy capture of the legal system by the Nazis and facilitated its modification to meet evil Nazi goals.

With the apparent discrediting of positivism and the yearning for a normatively grounded theory of law, mainstream scholarly activity turned toward a revival of natural law. This took three paths: a new Thomism sponsored primarily by Roman Catholic scholars, a secular version of natural law based on the "material value philosophy" and the "Radbruch Formula."

Thomistic natural law had been cultivated in various intellectual circles ever since the great saint produced his *Summa Theologica* in the thirteenth century. After 1945 it had great appeal to some German academics as a mature philosophy that based the validity of all law on universal moral principles. Expectations were high that natural law would provide a framework for the new post war society, that it would answer difficult moral and political questions both great and small, and that it would provide a defense against the establishment of evil law. Even the new German constitutional court flirted for some time with the use of natural law as a justification for decisions, and this trend has not entirely ceased.[2] However, as time passed it became apparent that the expectations for natural law had been too high. The answers were not there, or were not convincing. Some found Thomism unacceptable because it required the philosophical support of a particular metaphysics and of certain religious assumptions. It was a "confessional" philosophy.[3] Of course, it still retains some adherents in the contemporary scholarly world.[4]

A variation, not subject to the religious objection, was a natural law based on what was called the "material value" philosophy originally worked out by Max Scheler and developed further by Nicolai Hart-

2. See Donald Kommers, *The Constitutional Jurisprudence of the Federal Republic of Germany* (Durham, N.C.: Duke Univ. Press, 1989), 54, 312, and cases cited therein.

3. Typical of this work is Josef Fuchs, *Lex Naturae: Zur Theologie des Naturrechts* (Düsseldorf: Patmos, 1955). Of lesser impact was some Protestant-oriented work along the same lines. See Hermann Weinkauff, "Das Naturrecht in evangelischen Sicht," *Zeitwende* 23 (1951): 95. For a collection of works from this period dealing with the question of natural law, see Werner Maihofer, ed., *Naturrecht oder Rechtspositivismus* (Darmstadt: Wissenschaftliche Buchgesellschaft, 1962).

4. See Kommers, supra note 2 at 48–60.

mann. Like Thomism, this view asserted a pre-ordained objective order of values that could be known by human beings.[5] This order of values grounded the validity of law and presumably would guide legislative and judicial decisionmakers to right solutions. But just as with Thomism the problem of the generality of principles, the practical difficulty of dealing with conflicting values, and the metaphysical basis of the pre-ordained order led to diminishing enthusiasm for this philosophy as the years went by. In addition, both this version of natural law and Thomism were interpreted so as to emphasize the values of security and stability, thereby reinforcing authoritarianism rather than strengthening individual rights. Both began to disappear from mainstream legal philosophy in the late 1950s.[6]

The other alternative that sought to resolve the problem of the morality of law was offered by Gustav Radbruch, a noted politician and scholar in pre-Hitler Germany. The third edition of his major work in legal philosophy was published in 1932 on the eve of the assumption of power by Hitler. In 1933 Radbruch was dismissed from his position as professor at Heidelberg for his political views. He experienced the entire Nazi ordeal in Germany and was restored to his professorship in 1945.

Radbruch's pre-war philosophy was a positivist one. Following Kant he recognized the distinction between the world of fact and the world of value. His attempt to deal with the latter seems to have a Weberian orientation. Immediate ends could be justified in terms of more abstract goals, but a clash of these ultimate goals could not be rationally resolved because of the fundamental difference between empirical reality and value. The Ought could not be derived from the Is. For Radbruch the idea or concept of law consisted of three dimensions or antinomies, each in tension with the others: certainty, expediency, and justice. Certainty, or legal security, was the most important of these, the others secondary. It is the law's primary function to lay down a rule of conduct for all situations (establish a Legal Order) so that people can conform their behavior to it, that is, they can know exactly what they and others can and cannot do. If this basic function is not satisfied, no law exists.[7] Of course, the law should strive to do justice and to accomplish the immediate goals of society (expediency), but this will not always occur. While justice and

5. See Helmut Coing, *Grundzüge der Rechtsphilosophie*, 2d ed. (Berlin, de Gruyter, 1993), 61, 71, 127–129, 153–161, 240–242, 290–295.

6. A well-recognized critique was given by Hans Welzel in *Naturecht und materiale Gerechtigkeit*, 4th ed. (Göttingen: Vanderhoeck and Ruprecht, 1990).

7. There is a significant parallel here between Radbruch's notion of the fundamental requirements of law and the "morality of law" discussed by Lon Fuller. See Lon Fuller, *The Morality of Law* (New Haven, Conn.: Yale Univ. Press, 1964).

expediency are incorporated in the idea of law, they remain partly ideals to be pursued; legal security, on the other hand, is essential.

As a result of the Nazi experience, Radbruch changed his views. He, too, thought that positivistic legal philosophy had been an ally of the Nazi regime. He was also concerned with a further problem. Many laws formally enacted by the Nazis had to be retroactively invalidated after 1945. This presented a fundamental challenge to a positivistic viewpoint. How could one maintain respect for and fidelity to law, maintain the rule of law, while at the same time assert that selected prior laws, because of their evil character, were not laws? Radbruch saw the conflict as one between justice and legal security. He reversed the priority of his three antinomies. Justice was, after all, the most basic; indeed, legal security was itself a requirement of justice, very important but not fundamental. Thus justice could come in conflict with itself. The problem was therefore to devise a principle to determine when the normal obligation to obey and enforce properly enacted law must give way to considerations of a higher justice. Radbruch drew on the learning centering around an old concept in German law called "The Nature of the Thing," and he formulated his principle as follows:

> Preference should be given to the rule of positive law, supported as it is by due enactment and state power, even when the rule is unjust and contrary to the general welfare, unless the violation of justice reaches so intolerable a degree that the rule becomes in effect "lawless law" and must therefore yield to justice.[8]

As to defining the meaning of the term "justice" in this principle (called the "Radbruch Formula" in subsequent debate), Radbruch was willing to turn to older ideas of natural law. He recognized that the efforts made in the course of history to formulate a higher law by which positive law could be evaluated answered a legitimate need. By reconceiving the concept of law in terms of the three antinomies, but this time with justice as paramount, the positive law itself was given its essential moral element. By using his formula one could determine when law ceased to carry its usual obligation—when law became non-law.

The Radbruch Formula was debated in scholarly circles for several years.[9] It had an appeal to those scholars who wanted to preserve the advantages and benefits of a positivistic approach while acknowledging the priority of justice in extreme circumstances. Like the revival of tradi-

8. Gustav Radbruch, "Gesetzliches Unrecht und übergesetzliches Recht," in Gustav Radbruch, *Rechtsphilosophie*, 4th ed. (Stuttgart: Koehler, 1950), 352.

9. It also received attention in the Anglo-American world in the so-called Hart-Fuller debates of the late 1950s. See James Herget, *American Jurisprudence 1870–1970: A History* (Houston: Rice Univ. Press, 1990), 292–299 and sources cited therein.

tional natural law theory, however, the interest in the Radbruch Formula faded in subsequent years as newer philosophical concerns occupied the attention of scholars.

The current discussion of the morality and legality of punishing border guards and others involved in the killing of East Germans fleeing into West Germany in recent years (*der Mauerschütze*) has stimulated new interest in natural law and also in the Radbruch Formula.[10] As was the case in the early post-war years, the authorities of the Federal Republic of Germany in the 1990s have drawn into question the killing of would-be escapees from the former East Germany done at the direction of the East German military authorities. Two recent decisions of the Bundesgerichtshof have upheld the punishability of the border guards, suggesting, at least, a Radbruchian justification.[11] Some of the same moral-legal questions that emerged in the immediate post-Nazi era have again been presented, and theorists have again begun to debate the value of natural law or the Radbruchian formula. Can the problem be theoretically resolved? It would appear that the traditional positivist-natural law controversy will continue with a new chapter.

Critical Theory and Marxism

Somewhat outside the mainstream of intellectual development, another significant line of thinking unfolded in Germany in the early post-war period; this was known as critical theory.[12] Critical theory began at the Institute for Social Research at the University of Frankfurt in the 1920s. When Hitler came to power the members of the Institute migrated abroad, mostly to the United States, where they continued their scholarly efforts. In 1950 three of these theorists, Max Horkheimer, Theodor Adorno, and Friedrich Pollock, returned to Germany to reestablish the Institute in Frankfurt. Unlike the newer intellectual movements in Ger-

10. The most extensive work on this subject appears to be Frank Saliger, *Radbruchsche Formel und Rechtsstaat* (Heidelberg: C.F. Müller, 1995). See also, Michael Pawlik, "Strafrecht und Staatsunrecht," *Goltdammers Archiv für Strafrecht* 10 (1994), 472; Helmut Lecheler, *Unrecht in Gesetzesform? Gedanken zur "Radbruch'schen Formel"* (Berlin: de Gruyter, 1994); Ralf Dreier, "Rechtsphilosophische Aspekte juristischer Vergangenheitsbewältigung," *Zeitschrift für Gesetzgebung* 8 (1993), 300; Michael Pawlik, "Das positive Recht und seine Grenze," *Rechtsphilosophische Heft* 2 (1993), 95; Robert Alexy, "Mauerschützen: Zum Verhältnis von Recht, Moral und Strafbarkeit," *Berichte der Joachim-Jungius-Gesellschaft* 3 (1993), 28; Klaus Lüderssen, *Der Staat geht unter—das Unrecht bleibt? Regierungskriminalität in der ehemaligen DDR* (Frankfurt: Suhrkamp, 1992).

11. See the explanation of these decisions in Pawlik, supra note 10.

12. On critical theory, see Thomas B. Bottomore, *The Frankfurt School* (Chichester: Horwood, 1984); David Held, *Introduction to Critical Theory: Horkheimer to Habermas* (Berkeley: Univ. of California Press, 1980).

many in the 1950s and 1960s, their work was a continuation of scholarship from earlier decades.

Critical theory was a neo-Marxist intellectual approach that combined elements of philosophy, sociology, and psychology. Its major tenets included the following ideas: most persons in capitalist society are exploited and repressed by the social system; this oppression is masked by ideology, but liberation can be achieved through a transformation in social institutions and ways of thinking. The task of the scholar is to expose the ways in which dominance is perpetuated. Such exposure leads to emancipation by raising consciousness of true social reality. In this view law serves two functions; it is an instrument of dominance and repression, but at the same time it appears to legitimate unjust societal relationships.[13]

Horkheimer and Adorno continued to write into the early 1970s, and the Marxist position was given new support in West Germany from the work of Ernst Bloch. But it was a brilliant young scholar at Frankfurt by the name of Jürgen Habermas who picked up the themes of critical theory and breathed some new life into the tradition. Habermas' early writings reflect concern with dominance and the masking role of ideology, and the problem of emancipation. However, in the mid-1970s his thinking took a turn toward language-philosophy, and he ultimately abandoned, or at least greatly modified, his critical theory. The language-philosophy development is discussed below.

While critical theory was basically Marxist in orientation, a more traditional Marxism-Leninism was reflected in the work of scholars in the German Democratic Republic. Following a conference of scholars and government officials at Babelsberg in 1958, an official legal philosophy was settled upon; thereafter most of the East German scholarship simply followed the party line.[14] Legal scholars in the Federal Republic showed some sporadic interest in Marxist views, particularly in the mid-1970s, but this was definitely a minor movement.

Existential Legal Philosophy

Another and less influential philosophical theme in the early post-war period with affinities to Marxist thought should also be noted; this was

13. These ideas are, of course, central to the critical legal studies movement in the United States, which derived in large part from German critical theory. See Herget, supra note 9 at 276ff.

14. See Karl Mollnau, "Die Babelsberger Konferenz oder: vom Beginn der Niedergangsjurisprudenz in der DDR," *Archiv für Rechts- und Sozialphilosophie* Special Edition 44 (1991), 236.

existentialism. The strong theoretical influence of Martin Heidegger and Karl Jaspers in Germany led to Werner Maihofer's attempt to work out an existential legal philosophy.[15] This work stood in the shadow of more dominant movements in scholarship and never gained many adherents in the legal world.

The Turn to Method

Beginning around 1960 interest in the normative basis of the legal system was replaced by a new inquiry into the methods of legal science. Perhaps partly because of the perceived failure of the attempts to reconstruct natural law theory, legal philosophy began to ask questions about itself: How should discussion of the law proceed? What is the method that will be most fruitful? The foundational thinking for this self-examination came from several sources. Within Germany the pioneering work on "Topics" by Theodor Viehweg began to be taken seriously, and the "Mainz School" of rhetorical theory came into existence.[16] The early seminal works on legal logic by Karl Engisch[17] and Ulrich Klug[18] were rediscovered and published in new editions. The Heidegger-inspired philosopher Hans-Georg Gadamer also published his highly influential *Truth and Method* in 1960, stimulating the rise of a school of legal hermeneutics.[19]

Stimulus from outside Germany, however, probably had the greatest influence. A group of theorists, including Friedrich Hayek, Karl Popper, and the "Vienna Circle" of logical positivists, had migrated from Austria to England during the Nazi period. They continued their work and began to publish in English or English translation after the war. Ludwig Wittgenstein's labors in the field of language analysis and Karl Popper's achievements in the philosophy of natural science were particularly influential in the Anglo-American world and began to be received in Germany in the late 1960s.[20] In addition, the British tradition of language

15. See Werner Maihofer, *Recht und Sein* (Frankfurt: V. Klostermann, 1954).

16. See Theodor Viehweg, *Topics and Law* (translated by Cole Durham, Frankfurt: Peter Lang, 1993). Original German edition: *Topik und Jurisprudenz* (1953).

17. Karl Engisch, *Logische Studien zur Gesetzesanwendung* (Heidelberg: C. Winter, 1943).

18. Ulrich Klug, *Juristische Logik* (Berlin: Springer, 1951).

19. Hans-Georg Gadamer, *Truth and Method*, 2d. rev. ed. (translated by Joel Weinsheimer and Donald Marshall, New York: Crossroads, 1989). Original German edition: *Wahrheit und Methode* (1960).

20. The most influential works by these authors were Karl Popper, *The Logic of Scientific Discovery* (New York: Basic Books, 1959), original German edition: *Logik der Forschung* (1935); Karl Popper, *The Open Society and Its Enemies* (Princeton, N.J.: Princeton Univ. Press (1950); Karl Popper, *Conjectures and Refutations: The Growth of Scientific Knowledge* (New York:

analysis in philosophy—which traces back to Bertrand Russell and includes the work of scholars like A. J. Ayer, Suzanne Langer, John L. Austin, G. E. M. Anscombe, and Gilbert Ryle—was flourishing in the 1940s and 1950s.[21] It should be emphasized that these developments were taking place in the fields of language-philosophy and philosophy of science and did not initially impact on jurisprudence; in fact, the implications of these language-philosophy developments for legal philosophy were only beginning to be realized in England. The pioneering work in this direction was Herbert Lionel Adolphus Hart's masterful exposition, *The Concept of Law*, published in 1961.[22]

The methodological concern took German legal philosophy in what can now be seen as two major "positivist" directions: the social science of law, and legal analysis. The latter category would evolve into the schools of legal hermeneutics, rhetorical theory, and analytical jurisprudence. The main concern of these three modes of inquiry was to articulate a theoretical method for understanding and explaining such legal phenomena as interpretation of statutes, application of law by judges, legal argumentation, the use of logic in law, the problem of legal sources, and the autonomy of law. These modes of inquiry were only incidentally concerned with questions of justice, public policy, morality, or ideal systems of law; they were directed toward the methods of legal explanation and understanding. To make this distinction clear the term "legal theory" (*Rechtstheorie*) was used to describe the new scholarship in contrast to the previous "legal philosophy" (*Rechtsphilosophie*).[23] Most of the scholars operating in this vein considered their work to be scientific.

The social science of law, on the other hand, rejected such law-specific methods and attempted to bring the methods of the natural and social sciences ("true science") to the field of law. The major influence here was the work of Popper, whose approach was carried over to social science

---

Basic Books, 1963). It is the later work of Wittgenstein that most influenced both the British and Germans. Ludwig Wittgenstein, *Philosophical Investigations* (in both English and German translated by Gertrude E. M. Anscombe, Oxford: Basil Blackwell, 1953).

21. Representative works would include Alfred J. Ayer, *Language, Truth and Logic* (London: Gollancz, 1946); John L. Austin, *How to do Things with Words* (Cambridge, Mass.: Harvard Univ. Press, 1962); Suzanne K. Langer, *Philosophy in a New Key* (Cambridge, Mass.: Harvard Univ. Press, 1942); Gilbert Ryle, *The Concept of Mind* (New York: Barnes and Noble, 1949); Gertrude E. M. Anscombe, *Intention* (Oxford: Basil Blackwell, 1957).

22. This was published in German translation in 1973. An important earlier contribution by Hart was H.L.A. Hart, "Definition and Theory in Jurisprudence," *Law Quarterly Review* 70 (1954), 37.

23. A new journal called *Rechtstheorie* was founded in 1969 to publish scholarship of the new kind. The founders were Karl Engisch, H.L.A. Hart, Hans Kelsen, Ulrich Klug, and Karl Popper.

and law by Hans Albert.[24] This empirically oriented scientific method became known as critical rationalism. Systems theory, an alternative sociological approach, was developed somewhat later by Niklas Luhmann under the inspiration of the American sociologist Talcott Parsons.[25] Systems theory also made claim to social-scientific validity. The rivalry between these schools of social science and the varieties of legal analysis continues to the present as indicated in subsequent chapters of this book, although some of the issues seem to have been resolved.

The Role of Jürgen Habermas

As suggested above, in the 1960s and 1970s many of the important intellectual developments that have influenced present-day legal philosophy were taking place in the separate disciplines of sociological theory and philosophy (sometimes simply called "social theory"). A key figure in transmitting many of these ideas to the German philosophical discussion and of synthesizing them and advancing them further was Jürgen Habermas. As we have noted, originally influenced by Martin Heidegger, Habermas started his academic career as a member of the Frankfurt school of critical theory. As such, he debated in the academic literature first Hans Albert, foremost exponent of Popper's critical rationalism, then later Niklas Luhmann, the main proponent of systems theory.[26] In order to meet criticisms encountered in the course of these exchanges Habermas modified his views and rethought his position. In doing so he drew heavily on the thinking of the language-philosophy theorists.

Two key ideas shaped Habermas' thinking in the 1970s. The first was an epistemological approach known as the consensus theory of truth.[27] This view rejects the older idea of truth (going back at least to Aristotle) as a correspondence between statements (or knowledge) and reality,

24. Also important as an influence on the German philosophy of science was the seminal work of Thomas Kuhn, *The Structure of Scientific Revolutions* (Chicago: Univ. of Chicago Press, 1962).

25. Luhmann studied under Parsons at Harvard in 1960–61.

26. For a collection of essays from the early part of the debate, see Theodor Adorno et al., eds., *The Positivist Dispute in German Sociology* (translated by Glyn Adey and David Frisby, New York: Harper Torchbooks, 1976). Original German edition: *Der Positivismusstreit in der deutschen Soziologie* (1969). For essays relating to the Habermas-Luhmann debate, see Jürgen Habermas and Niklas Luhmann, eds., *Theorie der Gesellschaft oder Sozialtechnologie: Was leistet die Systemforschung?* (Frankfurt: Suhrkamp, 1971). See also, Franz Maciejewski, ed., *Beiträge zur Habermas-Luhmann Diskussion* (Frankfurt: Suhrkamp, 1973) and Franz Maciejewski, *Neue Beiträge zur Habermas-Luhmann Diskussion* (Frankfurt: Suhrkamp, 1974).

27. This was first articulated by Habermas in "Wahrheitstheorien," in *Wirklichkeit und Reflexion*, ed. Helmut Fahrenbach (Pfullingen: Neske, 1973), 211.

that a statement is true if it corresponds with what actually is. It also rejects the idea of truth (traceable to Spinoza and Leibniz) as coherence, that a statement is true if it is consistent with the rest of our knowledge. Rather, the consensus theory holds that what is true is what people would agree upon if they were to debate a proposition. Who the "people" are and what the conditions would be for this ideal debate are matters that Habermas was to work out, along with his colleague at Frankfurt, Karl-Otto Apel, in the late 1970s and 1980s.

The second key idea advanced by Habermas was that a philosophy of social science (or social theory) must be based on a theory of communication. In developing this notion Habermas relied heavily on Wittgenstein, the English language-philosophy theorists (especially the idea of a "speech act") and on the work of the American psychologist George Herbert Mead.[28] Habermas was able to work out this philosophy of social science (or social theory) most completely in a two-volume treatise published in 1981 called *The Theory of Communicative Action,* considered by some to be his opus magnum. This was Habermas' answer to critical rationalism and systems theory.

Subsequently Habermas has turned his attention to the question of moral justification.[29] Combining the consensus theory of truth with the notion of grounding social theory in the transcendental aspects of language, he was able to formulate a philosophy now called discourse theory (discussed in chapter four below), and he was finally able to bring his theory to bear on law and government in *Facticity and Validity,* published in 1992.[30] In the course of his philosophical journeys Habermas has seemingly moved from a Marxist-Hegelian oriented critical theory aimed at the goal of human emancipation to a Kantian oriented theory aimed at the universal justification of moral and legal values. It is perhaps even more amazing that, in making this remarkable transition, Habermas has nevertheless apparently been able retain the major philosophical positions he has taken over the years, combining them in a new synthesis.

28. The seminal work by Mead is *The Philosophy of the Act* (Chicago: Univ. of Chicago Press, 1938). See also Andrew Reck, *George Herbert Mead: Selected Writings* (Chicago: Univ. of Chicago Press, 1964).

29. In this Habermas has drawn some seminal ideas from the American developmental psychologist, Lawrence Kohlberg. See Lawrence Kohlberg, *Essays on Moral Development* (San Francisco: Harper and Row, 2 vols., 1981–84).

30. Jürgen Habermas, *Between Facts and Norms: Contributions to a Discourse Theory of Law and Democracy* (translated by William Regh, Cambridge, Mass.: MIT Press, 1995). Original German edition: *Faktizität und Geltung* (1992).

Legal Analysis and the Contribution of Koch and Rüßmann

Meanwhile the pursuit of various kinds of legal analysis was continued by other scholars. Otmar Ballweg and Waldemar Schreckenberger made innovative contributions to rhetorical theory.[31] Robert Alexy, a student of philosopher Günther Patzig and jurist Ralf Dreier at Göttingen, combined ideas of Jürgen Habermas with some principles of logical argumentation and formulated a much celebrated theory of legal discourse.[32] Karl Larenz and Arthur Kaufmann extended the exploration of legal hermeneutics.[33] Martin Kriele published his American-influenced and highly acclaimed *Theory of Legal Derivation*.[34] A milestone was reached in 1982 with the publication of *Theory of Legal Reasoning: An Introduction to Basic Problems of Legal Science* by Hans-Joachim Koch and Helmut Rüßmann.[35] Although this work was styled a "textbook" intended to be read and understood by students who were not versed in the subtleties of legal philosophy, it was nevertheless a penetrating treatise that drew on many areas of learning and synthesized a new approach, becoming a classic in a very short time. It treats many of the themes characteristic of German legal philosophy in the late 1970s and 1980s.

Koch and Rüßmann acknowledge the influence on their thinking of both language-philosophy and American jurisprudence. Both scholars served as judges in appellate courts, giving them an unusual first-hand knowledge of judicial decisionmaking. The objective of their book is to describe and explain what could constitute good grounds for judicial decisions. This breaks down into three sub-inquiries. First, what are the tasks that the furnishing of legal reasons are supposed to accomplish? Second, what difficulties stand in the way of these tasks, or what boundaries exist to their successful accomplishment? Third, what approaches would be fruitful in overcoming these difficulties?

Koch and Rüßmann expand the more traditional methods of analytic jurisprudence by instituting a new (for Germany) focus on fact-finding, by recognizing that judges assume certain value judgments in the discharge of their duties, and by inquiring into the ways that judges use the leeway or discretion that inevitably is given them. In addition to using the traditional logical analysis of the law, the authors employ insights from

31. See chapter five.

32. Discussed in chapter four.

33. See chapter two for a brief account.

34. Martin Kriele, *Theorie der Rechtsgewinnung* (Berlin: Duncker and Humblot, 1967).

35. Hans-Joachim Koch and Helmut Rüßmann, *Juristische Begründungslehre: Eine Einführung in Grundprobleme der Rechtswissenschaft* (Munich: Beck, 1982).

language-philosophy to deal with questions of interpretation and application, and they use symbolic logic to reconstruct the legal syllogism in a new form. They also try to incorporate metaethics in relation to the problem of substantiating legal values, and they attempt to use scientific theory, mathematics, and statistics in dealing with experience-based legal arguments. Unlike most German theorists, Koch and Rüßmann pay considerable attention to the individual case, and they frequently introduce cases to illustrate their presentation. Their work certainly did not answer all questions, and it provoked disagreement in some quarters. However, it did set the tone and shaped the dialogue for much of the discussion in the years to come.

Although there remains a wide variety of scholarly enterprise today, including neo-Kantian, neo-Aristotelian, and natural law theory, we can see from the foregoing brief history that the course of thinking in the past few decades has given most contemporary German legal philosophy certain defining characteristics. First, there is a concern for explaining legal reasoning and providing a basis for criticizing its results, or, in the alternative, for demonstrating that law can be explained through the methods of social science. Second, there has been a great absorption of ideas from abroad, notably British (including Wittgensteinian) language philosophy and various American philosophical ideas. Finally, there is a tendency to avoid any reliance on metaphysical or religious foundations. These themes will be explored in the following pages.

Chapter 2
A Summary Catalog of Contemporary Scholarship

> To a multitude of writers who . . . flourish in Germany the . . . object of political government [is] the extension over the earth of the empire of right or justice. . . . It would seem that this right or justice is not a creature of law; that it was anterior to every law; exists independently of every law; and is the measure or test of all law and morality. . . . It rather is a something, perfectly self-existent, to which [God's] law conforms. . . . I, therefore, cannot understand it.
>
> —John Austin[1]

In this chapter we will catalog some of the scholarly activities currently being undertaken in German legal philosophy. Thumbnail sketches of these various lines of thinking will be presented without critique or evaluation. The reduced attention paid to these views, in comparison with the treatment of other views in later chapters, does not, of course, necessarily reflect their historical importance, the skill and art of exposition and scholarship that they represent, or their inherent value. As indicated in the preface, because of time and space limitations a full evaluation of all of the ongoing work in this very active field is not possible. I have used as the criteria for full treatment of a legal philosophy that it (1) be relatively unfamiliar in American legal circles, (2) be connected to contemporary developments in other disciplines, and (3) be characteristically German in some way. The views summarized in the following catalog do not fully meet one or more of these criteria.

1. John Austin, *The Province of Jurisprudence Determined* (London: J. Murray, 1832), lecture VI.

Analytical Jurisprudence

The term analytical jurisprudence is broad and somewhat imprecise; it is therefore appropriate for use here to designate the work of a variety of scholars whose efforts follow a common thread but differ in a number of ways. This scholarship could also be designated "rational argumentation," "juristic reasoning," "modern positivism," "theory of argumentation," "rational legal method," or something similar. In the work of Norbert Hörster it includes the exposition of classic positivism combined with a utilitarian moral theory. The scholarship of Robert Alexy, discussed in chapter four, could also be included under this rubric; however, the uniqueness of the function of discourse in his approach warrants independent treatment in that chapter. Likewise, rhetorical theory, treated in chapter five, is closely related; however, the skepticism of rhetorical theory and its complete rejection of system demand separate consideration.

What, then, is the common theme that runs through contemporary analytic jurisprudence? It is to provide an answer to a problem that the process of judicial decision often brings to our attention. Can a court's decision be rationally justified? All theorists recognize that judges do not decide cases by simply subsuming the facts of a case under a rule of law, that is, that the classic Aristotelian syllogism does not provide an adequate explanation of judicial decisionmaking. However, this does not necessarily lead to the conclusion that judicial decisions are completely arbitrary and subjective. Indeed, they are often predictable, and judges themselves do not think that they decide arbitrarily.

In German thinking the matter of justification of decision is bound up with rationality in argumentation. Therefore, the analysts attempt to provide a theory of argumentation, or an explanation for decision that will demonstrate that judicial decisionmaking can be in some sense rational, objective, and free of external (non-relevant) influences. The approaches taken by various theorists differ. Some are led into the question of the validity of legal sources; others seek to reconstruct the model of formal argument using the tools of modern symbolic logic; still others seek to classify and prioritize types of arguments. Questions arise about what is meant by rationality, whether there are different kinds of rationality, and what standards are required to be met by a rationally justified decision. As one author puts it, "Three areas of legal rationality are central: derivation of law, justification of decision, and concept and system building."[2]

2. Delf Buchwald, *Der Begriff der rationalen juristischen Begründung: Zur Theorie der juridischen Vernunft* (Baden-Baden: Nomos, 1990), 21.

The ultimate importance of this theoretical work is political. If court decisions are arbitrary or subjective, a number of consequences follow. First, the democratic process is undermined because legislative acts, enacted through the majoritarian process, do not control the application of law in individual cases. The principle of separation of powers is violated because judges would be legislating. The principle of the rule of law becomes illusory. And the idea of fairness in judicial proceedings (due process) is equally undermined. Hence, there is a lot at stake. However, intuition and experience tell us that judicial decisionmaking is usually not arbitrary. The problem is to develop a theory that will adequately account for this intuition.

> If we undertake to develop a concept of rational legal justification systematically from a general, integrative conception of theoretical and practical rationality, this must rest upon the acceptance that talk of "rationality," "reason," "mind," at least in special areas, is thoroughly *meaningful.* Such investigation can prove whether this intuition is not an expression of an optimistic but unrealizable hope.[3]

A good example of this type of investigation is illustrated by the recent writing of a young scholar at Göttingen, Delf Buchwald, a student of philosopher Günther Patzig and jurist Ralf Dreier, both of Göttingen (the same mentors to Robert Alexy). Buchwald has advanced a two-tier theory of rational justification. To be rationally justified a judicial decision must meet requirements of "core justification" and "cover justification."

The core justification refers to the ordered set of sentences that constitute the judgment. In Buchwald's theory these must meet four requirements: they must follow logically; they must be premised on at least one norm of the legal system; the description of facts must fit the conditions for the application of the norm; and all premises must be necessary and sufficient to decide the case. The cover justification relates to an ordered set of arguments that support the decision. The requirements for cover justification are that the argument must follow logically (deductively), that each norm used can be morally justified (legitimacy), that the empirical facts and principles of causality are true and sufficiently informative, that the argument must be normatively specific (concrete), and that the argument must be compatible or coherent with the legal system as a whole. These specific requirements are, of course, further elaborated upon and analyzed.

To simplify, Buchwald has attempted to explain the conditions under which a judicial decision can be said to be rationally justified. It must be internally justified through the selection and use of the proper norms

3. *Id.* at 20.

and their logical application, and it is externally justified through consistency with the body of valid law, compatibility with the fundamental requirements of justice, and coherent with well-established empirical laws and a correct description of the facts. Unfortunately, Buchwald's discussion tends toward the abstract and is sometimes hard to follow. However, in an attempt to meet this difficulty, he gives a step-by-step explanation of legal justification in a particular legal case in an appendix to his book.[4]

The way in which the rationality of legal decisions can be demonstrated through analyses of this type is also being pursued by other scholars, as indicated in the bibliography.

Anthropological Jurisprudence

Anthropology is a social science; so, a philosophy of anthropology would presumably be a philosophy of science. Nevertheless, the study of legal anthropology easily leads to inquiries about the universality of norms among the various cultures of the world, to the problem of relating and assessing values between dissimilar societies, and to the question of whether obligation can be inferred from social practices or other empirically observed phenomena. This has led to scholarly work that we will characterize as anthropological jurisprudence. Two theorists in particular deserve our attention, Ernst-Joachim Lampe and Thomas Rentsch.

Lampe has developed a form of anthropological jurisprudence that he calls the "genetic legal theory." The objects of study are the historical factors, biological and cultural, that create, determine, and interact with the law. This theory answers the question "why law is." Lampe uses the empirical work of various anthropologists, psychologists, and historians to reconstruct the original development of what comes to be the law. Unlike more rationalist philosophies, his view is that present-day legal systems were not created at particular times and places, but are the result of a continuing process of biological and cultural evolution which began in the mists of prehistoric times. The latest major step in this evolution was the differentiation of law out of a more general and diffuse religious-ethical normative system.

One of the consequences of Lampe's theory is that, because of the way it has evolved, law is tied to the maintenance of certain "anthropological constants." These are basic human needs that have been constant throughout the prehistory and history of the species. They include such things as the needs for self-preservation, for security, for family, and for

4. *Id.* at 331. See also a recent article in English by Buchwald in which the idea of coherence in legal decisionmaking is explored: Delf Buchwald, "Statutory Interpretation in the Focus of Legal Justification: An Essay in Coherentist Hermeneutics," *Univ. of Toledo Law Review* 25 (1994), 735.

social interaction. Any legal system that fails to sustain these needs will itself fail.

> Every law, whether in the past, present or future, must be based upon the essential characteristics of the human being and must arrange its norms accordingly. A law which does not do this, which, for example, does not proceed on the assumption of the self-reproducing individual existence of the human being, would be irrational and thereby unlawful.[5]

Indeed, it is suggested that there should be a correlation between the anthropological constants and the basic rights protected by modern constitutions. While many thinkers draw from anthropology a worldview of cultural relativism, Lampe draws a more unified view, almost a natural law view, which emphasizes the basic similarities that all persons and cultures exhibit.[6] In this view the force of obligation or the legitimacy of law (assuming it sustains basic human needs) is derived from evolutionary need.

Rentsch's approach is somewhat different. While trained neither as lawyer nor anthropologist, he presents a "transcendental anthropology" which has significant ramifications for legal theory. He also emphasizes the similarity and uniformity of the human experience rather than diversity. Drawing upon strands of thinking from Heidegger and Wittgenstein, Rentsch presents a novel epistemological approach to the understanding of social life. In his view human beings construct their understanding on the basis of immediate life experience. The starting point for knowledge is the everyday world (called primary world by Rentsch) in which we find ourselves attempting to fulfill limited goals in the context of both fact and value. Although science and philosophy seek to find truth, the ultimate confirmation of knowledge leads back to the primary world. Scientific analysis abstracts from this world and loses something in the process. One of the important things lost is the indivisibility of fact and value. The basic human experience is one in which objects and processes are understood in relation to multiple goals and types of fulfillment.

One is born into and raised in a particular primary world leading to the absorption of certain ways of acting and speaking. These forms of living are not optional, but are determined by the community. Expanding Heidegger's notion of "existentials," Rentsch calls these forms "in-

5. Ernst-Joachim Lampe, "Rechtsanthropologie heute" in *Archiv für Rechts- und Sozialphilosophie* Special Edition 44 (1991), 222, 232.

6. Lampe uses the concept of "negative natural law," which is somewhat paralled by H.L.A. Hart's idea of the "minimal content of natural law." See H.L.A. Hart, *The Concept of Law* (Oxford: Clarendon Press, 1961), 189–194. See also Philip Selznick, "Sociology and Natural Law," *Natural Law Forum* 6 (1961), 90–94.

terexistentials." Examples are family, love, sexuality, work, religion, aesthetics, and law—all culturally imprinted life forms around which human beings orient their vision of successful life. Language mediates and reinforces these interexistentials. In this context Ought and Being cannot be separated. A basis for morality, and hence a basis for the critique of law, can be found in the need to orient one's behavior toward fulfillment of universal life forms. Rentsch claims that a critical legal philosophy must be developed based on his transcendental anthropology.

> The law originates in practical life in the pre-legal community of the primary world and touches upon the communicative interexistentials of the human being as they can reveal the analysis of the constitution of morality. The legal power of judgment must be drawn back so as to remain on the primary world.[7]

Aristotelian Theories

Aristotle's influence over the centuries has perhaps been greater than that of any other philosopher. Today neo-Aristotelians in the United States, Great Britain, and other countries as well as in Germany continue to mine the Stagirite's vast philosophical works for new yields. The current interest in the ancient Greek's thinking seems to originate in what is perceived as the failure of enlightenment and post-enlightenment philosophy to provide a satisfactory account of justice, government, and social life in general. Tied to these questions is, of course, the justification of the coercive power of law. With regard to morality and justice, many neo-Aristotelians assert that enlightenment philosophy, one-sidedly oriented to explain natural science, leads to cultural relativism while existential and "postmodern" philosophy lead to complete subjectivism.

The way out of these difficulties is to return to the teleologically oriented thinking of Aristotle. The Philosopher established a method of explanation based on purpose. Relating this to the world of values, principles of human action or rules of behavior can be derived from the overall purpose or end of mankind. This is happiness, or the good life. The good life is attained by the exercise of virtue. The virtues consist of such things as bravery, temperance, generosity, friendship, pursuing the contemplative life, and justice, among others. One who develops the habit or disposition of being virtuous, appropriately supported by family and by the state (city-state for Aristotle), can achieve the good life. What is right depends on what leads to the good life, that is, the good is prior to and determinative of the right.

While this short characterization of the Aristotelian approach might suggest an individualistic philosophy, that is not the case. The state, and

7. Thomas Rentsch, *Die Konstitution der Moralität* (Frankfurt: Suhrkamp, 1990).

the law that it creates, are necessary for the attainment of the good of both the individual and the community. The human being is social by nature and cannot fully achieve individual potential without the support of organized society. The state is therefore also natural. Indeed, participation in the activity of government is a part of the good life in a well-founded state.

Justice is one of the most important virtues, and Aristotle makes his classic distinction between distributive justice and corrective justice. The latter consists in correcting a wrong, or making whole one who has suffered harm, and is the operating principle of adjudication. The principle of distributive justice awards those goods of society to those who are entitled to them. This is not an egalitarian principle, but one based on merit.

Aristotle also recognizes a distinction between conventional law and natural law. The former is local and distinctive of a particular people, while the latter is common to all human beings. This is because of the common nature—common needs, common ends—of all human beings. This idea has been, of course, greatly elaborated upon by subsequent philosophers in ancient, medieval, and modern times.

Most of the contemporary German work in the Aristotelian mode would be considered political philosophy and so somewhat outside the focus of this book. For instance, Arno Baruzzi has written several books that attack the Kantian-Hegelian idea of freedom as autonomy and only autonomy, suggesting an Aristotelian alternative. He and Robert Spaemann have both been critical of the justification of values through a theory of evolution (Niklas Luhmann, for example), proposing instead a teleologically based approach.

Hegelian Theories

Georg Wilhelm Friedrich Hegel was a giant in the field of philosophy in the nineteenth century, perhaps one of the two most influential philosophers, along with Kant, in German history.[8] He developed a comprehensive theoretical schema that included a philosophy of law. Since his work is at a very high level of abstraction and quite metaphysical, it has not had much direct influence on lawyers, judges, or even law professors. However, some of his ideas were very powerful, and Hegel's indirect influence on anthropology, history, and legal theory has been substantial. In Germany there have been neo-Hegelians ever since the master died in 1831.

8. Of course, Karl Marx would have to be added here if one considers Marx a full-fledged legal philosopher.

As suggested, Hegel's theory of law is abstruse and theoretical, and it is to some extent dependent on other aspects of his philosophy. It would not be possible to do it justice in the short confines of this chapter, so we must be content to mention some of its outstanding features.[9] The subject matter of the philosophy of law is the idea of Right, that is, the concept of right and the actualization of that concept. Right in turn is the realization of the freedom of the will, a key notion carried over from Kant's philosophy. Individuals are capable of being conscious of themselves and of their capacity to exercise their freedom. This constitutes personality. Of course, people in any society are interdependent and must recognize each other's personalities through reciprocity. Each person is inherently capable of possessing rights (this is abstract Right), but when this abstract Right is objectified into something universally recognized and willed (becomes actualized by the state), it becomes positive law. The positive law is the result of the universal concept of Right being applied to particular objects and persons in a historical context. The three major categories of law that can be logically derived from these beginnings are property, contract, and wrong (crime-tort). Positive law, especially its more specific rules, is conditioned by the particular spirit or character of a nation and requires a judicial apparatus, created by the state, to make it concrete.

Right (law in the broad metaphysical sense) thus becomes a unified whole, an order or set of principles derived from the idea of Right or freedom which governs the relationships of persons in a society such that their freedom is secured and maximized. These principles and relationships will vary from society to society and will change over time because of different social and cultural circumstances. The entire legal structure is essentially autonomous and logical; at the highest levels of the dialectic process feelings, emotions, attitudes, and interests play no role. Common morality is subjective and different from Right. Right is an objective order, not invented, that has a determined logical structure. Although the legal order is based on the principle of individual freedom, this freedom can only be realized in the context of particular human relationships. Here matters of common morality, emotional feelings, traditions, and other factors in social relationships become important. These communal considerations mean that the legal order must prevail when a claimed exercise of individual freedom runs counter to it. The individual will is subordinate to the fundamental order of the state.

9. For a contemporary American view of some important aspects of the theory, see Fred Dallmayr, "Rethinking the Hegelian State," *Cardozo Law Review* 11 (1989), 1337. See also, Andrew Arato, "A Reconstruction of Hegel's Theory of Civil Society," *Cardozo Law Review* 11 (1989), 1363, and Terry Pinkard, *Democratic Liberalism and Social Union* (Philadelphia: Temple Univ. Press, 1987).

From the standpoint of present-day thinking, we can perhaps single out three important contributions to jurisprudence made by Hegel. Unlike his predecessors (and some of his successors) in the field of legal theory, Hegel recognized the significance of historical development for law; although his particular theory of historical development (unfolding of the Idea of Spirit) has been largely discredited, he did direct attention to the phenomenon of legal evolution. His philosophy (borrowing here from Montesquieu) also pointed out that law's form, legitimacy, and effectiveness can only be understood and assessed in relation to the other cultural phenomena existing in a particular society. Finally, he provided a counterthrust to the excessive individualism of the eighteenth century and brought to the forefront the importance of community and cooperation.

The current efforts being made in German legal philosophy in the Hegelian mode attempt to reformulate Hegel's ideas in a way more acceptable to thinking in a less metaphysically oriented world and to apply some of his insights to changed modern, conditions. We now live in a welfare state, yet much of the theoretical justification of government ("democratic theory") still rests on individualistic political philosophies. Although in his day private law was much more prominent than public law, Hegel's ideas may suggest some ways to justify minimum social conditions and entitlements.[10] Other aspects of the tension between individual rights and community welfare may also be illuminated by his thinking. Some scholars have also found valuable his insights regarding property, contracts, and the idea of an ethical community.[11] Hegel's influence in the form of Marxism is discussed briefly below.

Hermeneutics

The term hermeneutics (from Greek Hermes, the messenger-god) was first used to describe the critical interpretation of scripture employed by biblical scholars in past centuries. It was subsequently carried over into the field of literary interpretation and finally into all fields in which texts are interpreted. In Germany under Martin Heidegger and Hans-Georg Gadamer the interpretive approach was elevated to a full-fledged philosophy called "universal hermeneutics." Gadamer's most important work, *Wahrheit und Methode*, was published in 1960, and it had a substantial impact on legal theorists in Germany. The foremost scholar to apply the new approach to law was Josef Esser whose 1970 work, "Pre-

10. See Ludwig Siep, "Verfassung, Grundrechte und soziales Wohl in Hegels Philosophie des Rechts" in *Archiv für Rechts- und Sozialphilosophie* Special Edition 44 (1991), 361.

11. See Wolfgang Schild, "Rechtswissenschaft oder Jurisprudenz" in *Archiv für Rechts- und Sozialphilosophie*, Special Edition 44 (1991), 328.

understanding and Choice of Method in Legal Interpretation: Principles of Rationality in the Practice of Judicial Decision,"[12] became a classic.

The key point for understanding legal hermeneutics is the idea that every interpreter has a unique horizon, that is, sees things from his or her own point of view. One's horizon is determined by what one already knows, senses, feels—by what is in one's mind. This in turn is the product of education, socialization, and all of the experience one has undergone. A judge interpreting the law brings all of this to bear in forming his or her own unique horizon. The judge engages the text of the law by mentally questioning it, "playing" with it, moving back and forth between the text and his or her own perspective (*hin- und herwenden des Blicks*). Because the answer to a question is sought (usually related to a specific situation under consideration), the judge is open to its meaning. As this mental process is carried through, the judge's horizon is expanded (prior ways of thinking in this area are modified), and an interpretation of the text is reached that the judge deems to be the genuine one. There is a fit; understanding is achieved.

One of the consequences of this view is that there can never be a single, authoritative, "true" interpretation of a text. The interpretation is always a product of the interaction of interpreter and text, and every interpreter brings different knowledge, a different background (different horizon), to the task. This does not mean that persons who interpret a text differently can never come to agreement. Such agreement can, at least in some cases, be reached through a dialogue in which the presuppositions of one's own position (and of the other's position) are exposed, questioned, and reformulated. This is a form of rational argumentation. Such agreement, of course, does not mean that the agreed-upon interpretation is objective in some absolute or universal sense. Further, from this point of view it goes without saying that an interpretation once arrived at can be seen at a later time to be erroneous because new knowledge and understanding have been achieved in the interim.

While no two persons' horizons are the same, many texts pose no serious interpretive problems because there are similarities of horizon among the interpreters. Judges are all trained in much the same way and are usually drawn from similar social and intellectual backgrounds. Hence, many texts have a "plain meaning."

This Gadamerian viewpoint as advanced by Esser and others has found considerable acceptance in German legal philosophy. It has led to an inquiry about how rational argumentation in law works, how differing interpretations can be reconciled. It serves for some as a basic framework

12. *Vorverständnis und Methodenwahl in der Rechtsfindung: Rationalitätsgrundlagen richterlicher Entscheidungspraxis* (Frankfurt: Athenäum, 1970).

or point of departure from which rationality in law can be explored. With the possible exception of the work of Arthur Kaufmann, there is little contemporary discussion among legal scholars about the philosophical concept of hermeneutic interpretation itself; rather, the viewpoint is implied in the work of some of those scholars who are pursuing the problem of rational argumentation. This is discussed in chapters four and seven; see also the following discussion of "Integrative Jurisprudence."

Integrative Jurisprudence

There is some recognition in Germany today that legal philosophy may be made more useful for judges and other students of the law if some of the different traditional approaches can be integrated into one comprehensive method.[13] Work along these lines has been pioneered by Winfried Brugger. Brugger's starting point is the problem of interpretation of the law; in this respect his aims parallel those of Ronald Dworkin and other scholars who have advanced the American Legal Realist tradition. The challenge is to formulate a theory that will describe how legal decisionmaking works and also prescribe how it should work.

Brugger's starting point is a collection of propositions about human culture that have been more or less well established by anthropology. We must make choices in life in accordance with our own understanding of who we are; this in turn is dictated by the phenomena that we perceive. We have a sense of time, and therefore we are aware of history and of possible developments in the future. Our culture stamps us with certain conceptual ideals, and we in turn modify those ideals; of course, we are also aware of our basic needs. Brugger places these phenomenological factors into a four-dimensional pattern that might be called the "anthropological cross." In the vertical dimension we have at the top our ideals, cultural values, and goals; at the bottom are our biological needs and self-interest. The horizontal dimension is time, with the backward direction being our history and past experience and the forward direction being those presently foreseeable and seekable goals to be achieved. We define ourselves in accordance with our "reading" of the two dimensions.

In Brugger's view the interpretation of the law shares the same characteristics as the interpretation of the self. We define or interpret what the law is or what it should be with reference to the same four directions.

13. For American invitations to engage in this type of effort, see Harold Berman, "Toward an Integrative Jurisprudence: Politics, Morality, History," *California Law Review* 76 (1988), 779. Jerome Hall, "Integrative Jurisprudence" in *Interpretations of Modern Legal Philosophy*, ed. Paul Sayre (New York: Oxford Univ. Press, 1947).

Both are instances of judging in a structured context. To do an adequate job the interpreter must take the necessary reflective steps—forward, backward, upward, and downward.

> Upward arguments rely upon either explicit or implicit constitutional ideals of the political community, such as "justice for all." Downward arguments are based on the perceived urgency of needs and interests. Or, to put it more crudely, looking downward, what we want is what counts, while looking upwards, what we legitimately can and should expect or do is of greatest weight. These perspectives are intertwined with the backward and forward relationship of legal interpretation. The meaning of text and context always expresses past experiences of which the words themselves form a part; the past is constantly present in the meaning of words. The past, however, does not necessarily determine and constrict their essence. Words possess open-ended significance; contemporary developments in the real or ideal world shape their past purport so that the traditional understanding of the word is affirmed, broadened, or narrowed. These new speech conventions then in time become part of the modern "tradition" of the words' meaning. This is the forward-looking perspective in which contemporary goals and purposes become primary roots of reference.[14]

Brugger suggests that the traditional schools of thought have tended to concentrate on only one aspect of the law. For example, natural law-type theories have been mainly concerned with the "up" or ideal direction; anthropological, sociological, and interest-balancing theories have mainly looked "down"; historical theories have generally been directed to the temporal dimension; positivist theories have dwelt upon the "backward" direction through analysis of historical language; and utilitarian, pragmatic, and "law and economics" theories have been mainly concerned with the "forward" direction.

Brugger sees a need to reconstruct the relationship between legal philosophy and actual legal decisionmaking, and his approach is essentially a hermeneutical one, bearing some resemblance to the work of Ronald Dworkin.[15] In using this approach the insights of the various schools of jurisprudence should be integrated so as to be of value to judges and legislators. His four-directional model is a first step toward establishing such an integrative jurisprudence.

Kantian Theories

Kant still exercises a considerable influence over German philosophical thinking. This seems to be partly because the Germans often regard

14. Winfried Brugger, "Legal Interpretation, Schools of Jurisprudence, and Anthropology," *American Jour. Comparative Law* 42 (1994), 395, 415.

15. See Ronald Dworkin, *Law's Empire* (Cambridge, Mass.: Harvard Univ. Press, 1986), 45–86.

Kant's thinking as the culmination of enlightenment theory. That is, ideas that might historically be attributable to Locke or Leibnitz or others were incorporated into Kant's theory and have perhaps their most sophisticated statement there, rather than in the works of the earlier thinkers. Kant's core idea in the area of moral philosophy, the idea of universalizability of maxims of action, also seems to fulfill a need in some German thinking for a justification of duty and an ultimate grounding of morality which then also serves as the basis for critique of law. The current interest in reviving Kant's thought appears to be motivated by a dissatisfaction with what is perceived today to be a widespread moral relativism and a cynicism toward "rational" theories of morality.

The Kantian starting point[16] is the idea of freedom. Human beings possess, contrary to instinct-bound animals, the capacity of conscious choice of action, or free will. We cannot conceive of ourselves without free will. Humans also have, of course, natural needs for nourishment, shelter, physical security and so forth. These natural needs have been expanded and modified, through culture (as a sort of "second human nature"), leading to the desire for companionship, artistic expression, charity, love, and justice, among others. The satisfaction of these needs and interests is dependent on social cooperation. Social cooperation is achieved through the operation of social norms. Because of free will and the rational faculty possessed by the human animal, an individual can act in accordance with specific rules of thumb, or in accordance with more general maxims. In the moral realm one can legislate for oneself.

According to Kant, such maxims should be universalizable, that is, they must be compatible with the freedom of every person. An individual may arbitrarily choose those maxims of conduct that lead to a desired form of life; however, those subjective maxims must be limited to their general compatibility with the maxims of others seeking their own forms of life. This faculty of limited freedom is the "practical will," the individual's law-giving and action-motivating authority.[17]

The concept of law complements this moral theory. Law responds to the problem of threatened reciprocal impairment in the empirical social world. Thus laws relate not to inner attitudes or virtues but to external actions that can endanger other people. Correspondingly, laws neither coerce the will nor regulate moral sentiments, but control the legality of actions. Law can and should, because it aims at the limitation and coor-

16. For a somewhat lengthier but nevertheless brief exposition of Kant's jurisprudence, see Winfried Brugger, "Grundlinien der kantischen Rechtsphilosophie," *Juristenzeitung* 19 (1991), 893.

17. For a good discussion of practical reason contrasting Weberian instrumental reason and Aristotelian ethics with Kantian morality, see Jürgen Habermas, *Faktizität und Geltung* (Frankfurt: Suhrkamp, 1992), 542–562.

dination of human actions, determine and guarantee equal freedom in external relations of human beings with one another. Law can be regarded, in Kantian terms, as the quintessence of the conditions under which the choice of one with the choice of another can be united according to a general statute of freedom. The positive legal system must be constructed according to this moral principle. To put it another way, law implements the conditions of general freedom, of equality, and of reciprocal obligation.

Individuals pursuing their own interests egoistically can presumably understand that an advancement of individual choice of action comes about through the reciprocal security of spheres of freedom. This pragmatic level of argumentation is integrated into the Kantian course of thought. The capacity of the law to adjust the general securing of freedom and respect for equality makes it possible for the legal subject to understand and act responsibly. For the reasonable person legal compulsion is not necessarily onerous. If one takes the purposes of the law as one's own internally and acts on them out of respect, then an obligation to strangers becomes self-obligation; coercion becomes consensus.

The principle of freedom from coercion by others is owed to everyone equally; so the law of equality follows from the law of freedom, which depends not upon status, ability, power, or riches, but upon the capacity for reason in human beings. Humans can set themselves goals, act rationally to achieve them, and act responsibly to limit their actions. Equal capacity for rationality is the basis for moral and legal equality.

Kant's concept of law and the ideas of freedom and equality for every person lead to the question of how institutions can be devised to make these principles work. Kant distinguishes analytically a natural state and a civil state. In the hypothetical natural state the possibility of a natural law governing the relationship of private individuals is present in conditional form, but only in the civil state can the respective mine and thine be established and secured through official organization and public laws. Individual rights against other individuals are logically prior to the legal organization of the state, but require the latter for implementation. An organized legal system is therefore a necessity.

Kantian morality and his complementary view of law can perhaps best be used to evaluate an existing constitutional order or parliamentary legislation.[18] Of course, highest principles do not determine specific rules and details of the legal system by themselves. Such principles should be reflected, however, in the basic elements of a legal order, thus enabling critical reflection on the positive law.

18. Kant suggests a four-level model that is essentially paralleled in Rawls' theory. See John Rawls, *A Theory of Justice* (Cambridge, Mass.: Harvard Univ. Press, 1971), 195–201.

Some of the neo-Kantian scholarship in legal philosophy attempts to relate Kant's ideas to contemporary circumstances, particularly as a justification for the claim of universal human rights.[19] Other scholars have used Kantian orientations to resolve problems in particular areas of the positive law such as civil law, criminal law, and international law.[20] Still other works attempt to reinterpret or "rehabilitate" Kant in light of contemporary needs and ideas. Perhaps the most prominent proponent of neo-Kantianism in this respect is Otfried Höffe. Höffe takes the position that the social sciences which provide us with our understanding of human nature cannot legitimate legal principles. In his view these sciences must be supplemented by a legal categorical imperative based on the Kantian notion. Such an imperative provides a basis of obligation that transcends human needs and interests. He suggests a legal ethics that combines metaphysics and anthropology.

Neo-Kelsenism

Hans Kelsen has been the archtypical scholar of German legal philosophy. The durable Austrian published some of his main ideas in the second decade of this century and continued to refine his theory into the 1960s. He proposed a "pure" theory of law that had as its subject the positive law itself, free of empirical data, unencumbered by natural law or any other moral theory, and uncontaminated with sociology, economics, or other social sciences.

Kelsen's approach owes much to neo-Kantian philosophy. It is abstract, demands rigorous logic, and provides a comprehensive perpective of the legal order as an autonomous body of norms. As such, it has held, and still holds, great appeal to jurists educated in the German tradition. An institute for legal philosophy named for Kelsen exists at the University of Vienna, and several scholars there are continuing work in the mold of the master. The American scholar Stanley Paulson has also written extensively on Kelsen, as have scholars in Japan and Latin America. The aims of Kelsenian scholarship are to provide a theoretical framework for understanding positive legal systems in a way that promotes clarity, facilitates analysis, and avoids confusion with nonlegal discourse from related fields such as moral theory or sociology. Specifically, Kelsen rejects any notion that the validity of law is dependent on morality (a central theme

19. See Martin Kriele, "Die demokratische Weltrevolution: Warum sich die Freiheit durchsetzt," *Archiv für Rechts- und Sozialphilosophie* Special Edition 44 (1991): 201.

20. See the discussion in Kristian Kühl, "Rehabilitierung und Aktualisierung des kantischen Vernunftrechts," *Archiv für Rechts- und Sozialphilosophie* Special Edition 44 (1991), 212, 219.

of natural law thinking) or any notion that the norms of law can be reduced to fact (one type of positivism).

With these aims, Kelsen sets a limited task for jurisprudence. He views his theory, and presumably competing legal-philosophical theories, as a science. As such, it is intended to reduce chaos to systematic knowledge; it deals only with knowledge, not volition or ideal models. The pure theory is a science of what law is, not of what law ought to be; the latter task is reserved to political science, moral philosophy, or religion. Unlike the natural sciences, legal theory has as its object norms and their relationships. The existence and validity of norms are the same thing. Ultimate validity of all of the norms of a legal system rest upon a *Grundnorm.* This *Grundnorm* is not subject to empirical verification as in the theory of Hart (ultimate rule of recognition), but must be presupposed along Kantian transcendental lines. The correlation of the theory to particular systems of law is that of the possible to the actual. The theory is formal, and the theorist is essentially a logical analyst. Kelsen's theory, or something like it, underlies the work of many of the theorists who are exploring the rationality of law discussed above under the title "Analytic Jurisprudence" to which the reader is referred for further discussion.

Kelsen's last and unfinished work, *The General Theory of Norms,* was published in German in 1979 and translated into English in 1991.[21] In this work Kelsen seems to undo much of the theory that he had previously constructed. Contrary to his earlier view, a legal norm is considered the meaning of an act of will, and, instead of being a presupposition or assumption, the *Grundnorm* becomes a fiction, known to be false (not corresponding to reality). He is also skeptical of the role of logic in law.[22] These changes in his theory have given Kelsen scholars much grist for their mill.

Communitarianism, Feminism, Marxism, Law, and Economics

This improbable foursome has been lumped together here because there is not much to be said about any of them in relation to the current German scene. Some literature has appeared discussing what communitarianism is or is supposed to be. The work of the American Alasdair MacIntyre has claimed the attention of philosophers and a few legal

21. Hans Kelsen, *The General Theory of Norms* (translated by Michael Hartney, Oxford: Clarendon Press, 1991). Original German edition: *Allgemeine Theorie der Normen* (1979).

22. See Stanley Paulson, "Kelsen's Legal Theory: The Final Round," *Oxford Jour. Legal Studies* 12 (1992), 265.

scholars.[23] Other discussions that reflect some of the orientation of communitarianism can be found under the headings of anthropological jurisprudence and neo-Hegelianism discussed above.

Feminist jurisprudence, or what passes by that name in the United States today, has not yet found a home in Germany (except to the extent that it is a modified version of critical theory or Marxism). A number of articles have appeared that are critical of the law for its failure to provide sexual equality in particular areas, but not much in the way of theory. Some of the work of American protagonists of feminist jurisprudence, particularly Catherine McKinnon and Carol Gilligan, have been the subject of some commentary.

Of course, Marxist legal philosophy flourished in the former German Democratic Republic; however, it was generally regarded by the West Germans as ideological doctrine intended to support the legitimacy of the Communist regime. Since reunification the remaining advocates of Marxist jurisprudence have had little following, although a few are still advancing a modified and diluted version of the old theory.

Law and economics has been slow to take hold in Germany. There are a handful of scholars who are pursuing the economic analysis of law, and some texts have been written. However, the German legal profession and especially the law faculties have resisted the movement. This has been attributed to the long tradition in Germany of the autonomous legal subject, that is, the notion that law is essentially independent from economic considerations. In the United States, ever since Roscoe Pound advanced his sociological jurisprudence, ideas and theories from the social sciences have generally been welcomed in legal circles when they could be made applicable. This reflects an instrumental notion of law, a notion that law, and especially particular laws, serve particular social objectives. Such a notion runs counter to the German tradition which emphasizes an independent, abstract legal order with its necessary and logical connections. The widespread (but certainly not universal) acceptance of law and economics scholarship in the United States also reflects the general acceptance among the legal profession of the proposition advanced by the American legal realists that rules and doctrines do not decide hard cases; therefore, decisions based on demonstrable economic consequences are an acceptable alternative where doctrine fails. So far, only a few German scholars have been willing to follow this lead.

23. In particular, Alasdair MacIntyre, *Whose Justice? Which Rationality?* (Notre Dame, Ind.: Notre Dame Univ. Press, 1988).

Chapter 3
Critical Rationalism

> Critical rationalism is not an invention of our time, but a style of thought that humanity in its history at various times forgets to its detriment.
>
> —Peter Schwerdtner[1]

Background

Critical rationalism is a philosophical viewpoint usually associated with the name of Hans Albert (1921–). Another leading contemporary proponent of critical rationalism is Reinhold Zippelius, although his work has not been concentrated in this area of jurisprudence. In the following discussion we will primarily discuss the views of Albert. After a brief period as an American prisoner of war, Albert was educated at the university of Cologne in the late 1940s and early 1950s. Although his background is sociology, his main work has been in the field of scientific method or philosophy of science, especially as that relates to social science. Albert appears to have been influenced early in his career by the ideas of Viktor Kraft, Hugo Dingler, and Theodore Geiger; however, when he was exposed to the work of Karl Popper, he became a convert to Popper's way of thinking. Along with most sociological theorists, Albert also owes a substantial intellectual debt to Max Weber.

Popper was one of a substantial number of philosophers who migrated from Austria to England in the 1930s. Unlike most of these scholars, however, Popper was not particularly concerned with language or formal logic. Building on the work of others, including some important English

1. Peter Schwerdtner, "Rechtswissenschaft und kritischer Rationalismus," *Rechtstheorie* 2 (1971), 224.

theorists,[2] he was able to refine a philosophy of natural science that has been very influential in both Europe and America. Popper also suggested the application of his approach to areas outside natural science. This is where Hans Albert took up his own labors. Albert completed the application of Popper's theory to social science and particularly to the field of law. He thus comes to the subject of legal philosophy from a background in philosophy of science.

Albert has published 23 books and numerous articles, and although he reached emeritus status at the University of Mannheim, he continues to be active, living and writing in Heidelberg. His two most influential works are *A Treatise on Practical Reason* (1968, fifth edition 1991) and *A Treatise on Rational Practice* (1978). Albert was a major participant in the so-called dispute over "positivism" in Germany in the late 1960s and 1970s, carrying on an extended debate with Jürgen Habermas and others.[3]

Aims

In the context of this book we can give only a limited sketch of critical rationalism, a philosophical approach that can be regarded as an epistemology or as a "method," a term often used by Albert.[4] It is an attempt to account for the way that scientific method operates, that is, to explain scientific explanation. It does not try to provide a special technique of legal interpretation or to analyze the meaning of law or the various components of legal systems as analytical jurisprudence does. Nor does it seek to provide a basis or foundation for moral, political, or legal theory as natural law thinking does. However, critical rationalism does give an account of how moral and legal decisions should be made.

My point of departure is the thesis that science can interpret and analyze law as social fact and that as a consequence it can be found also in theoretically sup-

2. This would include Norman Campbell, John Stuart Mill, and William Whewell. See John Losee, *A Historical Introduction to the Philosophy of Science*, 2d ed. (Oxford: Oxford Univ. Press, 1980).

3. See the discussion in chapter one.

4. The following discussion is based primarily on these works by Hans Albert: *Rechtswissenschaft als Realwissenschaft: Das Recht als soziale Tatsache und die Aufgabe der Jurisprudenz* (Baden-Baden: Nomos, 1993); *Traktat über rationale Praxis* (Tübingen: Mohr, 1978); "Critical Rationalism: The Problem of Method in Social Sciences and Law," *Ratio Juris* 1 (1988), 1; "Erkenntnis, Recht und soziale Ordnung," *Archiv für Rechts- und Sozialphilosophie* Special Edition 44 (1991), 16; "Erkenntnis und Recht" in *Rechtsphilosophie oder Rechtstheorie*, ed. Gerd Roellecke (Darmstadt: Wissenschaftliche Buchgesellschaft, 1988).

ported enlightenment. There can therefore be a legal science as a real science, and, to be sure, as a real science of the usual kind. [5]

In a way critical rationalism has an appeal to American readers that few other German theories do. Popper borrowed heavily from the English tradition of philosophy of science; in fact, he was labeled a "crude empiricist" by some of his critics. The mainstream sociologists in America have tended to subscribe to this kind of empirical-oriented view of social science.[6] In addition, critical rationalism offers an appealing theoretical foundation for freedom of speech, something many American constitutional theorists have been seeking.[7] The work of Popper and Albert can be considered in part as an extension of the efforts of Max Weber to explain how social science does and should work.

Main Ideas

The Popperian theory, as extended by Albert, concerns itself with the activity of problem solving through scientific method. It adopts a realist correspondence theory of truth, that is, statements about reality have a truth value; they are true if they do, indeed, correspond with reality. These statements may be simple descriptive sentences, or more abstract propositions, or generalized "laws" of nature. Of course, statements characteristic of science assume the operation of cause and effect, and they deal with the world of fact, not with metaphysical, spiritual, or supernatural entities, although the propositions of science themselves are not facts but hypotheses or theories constructed by scientists. They are abstract statements or "laws" about reality that have explanatory and predictive power. According to Albert this kind of discourse involving propositions describing reality is the only kind of rational discourse; thus, he rejects a distinction made in some philosophies between practical reason and speculative reason, as well as the distinction between scientific explanation and hermeneutical understanding.

A starting point from which to review Albert's philosophy is his critique of the two traditional philosophies of the enlightenment, rationalism and empiricism. Albert presents his critique of these earlier views through the "Münchhausen Trilemma." Any scientific statement can be challenged by asking, "Why?" That is, one can inquire as to the reason, basis,

5. Hans Albert, *Rechtswissenschaft als Realwissenschaft*, supra note 4.

6. See Richard Lempert, "The Autonomy of Law: Two Visions Compared" in *Autopoietic Law: A New Approach to Law and Society*, ed. Gunther Teubner (Berlin: de Gruyter, 1988).

7. Albert emphasizes the need to avoid dogmatism. As indicated below in the text, truth is gradually achieved by active inquiry in a critical spirit—an idea similar to Holmes' "marketplace of ideas."

or foundation of the statement or proposition. The basis will be another statement or set of statements from which the first can be deduced. This new statement in turn can be questioned. This process can be continued until one of three consequences results (the Münchhausen Trilemma). The first possibility is an infinite regression, and no final foundation is established. The second possibility is a circular justification, with the substantiating statements being statements used earlier in the chain of justification, obviously unsatisfactory.[8] Finally, the chain of substantiation can be cut off. Albert characterizes the basis for cutting off the chain of argument as "dogmatic." This dogmatic closure may be accomplished through religious doctrine, political ideology, and in other ways. To the extent that any field of inquiry is dogmatized, it fails to pursue the truth, and, indeed, may propagate falsity.[9]

The rationalist tradition, stemming from Descartes,[10] found the unquestionable final grounding in introspection or intuition, in reflection on self-evident truths that are immediately known to the mind: "I think, therefore I am." The empirical tradition, stemming from Bacon,[11] found the absolute certainty in fact, in the raw data of sense perception. Both philosophies attempted to account for the establishment of certain knowledge, particularly as that knowledge was accumulated in the natural sciences.

In the course of time, however, it became apparent that there were cracks in the wall of certainty. Our intuitions and self-knowledge obtained by internal reflection turned out to be unreliable. Psychology showed that, rather than producing certainty, self-reflection could yield illusion. Likewise, the hard facts of sense perception proved to be softer than expected. The senses could be fooled, and there was no way to predetermine when this might happen.

> Science progresses neither by the derivation of certain truths from self-evident intuitions with the aid of deductive processes, nor through the derivation of such truths from self-evident perceptions using inductive processes: it advances, rather, through speculation and rational argumentation, through construction and criticism.[12]

8. However, see Niklas Luhmann's view in chapter six.

9. For a lively and persuasive argument that Habermas' discourse ethics (chapter four) fail to survive the Münchhausen Trilemma, see William Fusfield, "Can Jürgen Habermas' 'Begründungsprogram' Escape Hans Albert's *Münchhausen Trilemma*?" *Rhetorik* 8 (1989), 73.

10. The classic rationalists would include Descartes, Spinoza, Leibniz, and Kant.

11. Major empiricists include Bacon, Locke, Berkeley, and Hume.

12. Hans Albert, *Treatise on Critical Reason* (translated by Mary Varney Rorty, Princeton, N.J.: Princeton Univ. Press, 1985), 62. Original German edition: *Traktat über kritische Vernunft* (1968).

And so the two rock-solid foundations of true (certain) knowledge came to be regarded as unreliable. The Münchhausen Trilemma again presented itself.

Albert asserts that the Münchhausen Trilemma cannot be resolved undogmatically as long as certainty is required as an attribute of knowledge. Here we reach a major tenet of critical rationalism: we can never have certain knowledge. This is sometimes called the principle of consistent fallibilism by Albert. Every proposition, every scientific law, every theory can be questioned. This does not mean, however, that there is no such thing as truth; rather, it means that all of the knowledge we have is tentative, subject to revision. But we can know that a proposition or theory is tentatively true, that our statements correspond to reality. Here is a second major tenet of critical rationalism. A proposition, statement, or theory about reality is true when it is subjected to rational critique and proves better than competing theories. In other words, theory "A" is better (truer) than theory "B" when it holds up better than "B" under critique and experiment, that is, it explains more specific instances, has better predictive value, accords better with other scientific knowledge, accounts for more factual variations, and has fewer exceptions.[13] It may be, of course, that theory "B" explains some things that theory "A" does not. Hence, a competing theory may not be entirely "untrue." Indeed, critical rationalism demands a pluralism of theories; in this view our knowledge increases and becomes more accurate through a process of critique and comparison with alternatives. If there is no comparison, a theory is poorly supported. The acquisition of knowledge is something that must be actively pursued; knowledge is not absorbed by us passively. In this view, of course, one does not and could not anticipate constructing an absolute theory "X" that will be true for all time (and therefore certain). No scientific proposition is immune from critique. Thus, the Münchhausen Trilemma is avoided by sacrificing certainty as a characteristic of knowledge. There is no final substantiation or ultimate grounding; everything is open to further critique.[14]

> The new concept of rationality embodied in the principle of critical examination differs from the classical doctrine principally in that it does not necessitate recourse to any dogma whatsoever, and does not allow the dogmatization of answers of any sort—of metaphysical or scientific theories, of ethical systems, historical theses, or practical and thus also political proposals. Simultaneously all

13. Of course, in some cases the question of which theory is better can become problematic.

14. This is the basis on which critical rationalism attacks the discourse theory of Jürgen Habermas, Karl-Otto Apel, and others. For an extensive critique of discourse theory by one of Albert's followers, see Herbert Keuth, *Erkenntnis oder Entscheidung: Zur Kritik der kritischen Theorie* (Tübingen: Mohr, 1993).

> claims for the infallibility of any court of appeal are rejected in favor of a thoroughgoing fallibilism.[15]

We may ask, how is a theory critiqued? This depends for the most part on the procedures and canons of the particular discipline, but in general scientists seek to deduce conclusions from a theory or proposition that can then be falsified. A fruitful hypothesis will produce inferences as to matters of fact that can be tested empirically, usually through experiment. When the inferences are empirically verified, the theory has support; when it is falsified, it cannot be true and must be modified or abandoned.

It has been recognized for some time that the facts which are deduced from scientific theories for verification or falsification of the theory are themselves determined, at least partially, by the theory.[16] Without a theory the scientist does not know what facts to look for. The recognition of this, according to Albert, emphasizes that alternative theories must also be considered by the scientist as a part of that critical work.

> The methodology of critical examination will . . . regard as necessary not merely the search for contrary facts, but above all the search for alternative theoretical conceptions, in order to facilitate the construction and application of competing frames of reference as well as novel solutions to problems.[17]

Albert agrees that the scientific enterprise involves making decisions that have no rational basis. For example, what is to be investigated? How is the area of investigation to be limited? What hypotheses will be proposed? Why will one theory be accepted as better than another?[18] Thus, the decision to use the method of critical rationalism in science and other areas is one which the method itself cannot justify. Methods are not true or false themselves, but more or less useful.

> That the process of cognition is shot through with regulations, valuations, and decisions seems to be an observation that needs only to be stated clearly to be assured of general recognition. We choose our problems, evaluate solutions to them and decide to prefer one of the available solutions to the others—a procedure that is certainly not lacking in components of an unambiguously evaluative character.[19]

15. Albert, supra note 12 at 47.

16. See Thomas Kuhn, *The Structure of Scientific Revolutions* (Chicago: Univ. of Chicago Press, 1962).

17. Albert, supra note 12 at 68.

18. See chapter three, "Erkenntnis und Entscheidung," in Hans Albert, *Traktat über kritische Vernunft*, 5th expanded ed. (Tübingen: Mohr, 1991).

19. Albert, supra note 12 at 77–78.

While these considerations may lead some to think that the scientific enterprise itself is on shaky grounds and has no claim to objectivity, Albert points out that such a conclusion rests on the fallacy of final substantiation, that is, a demand for absolute certitude.

Critical rationalism is, indeed, an interesting and persuasive account of what happens in natural science, but when we seek to apply it to moral or legal behavior, new questions are raised. For instance, the idea of a norm presents serious problems, yet norms are an important aspect of human activity.[20] A norm is a prescriptive statement, a statement about what ought to be. Rules of law, principles of morality, standards of justice are all norms. Obviously what ought to be and what is can be quite different things. Norms, at least in themselves, are not facts; they cannot be true or false. How then, can critical rationalism, which must deal with the "real" world, the world of fact, account for norms?

There are two possibilities here, both endorsed by Albert. First, normative behavior in a particular society can be a matter of fact,[21] that is, an observer can perceive that people in certain circumstances observe norms, state them, follow them, and take action to enforce them. From this viewpoint norms are facts just as much as opinions, intentions, motives, religious belief, and other phenomena that can be observed with respect to a given society. In the world of social science norms and normative systems are a part of the great complex of behavior that must be accounted for. However, while the description of norms, and of the relationships of norms to behavior, can yield information about society that is enlightening to us, it cannot yield an evaluation of the norms themselves. The "validity" of a norm, from this perspective, can only be described in terms of behavior—that it is followed, acknowledged, enforced, deviated from, and so forth. From such an observer's perspective, no "ought" can be derived from statements about behavior; there is no internal viewpoint.

According to Albert there is, however, a second way to deal with norms, a way in which norms can be evaluated and practical decisions made, and, incidentally, in the process the methods and results of social science can play an important part. Albert calls this approach to norm evaluation "social technology." It is in part a refinement on the methods first advocated by Jeremy Bentham. Bentham demanded that the consequences of any particular legislative policy be evaluated to determine its merits. Albert does not endorse Bentham's pleasure-pain utilitarian cal-

20. The term "norm" is used here in its broadest sense as any kind of standard by which something can be evaluated. This is consistent with the German usage of the term.

21. In this Albert generally follows Max Weber. See his discussion in Albert, supra note 18 at 75.

culus as the standard of evaluation, but instead proposes a pragmatic approach very similar to that put forward many years ago by the American philosopher, William James.[22] Social science methods can be used to determine the consequences of alternative legal norms or policies. Such consequences are, of course, facts. These alternative consequences can then be measured by standards advanced as hypotheses. Drawing upon the terminology of Rutledge Vining, Albert calls these hypothetically advanced standards "performance characteristics."[23] At other points Albert refers to "goal-setting." Thus, norms are accounted for and evaluated in a purely instrumental way. Norm "A" is better than norm "B" if the consequences of following norm "A" satisfy standards "X" and "Y" (or achieve goals "X" and "Y") better than norm "B," where "X" and "Y" are advanced as hypotheses (performance characteristics).

How are such hypotheses generated? In theory, any performance characteristic can be advanced—reduction of poverty, freedom of choice in lifestyles, security from crime, or conservation of resources. As a practical matter in many cases these standards are likely to be uncontroversial, at least within a particular group. For example (mine, not his), if a legislature is considering a speed limit for highways in a particular context, the consequences of various alternative speed limits could be evaluated in terms of such considerations as (1) number of highway accidents likely to occur (with deaths, injuries, and damages calculated); (2) effect on roads in terms of difference in maintenance and construction costs; (3) satisfaction of drivers with the time it takes to make trips of varying length; (4) effects on the environment; (5) impact on commercial activity; and (6) effect on fuel costs. When these calculations have been made, the degree to which the various performance characteristics can be satisfied are known. A decision based on these considerations can then be made. Such decisions, in principle, will be rational and objective. Each policy maker or legislator will know what is, or is not, being gained. This is rational decisionmaking with the assistance of science.

It might appear that this type of "social technology" will work with fairly simple matters like highway speed limits but that it would be inadequate to justify more basic norms such as the prohibition against murder or the right of free speech. However, for at least two reasons Albert's position would appear to be that the same process must be employed even though more complex norms like the right of free speech would be much more difficult to evaluate. First, the performance characteristics or standards are not obvious and would be controversial; second, all of the

22. See William James, *Pragmatism: A New Name for an Old Way of Thinking* (New York: Longmans Green, 1907); *The Will to Believe* (New York: Longmans Green, 1897).

23. "Leistungsmerkmale." See Albert, *Traktat über rationale Praxis*, supra note 4 at 84.

consequences that follow from the acceptance of the free speech norm and from its alternatives would be difficult to trace. However, critical rationalism demands that these unarticulated assumptions and speculated consequences be brought into the open and tested in order to have a full understanding of the value of free speech. That the task is difficult does not mean that it is the wrong approach.

Albert suggests, with respect to the positing of major performance characteristics or social objectives, that we should use as a starting point those ideals or goals that our society has traditionally and consistently endorsed, for example, personal security, individual freedom, and economic welfare. We can draw on the proven resources of our social life; there is no reason to ignore the lessons of past experience, even though such experience is in part due to the accidents of history. At the same time, these ideals must be kept open to criticism and must be modified as further experience dictates.

This kind of evaluation of norms (social technology) is proposed as the method to be followed in the making of legal decisions.[24] To reach legal decisions, whether legislative, judicial, or administrative, hypothetical goals are to be advanced, and alternative means, legal norms, are to be evaluated in terms of how well they serve to achieve the postulated goals. Those norms, or that norm system, which best does the job is to be selected and implemented. Such goals are always open to criticism, modification, and replacement, again based on rational critique.

> An applied science of this kind can only point to possibilities of action and thereby to possibilities for achieving particular goals or combinations of goals through the use of particular means. . . . It can analyze the effects of various systems with respect to criteria formulated on the basis of certain values. It cannot, of course, supply any legitimation to a social order in the sense of the classical idea of justification. If one accepts the position of critical rationalism, justifications of this kind must be replaced by comparative evaluations of alternative solutions to the problems concerned.[25]

Critique and Reply

A number of objections have been raised against critical rationalism. The first deals with the attributes of norms from the sociological or behavioral viewpoint. This approach to norms as fact, while yielding potentially valuable information, cannot answer questions of obligation from the

24. There is a close similarity between the method of Albert and that of Roscoe Pound, who drew on the ideas of William James. See the discussion in James Herget, *American Jurisprudence 1870–1970: A History* (Houston: Rice Univ. Press, 1990), 164- 170.

25. Albert, "Critical Rationalism: The Problem of Method in Social Sciences and Law," supra note 4 at 17.

viewpoint of the participant in the social activity, such as: What should I do? Am I bound to follow this rule? Why do I have to pay this tax? According to critical rationalism, all scientific statements must have truth value. Therefore scientific statements are *about* norms; they cannot be normative statements themselves.

This point is the source of attacks on critical rationalism as well as the basis for criticism of other views by critical rationalists. Both traditional natural law theory and legal positivism treat law as a system of norms. The question of "validity" (meaning whether a norm conforms to another standard) is central in both.[26] Under these perspectives the legal scholar is concerned with identifying which norms are valid according to a higher standard and how those norms are to be interpreted in specific cases. These questions are not factual questions, but legal or moral ones. Advocates of traditional jurisprudence point out that critical rationalism does not allow for rational discourse with norms. It thereby fails to account for the whole of legal argumentation and thereby also fails to be of any assistance to the practice of law where most intellectual questions are matters of legal argumentation and interpretation. In addition, the natural law advocates maintain that failure to deal with norms means that critical rationalism cannot explain the normativity of law and the meaning of legal obligation.

On the other side, according to Albert, this insistence on a normative science implies that there is some kind of reality or world, different from that known to science, that is populated by entities such as norms and values. A norm that is valid "exists" in that world, but, of course, is not subject to scientific investigation which applies only to statements that can be true or false. Albert calls this "value-Platonism" and rejects it entirely. He points out that these ways of thinking always involve dogmatizing a body of knowledge and thereby immunizing it from criticism. In the positivist view the ultimate validity of the legal system must be "presupposed"[27] or is "accepted."[28] This means that the question of ultimate validity cannot be asked. A dogma is necessary to create this world of norms.[29] Under natural law thinking the ultimate validity of the legal

26. The German term used for validity by Albert and others is usually *Geltung*, although occasionally *Gültigkeit* is also used.

27. Kelsen's view. See Hans Kelsen, *The Pure Theory of Law* (translated by Max Knight, Berkeley: Univ. of California Press, 1967) 45–46.

28. The view of Hart. See H.L.A. Hart, *The Concept of Law* (Oxford: Clarendon Press, 1961), chap. 6.

29. An attempt has been made to graft the epistemology of critical rationalism onto Kelsen's "Pure Theory of Law." See Rudolf Thienel, *Kritischer Rationalismus und Jurisprudenz* (Vienna: Österreichischer Staatsdruckerei, 1991). Although not a direct response to Thienel's thesis, Albert's view of this is given in Hans Albert, "Zur Kritik der reinen Juris

system depends on ultimate moral principles (the natural law) that are the foundation for positive law. The natural law is either postulated through religious dogma or inferred from facts in violation of the naturalist fallacy. As to the ultimate grounding of the legal system and the meaning of normativity, these are purely metaphysical ideas that have no basis in reality. Of course, there can be no ultimate grounding of normative propositions any more than there can be ultimate grounding of the theories of the physical sciences. In Albert's view both natural law and normative positivism (analytic jurisprudence) are throwbacks to older ways of thinking that are entirely incompatible with scientific method.

While Albert's argument against value-Platonism is persuasive, it does not necessarily answer the charge that critical rationalism fails to deal adequately with the problem of interpretation of norms. This problem is a central one for legal philosophy as well as a practical one that confronts the lawyer and judge every day. It appears to involve the logical analysis of language and the hermeneutical investigation of judicial decision-making, neither of which is "scientific" according to critical rationalism. This may simply mean, of course, that interpretive activity is not science.

However, Robert Walter has suggested that Albert has failed to realize that modern positivism (in Walter's thinking, a Kelsenian-type pure theory of law) does in fact meet the demands of critical rationalism.[30] Positivism makes an initial assumption (the presupposed Grundnorm) relating to the norms that guide human behavior. According to Walter this is no different in substance than any other scientific hypothesis; it is value-free and testable, and the propositions of the science are about norms, not the norms themselves, and are hence truth-capable.[31] Therefore, positivism (or legal dogmatics in the German lexicon) is not "merely" a practical science as Albert contends; rather:

> Since it is based upon an hypothesis, it gives no directive to action, and to that extent it is not a practical science. . . . That legal dogmatics helps the practitioners does not rob it of its scientific character. Many sciences can serve practice; but they do not thereby lose their scientific character.[32]

It may be wondered, however, whether changing the label of the Kelsenian "presupposition" to a scientific "hypothesis" actually changes the nature of the theory.

---

prudenz," *Internationales Jahrbuch für Rechtsphilosophie und Gesetzgebung* (1992), 343. See also Albert, *Rechtswissenschaft als Realwissenschaft*, supra note 4.

30. See Robert Walter, "Bermerkungen zu Albert, zur Kritik der reinen Jurisprudenz," *Internationales Jahrbuch für Rechtsphilosophie und Gesetzgebung* (1992), 359.

31. *Id.* at 361.

32. *Id.* at 361–62.

A second objection to critical rationalism goes to Albert's alternative way of handling norms, the idea of postulating performance characteristics and then evaluating norms instrumentally. Certainly just any standard or performance characteristic cannot be chosen. Could one propose "increase in disease" as a standard to be sought after?[33] The postulation of standards seems, in principle, to be arbitrary. However, Albert presents some suggestions that take much of the bite out of this objection. First, as mentioned, we should not expect the standards proposed to be controversial, especially within a given culture. This is because many values are widely shared within a given society.[34] Second, Albert asserts that the principle of "realizability" must be observed. By this he means that aiming for utopias is not rational, and therefore only goals that are likely to be reached can be considered. This includes the requirement that all costs and benefits must be accounted for. It also means that in proposing performance characteristics or goals we do not write on a clean slate; we must take into account the situation into which history has brought us, that is, operate in the context of our present institutions. Third, the long history of the human race contains many "experiments" in social control that suggest that some policies are better than others. In the course of their development human cultures have devised regulative ideas that appear to have been successful and that could serve as appropriate hypotheses, always subject, of course, to critique and possible modification or rejection.[35] Thus, while we are in principle free to establish such goals as we think best, the practical alternatives may often be quite limited.

A further objection to the social technology approach is the problem of competing or conflicting standards or goals. To use the previous example of the speed limit legislation, how are the various standards (driver satisfaction, safety, fuel economy, etc.) to be weighed against one another? It is clear that whatever policy is decided upon will result in favoring or weighing some standards more than others, that is, any particular goal can be achieved only at the expense of others. Albert recognizes this problem, but does not deal with it very persuasively.[36]

33. This problem parallels the question in the physical sciences of what hypotheses can be advanced.

34. A similar approach, but perhaps more legally sophisticated, was taken by Myres McDougal and Harold Lasswell in their "Law, Science, and Policy." See the discussion in Herget, supra note 24 at 220–227.

35. In this line of thinking Albert has suggested, as major goals, personal security from violence and oppression, maximization of economic welfare, and maximization of individual freedom. See chapters four, five, and six in Albert, *Traktat über rationale Praxis*, supra note 4.

36. At one place he says, "The selection and the weighing of these criteria is, of course, a value problem: It depends on the standards of value one believes to be relevant for an

Presumably all permutations and combinations of a particular problem are to be assessed, but which are the better solutions still seems to remain a subjective and irrational matter; there is no obvious common denominator or scale. It may be that the weight attributed to any goal may have to be hypothesized just as the goal itself is.

The use of social technology in the legislative process as prescribed by Albert is certainly nothing revolutionary, and in fact it may describe what is actually done in the better instances of legislative action. But the method of critical rationalism becomes much more problematic when one attempts to apply it to judicial decisionmaking or the application of a law by a government official. Application is not legislation. At the level of the particular case the options open to the judge are severely limited by statute (the major policy decisions have already been made by a legislative body and are communicated in the form of legal norms). Albert recognizes that in many cases the decision for a particular factual situation has not been made by the legislator; judges often have some degree of leeway. Within this area of leeway, the same pragmatic approach can be taken, that is, establishing the consequences of alternative decisions and then evaluating those consequences against postulated performance characteristics.

Admitting that this technique might be used in some cases, it nevertheless has questionable value for practice. An initial objection is that judges are institutionally ill equipped to do the necessary kind of decisionmaking. They have no independent investigative facilities, they cannot undertake experiments, they cannot determine the consequences of alternative decisions. On the other hand, they can make use of the published findings of social scientists. In addition, judges cannot fashion whole new regulatory schemes in the context of individual cases, and they are not trained as social scientists. Furthermore, as Ronald Dworkin pointed out long ago,[37] judges do not decide cases in two steps, first determining that no official norm is applicable, then looking elsewhere for guidance. They try to apply "the law" as best they can understand it, even though the official norms are ambiguous. Although it is generally recognized that judges make law through their decisions in novel cases, they do not perceive their role as being lawmakers with the same kind of legislative freedom that legislatures have.[38] Their role and powers are

---

analysis of the adequacy of the social order." Albert, "Critical Rationalism," supra note 4 at 11.

37. Ronald Dworkin, *Taking Rights Seriously* (Cambridge, Mass.: Harvard Univ. Press, 1977), 31–39.

38. Dworkin has characterized and critized the approach suggested by Albert without, however, refering specifically to him, as "legal pragmatism." Ronald Dworkin, *Law's Empire* (Cambridge, Mass.: Harvard Univ. Press, 1986), 151–175.

otherwise under the prevailing political system. Perhaps Albert would suggest that the role of courts be changed in western culture, but this seems somewhat utopian, if desirable at all.

It seems clear that judges, administrators, and lawyers are concerned mainly with interpreting the meaning of legislative acts, previous court decisions, and the argumentation of scholars, and they do so from an internal point of view. Albert has been generally very critical of the hermeneutic approach on the grounds that it departs from scientific method and purports to create a special kind of knowledge of its own.[39] While he concedes that there may be a limited role for the "art" of hermeneutics in legal practice,[40] it is difficult to see how that fits into his method of social technology. Perhaps the work of the "law and economics" scholars in the United States is instructive on this point.[41] Their work is very close to Albert's idea of social technology;[42] however, their more important contributions to legal reform have been in the form of legislative suggestions rather than guidance for court decisions. Their work in the latter arena, like Albert's in theory, is also generally limited to those cases in which the court has considerable leeway due to the uncertainty or ambiguity of official legal norms. Neither approach gives much guidance on the general problem of interpretation and application of existing law.

We should not, however, end on a negative note in assessing the philosophy of critical rationalism. As the name would suggest, its critique of other legal philosophies has been very effective, and it has exposed some of the serious flaws in the methods and assumptions of natural law, positivism, critical theory (Frankfurt school), hermeneutics, and discourse theory. It has also established the science of the sociology of law on a firm epistemological basis, persuasively defending it from critics of all kinds. Because of its objective, realist, and critical characteristics, critical rationalism may make a plausible claim to be the only true "science" of law, even if that means that the practice of judges and lawyers is an art and not a scientific enterprise.

39. See Albert, "Critical Rationalism," supra note 4 at 6–9.

40. See Hans Albert, *Kritik der reinen Hermeneutik* (Tübingen: Mohr, 1994).

41. See generally, Richard Posner, *The Economic Analysis of Law* 4th ed. (Boston: Little Brown, 1992); Robert Cooter and Thomas Ulen, *Law and Economics* (New York: HarperCollins, 1988).

42. Albert has noted the similarity but rejects the notion that the "law and economics" movement is just the same as social technology, mainly on the ground that only one performance characteristic—wealth maximization—is used, and this performance characteristic is not subjected to critique but dogmatically accepted.

Chapter 4
Discourse Theory

> Different minds may set out with the most antagonistic views, but the progress of investigation carries them by a force outside of themselves to one and the same conclusion. . . . The opinion which is fated to be ultimately agreed to by all who investigate, is what we mean by truth.
>
> —Charles Sanders Peirce[1]

Background

Discourse theory began in the 1970s with the writings of Karl-Otto Apel and Jürgen Habermas. At first it was a purely philosophical theory, an attempt to provide an ultimate grounding for truth and moral values through a procedural technique. That it had implications for legal philosophy was, however, clear. These implications were seized upon by Robert Alexy whose doctoral dissertation, *Theory of Legal Argumentation*, was published in 1978.[2] Since that time there has been considerable discussion of discourse theory in the German literature of legal philosophy.[3] Alexy has continued to publish and remains the leading proponent of the theory.[4]

In order to understand what discourse theory can do for law and how

1. Charles Sanders Peirce, "How to Make Our Ideas Clear," in *Philosophical Writings of Peirce*, ed. Justus Buchler (New York: Dover, 1955).

2. The original work has been translated into English: Robert Alexy, *A Theory of Legal Argumentation* (translated by Ruth Adler and Neil MacCormick, Oxford: Clarendon Press, 1989). It has come into a second edition in German with some material added: Robert Alexy, *Theorie der juristischen Argumentation*, 2d ed. (1991).

3. Other proponents of legal discourse theory are Aulis Aarnio (Finland), Adela Cortina, Klaus Günther, Mattias Kettner, Wolfgang Kuhlmann, and Aleksander Peczenik. See the bibliography.

4. His latest books are Robert Alexy, *Recht, Vernunft, Diskurs: Studien zur Rechtsphilosophie* (Frankfurt: Suhrkamp, 1995) and *Begriff und Geltung des Rechts* (Freiburg: Alber, 1992).

it applies in that field, it will be helpful to give a brief sketch of the prior philosophical undertaking of Jürgen Habermas.[5] As suggested in chapter one, the reader should be alerted that Habermas' views have changed over the years. Originally an adherent of the philosophy of Martin Heidegger, he joined the neo-Marxist school of "critical theory" (the Frankfurt school) led by Max Horkheimer in the 1960s.[6] Habermas began to shift from this historical philosophy in connection with his debates over the "social science of law" with Hans Albert and Niklas Luhmann; he rethought his position, eventually downplaying or perhaps discarding the Marxist historical philosophy. Working with Apel in the early 1970s, and influenced heavily by English linguistic theory, the later work of Wittgenstein, and the theories of the American, George Herbert Mead, Habermas' efforts took a linguistic turn that culminated in his "theory of communicative action," a philosophical framework for social research and understanding. This in turn led to "discourse theory" and "discourse ethics," which Habermas has pursued to the present.

Aims

The general aim of discourse ethics, or practical discourse theory, is to provide a justification for political, moral, and legal argumentation. In this respect discourse theory is a substitute for the old natural law. However, it differs from natural law in that a different epistemological approach is taken, naturalistic arguments are rejected, the substantive content of moral or legal ideas is only secondarily considered, and the ultimate grounding is procedural, that is, only those substantive propositions (or norms) that emerge from the discursive process through consensus are valid.[7] In addition to the ultimate grounding of normative practice, discourse theory is concerned with the rational connection between such grounding and specific exercises of moral and legal judgment, including legal decisionmaking in legislation and judicial decision. It seeks to demonstrate that law can be rational in the sense that particular legal decisions can be supported through logical operations leading back to the original justified starting point. In this view neither legislative norms nor judicial decisions have to be arbitrary. They can be criticized and evaluated in the framework of discourse theory.

5. See also the discussion in chapter one.

6. On the Frankfurt school, see Thomas B. Bottomore, *The Frankfurt School* (Chichester: Horwood, 1984); David Held, *Introduction to Critical Theory: Horkheimer to Habermas* (Berkeley: Univ. of California Press, 1980).

7. The procedural grounding of principles of justice was successfully brought to fruition by John Rawls, whose ideas have had considerable impact in Germany. See John Rawls, *A Theory of Justice* (Cambridge, Mass.: Harvard Univ. Press, 1971).

According to Alexy the theory is intended to demonstrate how rational decisions can be made in the law. If the theory were worked out completely successfully, it would provide a code of practical legal reason. Starting from a position widely shared, viz., that legal argument (by lawyers, courts, scholars) employs extra-legal value judgments, the theory attempts to answer whether value judgments can be rationally justified, whether they are necessary, and how they relate to legal doctrine. Although we generally unconsciously assume the contrary, if legal conclusions, particularly those of the courts, are not rational, then the consequences are, indeed, scandalous.[8] For example, law teachers and their students are fooling themselves, the practice of law is of a kind with the practice of witchcraft, and legal compulsion is the disguised exercise of power by private interest. Thus, demonstrating that law is rational has significance for questions of justice, of political practice, and of professional accountability, among others.

Main Ideas

In his discourse theory Habermas proposes a consensual theory of knowledge.[9] Unlike the correspondence theory of knowledge adhered to by Hans Albert and others in which truth is a matter of the correspondence between statements and an objective reality, for Habermas truth is determined through a consensus of all persons. Facts cannot serve as the criterion of truth because "facts" are partly determined by what is in the world and partly determined by language, that is, facts are language dependent. Habermas does not deny the reality of a world independent of the mind which is the "object" of truth.[10] But truth does not consist of some sort of correspondence between statements and that world; rather, the truth of a statement lies in the possibility of its justification by consensus through discourse. Such a justification is theoretically sufficient for all peoples and all cultures in the world, including future generations.

8. The anti-rational position has been taken by Critical Legal Scholars, Legal Realists, and the Free Law Movement. On the Free Law Movement, see James Herget and Stephen Wallace, "The German Free Law Movement as the Source of American Legal Realism," *Virginia Law Review* 73 (1987), 399. On American Legal Realism, see James Herget, *American Jurisprudence 1870–1970: A History* (Houston: Rice Univ. Press, 1990) 147–227. On Critical Legal Studies, see Mark Kelman, *A Guide to Critical Legal Studies* (Cambridge, Mass.: Harvard Univ. Press, 1987).

9. Such a theory is traceable at least back to the work of the American Charles S. Peirce, as Habermas acknowledges.

10. He actually maintains that there are three "worlds." See Jürgen Habermas, *The Theory of Communicative Action,* vol. 1 (translated by Thomas McCarthy, Boston: Beacon Press, 1984). Original German edition: *Theorie des kommunikativen Handels, Band I* (1981).

This directs our attention to what is meant by "consensus" and "discourse." Habermas proposes an ideal speech situation in which all persons are entitled to participate in argumentation.[11] Any assertion can be made problematic and submitted for consideration. Arguments can be made for or against the proposition. Anything asserted is criticizable. However, coercion, broadly conceived, is not permitted. Parties to the discourse must act honestly and consistently; they may not engage in strategic behavior; they cannot threaten, promise, or otherwise try to persuade others on any basis except the soundness of their arguments. Parties must also be able to place themselves in the shoes of others in the debate in order to see things from their perspective. Anyone can introduce any relevant point at any time, and there is no time limitation on the debate.[12] If these rules of proceeding are carefully followed, the resultant discourse may eventually arrive at a consensus as to the truth of the proposition under consideration or an alternative. Such a consensus means that the proposition is true in a non-culturally relative way.

Although this method of establishing or accounting for truth and knowledge may strike one as bizarre at first, its great attraction lies in the fact that it can be used in the normative realm as well as the descriptive. It can be used to determine what ought to be as easily as what is. As Albert is fond of pointing out, the correspondence theory of truth leads one to look for a parallel world of "ought" when considering the validity of normative statements, that is, one may be led to think that norms are valid if they correspond to the "oughts" in the Platonic world of Ought just as propositions are true when they correspond to facts in the real world.[13] With Habermas' theory no problem of a phony world arises. A norm can be debated in the ideal speech situation just as well as a descriptive proposition, and its validity can be decided as correct or incorrect.[14] This kind of discourse dealing with norms is called pragmatic or practical (leading to human action or decision) in contrast to theoretical discourse, which deals with the truth of descriptive propositions.[15]

Since people drawn from different cultures and different societal roles

11. This idea seems to be an extension of Chaim Perelman's idea of the "universal audience" of all rational and informed human beings. See Chaim Perelman, "Fünf Vorlesungen über die Gerechtigkeit" in *Über die Gerechtigkeit,* ed. Chaim Perelman (Munich: C.H. Beck, 1967).

12. There are strong parallels between Habermas' ideal speech situation and the "initial position" and "veil of ignorance" in John Rawls' theory of justice. See Rawls, supra note 7 at 136–142.

13. See the discussion in chapter three.

14. The term *Richtigkeit* is usually translated as "correctness," although it may also be rendered as "rightness" or "rectitude."

15. This distinction parallels the division of reason into "speculative" and "practical" found in Kant, Aquinas, Aristotle, and others.

have different interests and values, it might be thought that the discourse carried on in the ideal speech situation would merely fragment into the confrontational assertion of the different interests. Here Habermas brings into play the principle of universalizability. Universalizability is a variation of Kant's categorical imperative, or it might be said that the categorical imperative is applicable to all parties to the discourse, meaning that those norms that have the possibility of being correct must represent generalizable interests. A norm that can be supported by all is such that everyone can accept its direct and indirect consequences for the satisfaction of the needs of each and every individual. Acceptability is the key.

What is Habermas' basis for these rules and procedures that constitute the ideal speech situation? At this point I will give only few remarks that indicate the direction of the argument.[16] Habermas says that the requirements of the ideal speech situation are presupposed in all communicative behavior. When one speaks, one enters into a game and accepts the rules of that game. The rules are valid because their validity is a condition of the possibility of linguistic communication. In this sense they are transcendental. The justification of the requirements governing the discussion of norms is called "transcendental pragmatics" by Apel and "universal pragmatics" by Habermas.[17] Thus, discourse theory solves the Münchhausen Trilemma[18] by finding an ultimate grounding in the presuppositions of linguistic communication.

The ideal speech situation is admittedly unattainable for many obvious reasons.[19] Any real speech situation is therefore fallible. However, according to its proponents, the ideal speech situation can serve as a "regulative idea" and therefore a basis for modeling and criticizing any real discourse. Both Habermas and Alexy acknowledge a distinction between ideal discourse and real discourse. In real discourse the answer to a practical question is sought under conditions of limited participation, limited absence of coercion, limited speech-conceptual clarity, limited empirical information, limited capacity to exchange roles, limited freedom from bias, and limited time. Nevertheless, ideal discourse serves as a model to which real discourse should approximate. Alexy further explains:

16. A fuller discussion follows below in connection with Alexy's theory of legal discourse and its critique.

17. There are a number of differences between the philosophical approaches of Apel and Habermas. Space limitations do not permit of their discussion here. For a thorough critique of both in German, see Herbert Keuth, *Erkenntnis oder Entscheidung: Zur Kritik der kritischen Theorie* (Tübingen: Mohr, 1993).

18. This is Albert's paradox. See the discussion in chapter three.

19. For example, persons entitled to participate in the discourse include all those who will be born in the future. There also might be a problem finding a large enough debating room.

These requirements [of discourse] can be formulated as rules of rational discussion. The rules of rational discussion do not relate only to statements as do the rules of logic, but reach out beyond them to govern the conduct of the speaker. To this extent they can be called "pragmatic rules." Observance of these rules does certainly not guarantee the conclusive certainty of all results, but it does nevertheless mark the results out as rational ones. Rationality is accordingly not to be equated with conclusive certainty. This characterizes the basic idea of the theory of rational practical discourse.[20]

Let us turn our attention now to the application of discourse theory to the law, the significant contribution of Robert Alexy.[21] As stated above, Alexy strives to demonstrate how law can be rational. However, Alexy does not simply attempt to prove a limited type of rationality. He does not merely seek to provide analytical and logical tools with which the argumentation from given premises to a legal conclusion can be explained and justified, presumably a main part of the work of many scholars in the general field of analytical jurisprudence. Rather, Alexy seeks to demonstrate that the premises of legal argumentation themselves can be justified as well. In other words, there can be an ultimate grounding of legal norms. It thus turns out that legal discourse theory not only demonstrates that law can be rational, but in the process defines what is meant by rationality. This broad view of the scope of rationality marks a deep divergence between discourse theory and other types of analytic jurisprudence.

Alexy's point of departure is to prove that legal discourse is a special case of general practical discourse. In the first place legal discourse, utilizing the specific structures and procedures of the law, is needed to correct one of the great deficiencies of general practical discourse: that it may lead to no conclusion or agreement. By institutionalizing the discourse procedure in such a way as to force a decision within a reasonable time, the legal system makes up for deficiencies of general practical discourse. Further, Alexy points out that legal discussions are concerned with practical questions, that is, what should be done. The questions are discussed with a view to their correctness (rightness, rectitude), and they take place under certain restraints peculiar to the legal system. This does not mean that discourse accounts for everything legal. Sociological or economic studies of the law as fact are not included, nor are studies of the psychology of judges, jurors, or witnesses. This alone substantially

20. Robert Alexy, A Theory of Legal Argumentation, supra note 2 at 179.

21. The following discussion is based primarily on these authorities: Robert Alexy, *Theorie der juristischen Argumentation*, 2d ed. (Frankfurt: Suhrkamp, 1991); Robert Alexy, "A Discourse-Theoretical Conception of Practical Reason," *Ratio Juris* 5 (1992), 210; Robert Alexy, "Idee und Struktur eines vernünftigen Rechtssystems," *Archiv für Rechts- und Sozialphilosophie* Special Edition 44 (1991), 30.

differentiates the purposes and aims of sociology of law, law and economics, and hermeneutical theory from discourse theory. It is recognized that many "legal" activities, such as arresting offenders, running a law office, determining the economic consequences of a new tax, maintaining a law library, and even rendering of a judgment in a specific case, do not directly involve argumentation. In the case of a trial in court as well, where there is certainly an interchange of communication, the discussion is so structured and roles so differentiated that it can only very roughly be characterized as a discourse. On the other hand, all of these phenomena are indirectly related to legal discourse with its claims to correctness and probably could not be understood without reference to legal argumentation. The claim of legal discourse theory is to elucidate this central aspect of legal life.

The requirements for legal discourse, like the requirements for general practical discourse, can be set out as rules. Alexy gives a set of 28 rules, divided into seven different types.[22] He summarily explains these rules as being of two different kinds:

> Rules relating directly to the structure of arguments, demand, among other things, freedom from contradiction, universalisability in the sense of a consistent use of applied predicates, linguistic and conceptual clarity, the truth of applied empirical premises, deductive completeness of arguments, consideration of consequences, prioritisation, the assumption of an exchange of roles or role reversal, and the analysis of the genesis of moral convictions.[23]

Rules like these are very likely to be found in one form or another in any theory of rational argumentation. They help to assure that the arguments made are sound. However, discourse theory adds to these rules some additional ones that relate only to participation in discourse. Their purpose is to assure the impartiality of argumentation.

> Rules serving this particular purpose may be designated "specific rules of discourse." The most important are as follows: 1. Everyone who can speak may take part in discourse. 2. (a) Everyone may question any assertion. (b) Everyone may introduce any assertion into the discourse. (c) Everyone may express his or her attitudes, wishes, needs. 3. No speaker may be prevented from exercising

22. The first group is basic and includes rules requiring consistency and honesty. The second group defines the "rights" of the speakers in the discourse, which include the right to participate, to challenge assertions, to be free from coercion. Next come weight and burden of argument rules of a more technical kind. The fourth group establishes the forms of argument, and the fifth deals with justification of positions. Sixth are transition rules governing the shifting of discourse from practical to another kind. Finally, there are rules governing internal justification and external justification. Alexy, *A Theory of Legal Argumentation*, supra note 2 at 297–302.

23. Robert Alexy, "A Discourse-Theoretical Conception of Practical Reason," supra note 21 at 210, 214.

> the rights laid down [above] by any kind of coercion internal or external to the discourse.[24]

In the process of discourse in which these rules are followed the validity or correctness of a norm may be reached by consensus. Such a correct norm has ideal moral validity.

Alexy divides the justification of norms into two types. Internal justification involves proving that the conclusion follows from the premises used to justify it. This is essentially an exercise in applied logic, and Alexy employs the tools of modern symbolic logic to demonstrate the requirements necessary to make internal justification rational, including the articulation of assumed but not explicitly stated premises. Alexy says:

> In more complex cases a whole range of premises . . . is needed in justification of legal judgments, premises which cannot be inferred from any statute. In many cases even the norm from which one starts is not a norm of positive law. The requirement of deducibility leads to precisely the opposite of a concealment of the creative element in the determination of law; those premises which do not derive from positive law are brought right out into the open.[25]

External justification involves establishing the rational basis for the premises of argument. These premises, whether empirical, legal, or neither, can be justified in various ways. Alexy suggests a classification of six forms of argument: interpretation, dogmatic argumentation, precedent, general practical reasoning, empirical reasoning, and special legal argument forms. He then analyzes how each of these forms should be used.

Because of the typical structure of governments that has evolved in western societies today, Alexy sees discourse theory applied to law at four levels.

> On the first step is found the procedure of general practical discourse, on the second that of the official law-making, on the third that of juristic discourse, and on the fourth that of judicial process. The second and fourth procedures, those of the official law-making and of the judicial process, are institutionalized. . . . The sense of the model consists of the step-wise grounding of the necessity of the four procedures as well as in the presentation of the relations existing between them.[26]

At each level the principles of discourse theory can apply. For a complete justification of rationality one would start at the pre-legislative level (including pre-constitutional level). There the correctness of govern-

24. *Id.*

25. Alexy, *A Theory of Legal Argumentation*,. supra note 2 at 228.

26. Robert Alexy, "Idee und Struktur eines vernünftigen Rechtssystems," supra note 21 at 30, 36.

mental procedures and substantive norms would be discussed as a preliminary to actual legislation. The legislative debate itself would follow in institutionalized form in which specific legislative (and constitutional) provisions are subjected to discourse. After legislation has been enacted, juristic discourse takes place, that is, discourse by scholars and lawyers over the meaning and application of legislation. Finally, the discourse of courts in justifying their decisions in specific cases, also highly institutionalized, completes the application of discourse procedures. The essential factors to be tested in this process consist not just of rules, but of principles and procedures as well.[27]

Our discussion has centered on Robert Alexy's work thus far, but the recent book, *Facticity and Validity*, by Jürgen Habermas should be noted here.[28] Apparently in response to the criticism that his discourse theory has no relevance to political or legal practice, Habermas attempts with this book, among other things, to provide a justification for basic human rights, democracy, and the principle of the rule of law. While this falls under the category of political philosophy, which we have generally attempted to avoid in this book, a brief statement of its most important thesis may be in order in view of Alexy's complementary work.

Habermas suggests that modern political theory has centered around two themes, liberalism and the social state. Both are flawed conceptions. Liberalism, deriving primarily from John Locke's theory, emphasizes negative liberties (human rights and participation in the market economy); it concedes the necessity for government and some degree of infringement on these rights. Democracy, or self-government through majority rule, is the preferred form of government because it serves as a check on the extent of infringement of basic rights through excessive governmental control. When human rights come in conflict with the authority of government and law, human rights should prevail. Thus, the legitimacy of the democratic process is subordinate to and derived from the notion of basic rights. But history suggests that the minimal government that this theory proposes leads to a society in which some are rich and powerful and others poor and helpless. Economically, the big fish eat the little fish.

The idea of the social state, on the other hand, resolves the tension in the other way. The basic right of every human being is a positive one: to achieve self-realization through a political process in which everyone is equal and respects the interests of others. This political self-realization through the democratic process produces a constitutional and legal re-

27. *Id.* at 43.

28. Jürgen Habermas, *Between Facts and Norms: Contributions to a Discourse Theory of Law and Democracy* (translated by William Rehg, Cambridge, Mass.: MIT Press, 1995). Original German edition: *Faktizität und Geltung* (1992).

gime that guarantees not only basic liberal rights but also rights to work, to leisure time, to housing, to health care, to security, and to retirement income. However, if individual basic rights come in conflict with the social regimentation of the regime, the government must prevail. Thus, economic justice prevails over individual rights. Basic rights are created only by law and are legitimated through their democratic origin. History suggests, however, that the kind of social state advanced by this theory leads at best to a smothering paternalism and at worst to a repressive authoritarianism.

The problem then is: how can these two great modern principles of government, human rights and democracy, be reconciled? Habermas says that discourse theory provides the answer. The political process must approximate the ideal speech situation. To the extent it does, both the ideals of democratic self-realization and individual human rights will be reached. The ideal speech situation in which all participate in an unselfish and fair argumentation is itself an idealization of what the democratic political process is. But, in addition, the results of this process in the form of constitutional and legislative norms will guarantee respect for the human rights that are necessary for a just society. This is because the norms so arrived at are *right.*

Indeed, Habermas posits an interesting solution to an old problem.[29] For a somewhat different attempt to justify constitutional rights through discourse theory, the reader is directed to a recent article by Alexy.[30] In *Facticity and Validity* Habermas also discusses many other facets of politics, law, and sociology which space does not permit us to explore here.[31]

Critique and Reply

After this brief sketch of the theory of legal discourse, we will note some of the major criticisms that have been leveled against it and the responses made to those criticisms.[32]

The first major criticism asserts that the idea of rationality espoused by discourse theorists is itself culturally relative to western society.[33] Many

29. The debate is carried further in Jürgen Habermas, "Human Rights and Popular Sovereignty: The Liberal and Republican Versions," *Ratio Juris* 7 (1994), 1; Robert Alexy, "Basic Rights and Democracy in Jürgen Habermas' Procedural Paradigm of Law," *Ratio Juris* 7 (1994), 227.

30. Alexy, "A Discourse-Theoretical Conception of Practical Reason," supra note 21.

31. See especially his discussion of feminism.

32. See Herbert Keuth, supra note 17, for a penetrating and comprehensive critique of the general philosophical theory of discourse (Habermas, Apel, Kuhlmann).

33. "Western society" or "western culture" as used here refers to the culture developed in Europe from the sixteenth century down to the present, and includes all those societies which essentially retain that culture, whether located in Europe, America, or elsewhere.

societies do not engage to any appreciable extent in the kind of argumentation that discourse demands. Coordination of societal functions as well as resolution of disputes can be and are accomplished in some societies through authoritarian command, through appeal to non rational (in the western sense) authority or procedures, through mediation of third parties based on bargaining, or through direct negotiation or bargaining. In none of these processes is argumentation in the discourse sense necessary. Indeed, in traditional far eastern cultures where interpersonal confrontation is viewed negatively, argumentation is something to be avoided. Some critics have also suggested that the Anglo-American common law is not rational; there is certainly some truth in that, especially if what is meant by rational is discourse theory's thoroughgoing demands for justification. Even in western society today argumentation is often terminated by appeal to religious authority, to a belief system. Could the "rationality" of discourse theory be just another such belief system?

In response to charges of this kind Alexy calls argumentation "the most general form of life of human beings,"[34] implying that all societies engage in it. While a claim might be made that speech in general is the most widely practiced human activity, it may be challenged empirically whether "rational" argumentation is all that widespread. This argument does no damage, of course, to the claims of discourse theory as a theory of rationality in the western tradition, especially the legal tradition. What it does damage, however, is the claim to universality throughout the world. If this critique is correct, then discourse theorists, in order to maintain their claim of universality, must show why western rationality in ordering the affairs of life is superior to other ways utilized in other societies. Why is "rational" better?[35]

34. Alexy, "A Discourse-Theoretical Conception of Practical Reason," supra note 21 at 220ff. See also Alexy, *Theorie der juristischen Argumentation*, supra note 21 at 417ff.

35. Alexy seems to admit this argument at one place. "These universals may in reality hardly be apparent because of the existence of taboos, traditions, or terror." Alexy obviously intends a negative connotation to "taboos, traditions, or terror." In fact, traditions that minimize strife and conflict (and therefore also argumentation) may perform very positive functions in a society. He goes on to say, "However, they would only disappear completely once the participants in any given form of life finally and completely lost the capacity to pose the question: 'Why?' It is for this reason that the rules of discourse do not define a particular form of life [culture], but rather something which has validity or relevance in any form of life whatsoever, albeit to a very variable degree. To this extent discourse theory is an indication of the potential for reason in human reality." The last sentence might be paraphrased, "To this extent discourse theory is an indication of the potential for non-western cultures to acquire the western characteristic of "rationality." Alexy, "A Discourse-Theoretical Conception of Practical Reason," supra note 21 at 221.

A second and related criticism of discourse theory is that the final grounding of discourse rules themselves is flawed.[36] The grounding of these rules is accomplished by characterizing them as following from the "necessary presuppositions" of speech.[37] In order to assert something there must be rules of speech about how assertions are or can be made. We do not create these rules; rather we are stuck with them because we learn them as we learn our natural language, and our natural language is beyond the control of any person or group of persons. But how far do these presuppositions take us?

According to discourse theory, assertions are "speech acts" that raise implicit claims to truth or correctness. This statement may be doubted; at least its basis is unclear. But, in addition, it is declared that "The claim to truth or correctness carries with it an implied claim to justifiability."[38] By justifiability is meant here a willingness to make "rational" arguments in support of the point being made. This, of course, is empirically not the case in most ordinary conversation and does not follow logically from the idea of an assertion. Perhaps more commonly what is implied by an assertion is an appeal to dogma or to facts (for one holding the correspondence theory of truth); or, indeed, the appeal may be to a hypothesis or tentative position adopted as valid for the particular circumstances (as a pragmatist might contend). Indeed, an assertion (of a proposition or a norm) can be made, and often is, on the basis of subjective feelings and attitudes. Justification through the kind of rational argument contemplated by discourse theory is only a requirement because discourse theorists prefer that kind of justification. It is true that in the history of western legal thinking, that kind of justification is traditional. However, such thinking has been called "legalism" and criticized as too narrow.[39] The insistence on rational argumentation seems to be dictated more by the preferences of the discourse theorists than by any presupposed rules of language.

A similar argument can be made against the rules calling for consistency. In everyday experience human beings are not consistent in what they maintain and believe. This is not necessarily due to stupidity or stubborness or lack of reflection. Our upbringing is such that subjective attitudes and beliefs are implanted in our minds. These can come into

36. Or at least no more successful than the grounding of Kant's categorical imperative, a thesis rejected by many philosophers today.

37. For an effective criticism of Habermas' efforts in "grounding" his theory, see William Fusfield, "Can Jürgen Habermas' 'Begründungsprogram' Escape Hans Albert's *Münchhausen Trilemma*?" *Rhetorik* 8 (1989): 73.

38. Alexy, "A Discourse-Theoretical Conception of Practical Reason," supra note 21 at 219.

39. See Judith Shklar, *Legalism* (Cambridge, Mass.: Harvard Univ. Press, 1964).

conflict in certain contexts; however, there is nothing in the rules of language that forces us to give up these incompatible attitudes.[40]

In the same vein of argumentation it may be asserted that the principle of universalizability incorporates certain western values. Although our everyday experience almost entirely disproves it, we in western society like to think that all persons are equal; it is a part of our belief system. When confronted with the myriad ways in which people differ, we must limit this contention to "morally equal." Both the categorical imperative and the rules of discourse theory maintain that this moral equality must be observed. But language and its presuppositions give no justification for this position. The fact that two persons can speak to one another does demonstrate a certain reciprocity, an ability on the part of each to understand the other, but not much more can be implied merely from the use of language. If we look at the entire scope of recorded history, we find that by far in most societies inequality among persons is not only maintained but is held to be justified in the thinking of the society, and of course those societies have managed to coordinate the activities of their members through linguistic communication. Are we to assume that inequality in those societies was due to some defect of language? History also shows that the idea of equality (in the eyes of God) is a judeo-christian doctrine that has been taken over, mostly uncritically, into philosophical and political discourse in western societies.[41] It is thus difficult to accept the position of discourse theorists that the universality principle which assumes equality is dictated by the presuppositions of language. "These attempts to show a universal validity of criteria of rectitude no longer convince us today." [42]

Another form of the argument raised above has been made in terms of "motivation." Put simply, discourse theory tells us that if we want to engage in argument, we must follow the rules of discourse to succeed. This is like telling someone that if he or she wants to play tennis, the rules of tennis must be followed. But what if one doesn't want to play tennis? It is quite conceivable that a person or group holding a position of advantage in society (wealth, power, influence) would see no need to engage in discourse to justify anything. Their communications

40. A scientific analogue to everyday experience here is the competing images of light in physics as waves or as particles.

41. In fact, both conventional democratic political theory and discourse theory insist on assuming not only some kind of moral equality, but that everyone is equally capable of making good political (and moral) decisions. This assumption goes far beyond the recognition of the equal moral worth of each individual. Plausible alternatives are that moral and political decisions can best be made by the wisest, the most experienced, the best educated, the most unbiased or disinterested, or the most faithful to the Truth, etc.

42. Waldemar Schreckenberger, "Notizen über rhetorische Semiotik," *Archiv für Rechts- und Sozialphilosophie* Special Edition 44 (1991), 348, 350.

may consist of commands, threats, pleas, or whatever strategic behavior may be dictated to serve their interests. It is also possible that persons disadvantaged in a particular society would not choose to engage in discourse because they thought it futile. Or, a particular religious sect may refuse to enter into argumentation with outsiders because it believes that they do not understand the true bases for human living. In each of these cases the parties do not want to play the game. This possibility has led Alexy to modify the claims of discourse theory: "It would therefore seem that the transcendental argument can only be used to justify the hypothetical validity of the discourse rules as follows: they are valid wherever and to the extent that there prevails an interest in discourse."[43] He goes on to offer a pragmatic argument that it would usually not be in the interests of any person or group to decline consistently to participate in discourse.

The foregoing criticisms have attacked the transcendental or ultimate justificatory aspect of discourse theory. A different kind of argument, not surprisingly brought by a Kantian, asserts that discourse itself is quite unnecessary.[44] If an individual accepts the Kantian categorical imperative, "Act only on that maxim through which you can at the same time will that it should become a universal law," then the individual must take into account the interests of others, that is, one must place oneself in the position of all other persons. Because of this, the "maxim" will be universal. Under discourse theory each of the participants in the discourse must also undertake this mental role exchange. But if one person can do this alone (monologically), why is a discourse needed? Taking this argument a step further, let us assume that a discourse has taken place and has validated a norm. If an individual later wants to know whether the rules of discourse have been observed, including the rule regarding role exchange, how can this be determined? Either one must do monologically what the Kantian would have done in the first place, or one cannot know whether the discourse was properly conducted. If the former, then why discourse in the first place? Put in a broader way, what does discourse theory add to Kantian morality?

Alexy answers this objection in two ways.[45] First, he says that the inclusion of all participants in discourse is necessary in order to give full recognition to the moral autonomy of others. This does not make clear why the Kantian approach does not also take this autonomy into account. Second, Alexy says that persons in the discourse often have con-

43. Alexy, "A Discourse-Theoretical Conception of Practical Reason," supra note 21 at 221.

44. This is the argument of Ernst Tugendhat discussed in Robert Alexy, *Theorie der juristischen Argumentation*, supra note 21 at 404ff.

45. *Id.*

flicting interests that must be balanced. By balancing, he presumably means that the parties concerned are willing to settle on a position that recognizes part of the interests of both. Since there are no objective standards by which to measure this "balancing," it becomes essentially a matter of reasonable compromise. One individual monologically attempting to reconcile the competing interests of others has no rational guideline and therefore cannot enter into or formulate a compromise. Therefore, according to Alexy, the discourse is necessary in order to furnish the opportunity for compromise in this kind of situation. This answer to the objection makes sense, but it raises a more serious question that will be considered in connection with the next criticism.

This objection asserts that discourse theory distorts the notion of correctness (rightness, rectitude) and thereby offers an artificial concept of rationality. Why should the consensus arising from a discourse determine correctness, other than by definitional fiat? A consensus might involve a compromise, as suggested above, but compromises are the result of negotiation and cannot be right (correct) in the usual sense of conforming to a standard. Consensus itself is not a standard. This objection takes on additional significance when the possibility of the validation of contradictory norms is considered. Alexy admits that the discourse procedure could result in both norm N and norm Not-N being correct (gaining a consensus).[46] This seems contrary to any intuitive notion of correctness. Thus, the argument is made that correctness has been artificially defined to suit the needs of the theory. Alexy's answer is that rectitude (correctness) has an absolute meaning as a "regulative idea," and a single right answer should always be pursued, but it cannot always be expected in real discourse.[47] Besides, legal discourse imposes institutional restraints that ameliorate the deficiencies of general practical discourse so that the problem of conflicting norms is unlikely. Whether this answer is sufficient may be questioned, however, since Alexy says that at all levels of legal discourse there may have to be resort to general practical discourse for supplementation.[48]

The problem of conflicting norms is also the basis for another argument against discourse theory, or to be more exact, for a modification of discourse theory. This comes from Klaus Günther who maintains that discourse theory alone cannot lead to conclusions in the application of the law.[49] He observes that often several "valid" norms that have been

46. Alexy, "Idee und Struktur eines vernünftigen Rechtssystems," supra note 21 at 34.

47. *Id.*

48. Alexy, *Theorie der juristischen Argumentation*, supra note 2 at 291.

49. See Klaus Günther, *The Sense of Appropriateness* (translated by John Farrell, Albany: State Univ. of New York Press, 1993). Original German edition: *Der Sinn für Angemessenheit: Anwendungsdiskurse in Moral und Recht* (1988). See also, Klaus Günther, "Critical Remarks

justified by the theory come into conflict in specific contexts. This problem of "colliding norms" requires another procedural technique that he calls "application discourse." Application discourse seeks to find the "appropriate" norm to govern a case from among those that are valid. The main method of finding appropriateness is to employ a coherence theory in which possible norms are evaluated in the light of all the circumstances, and that norm is found to be appropriate which is most coherent with other proven cultural norms. The foregoing is, of course, an extremely sketchy description of Günther's theory. It is significant, however, that Günther finds it necessary to move away from the method of justification through consensus in discourse to one of coherence. In his view the whole of legal discourse theory collapses as a practical matter unless supplemented by application discourse, which apparently does not involve consensus or the rules of discourse theory.

Finally we come to the principal debate between positivism (analytic jurisprudence) and discourse theory.[50] It should be noticed that Alexy's aims and the aims of positivism have a large area of congruency. Both want to make law rational, both are concerned with arbitrariness in the legal process, and both seek to use logical and linguistic analysis to clarify and explain legal decision. However, the positivists confine their activity to the positive legal system while Alexy applies discourse from the individual legal decision all the way up to the final grounding of moral principles. Alexy makes two major criticisms of positivism. First, he argues that the positivists offer no way to "ground" the legal system.[51] Thus, law becomes a sort of free-floating system of norms whose validity must simply be assumed—a non rational position. Second, he argues that an adequate concept of law must include the attribute of rectitude, thus requiring a necessary connection between law and morality.

The problem of grounding, of course, is only a problem for those who feel that compulsion to seek the intellectual security of an archimedean point. Few would be willing to ask seriously how the rules of tennis are "grounded." Yet the same intellectual problem is involved. For the positivist[52] the answer to the grounding question is the same for the rules of tennis as for the legal system. These normative structures (rules of law and tennis) have been presented to us by history; they are a part of our

on Robert Alexy's 'Special Case' Thesis," *Ratio Juris* 6 (1993), 143, and Alexy's reply thereto in "Justification and Application of Norms," *Ratio Juris* 6 (1993), 157.

50. This issue is the main subject of Alexy's book, *Begriff und Geltung des Rechts*, supra note 4.

51. Alexy gives most of his attention to Kelsen's version of positivism. Kelsen himself says that the *Grundnorm* must be "presupposed."

52. At least for the H.L.A. Hart variety of positivism. See H.L.A. Hart, *The Concept of Law* (Oxford: Clarendon Press, 1961).

inherited culture. This is not to say that we cannot, through collective efforts, change the rules of tennis or the legal system, or that we cannot evaluate them by whatever criteria we wish. However, there is an important difference between changing the rules of the game and inventing a new game. We are not called upon to reinvent all of the rules of law; they lie before us and must be dealt with, hopefully rationally. The problem of dealing with them, or, more accurately, understanding and using them, as well as the myriad other normative systems we encounter in daily life, does not have to involve the question of ultimate grounding.

Of course, there are ways to "ground" a legal system. Natural law theories insist on it. The Kantian approach characteristic of Alexy and Habermas also demands it; but that is because they insist on including a moral component in the law. Thus, the grounding question and the question of the separation of law and morals are intertwined. It becomes a matter of whose definition is more useful.

Alexy argues that the concept of law not only should be defined to include the notion of rectitude, but that it cannot adequately be defined otherwise. His main proof, following Ralf Dreier, consists of giving a number of examples of unjust laws to demonstrate that a non legal law cannot be legal. This seems to involve a semantic confusion that traces back to the use of different definitions. In particular Alexy's example of how non-law can become law within a gang of bandits appears to reveal a fundamental confusion. He claims that coercive orders can become law when the element of rectitude is added, that is, such orders carry "legality" when those issuing them and some number of those upon whom they are imposed think that they are right. But the attitude of people toward the law is really an empirical question to be dealt with by psychology or sociology. No doubt, as H. L. A. Hart suggests, many of the rules of a legal system are internalized by those who operate within it. This is no different from the internalization of the rules of tennis by the players of the game. It is possible for tennis players to recognize that the rules work well enough to make the game worth playing without imputing a notion of moral rectitude to them. Internalization creates no problem of rationality to distinguish rules of morality from rules of law or rules of tennis.

Alexy also adopts Ronald Dworkin's argument that the positivist cannot account for principles (as opposed to rules) within the law and therefore gives an incomplete account. This is a serious objection to positivism. Alexy, however, gives it a different interpretation from Dworkin's. For Dworkin the principles utilized in judicial decision belong to the conventional political morality of the particular society and its legal tradition. For Alexy the principles must carry true moral validity, that is, they must be morally right. There can be no distinction between the correctness of legal rules and the correctness of moral rules. Legal correctness for Alexy means moral rectitude. He argues that when a judge employs a principle in his decisional argument, he makes a claim of correctness for that principle. The claim of correctness implies that the claim is groundable (can be substantiated).[53] This carries us into the grounding process of discourse and ultimately (and ideally) to an absolute moral position. In contrast, positivists usually see these extra-legal principles as drawn from conventional morality.[54]

Alexy insists that defining law in a way that omits the element of rectitude is unacceptable. The reason for this is simple. He, like his natural law predecessors, thinks that it is crucial that law be grounded morally. He therefore insists on a concept of law that includes rectitude and therefore accounts for justice as well. Alexy's theory is consequently much more than just a theory of rationality; it is also a theory of justice.

So what are we to make of discourse theory? It is clear that ideal discourse theory is, because of its impossibility, just another aspirational model; in fact, it is so far into the realm of the abstract and utopian that it does not give useful answers to the questions of legal philosophy. Real discourse theory stands in the shadow of the ideal, and, to the extent that it fails to meet the requirements of the ideal, it loses its force and legitimacy. However, in spite of the many objections raised against it, many readers will feel that the rules of legal discourse as formulated by Alexy make considerable sense. They seem to grapple seriously with the problem of rationality in law. He has written a code for fair argumentation, although its basis is problematic. It seems that his suggestions could be useful within a more traditional analytic or rhetorical framework; but the theory as a whole tries to do too much. As has been pointed out, it turns out to be a theory of justice as well as a theory of rationality, and it is this aspect of the theory that seems weakest. Like earlier natural law theory, it demands a leap of faith to be convincing in the moral dimension.

We have known for a long time that a panel of judges who openly debate an issue are more likely to come up with a better decision than a single judge. Does legal discourse theory tell us anything more?

53. See Alexy, supra note 4 at 132.

54. For a defense of legal positivism against Alexy's attack, see Norbert Hoerster, "Zur Verteidigung der rechtspositivistischen Trennungsthese," *Archiv für Rechts- und Sozialphilosophie* 37 (1990), 27.

Chapter 5
Rhetorical Theory

> There, where today philosophy ends in speech skepticism, rhetoric has begun.
>
> —Otmar Ballweg[1]

Background

The current movement in German legal philosophy designated here as rhetorical theory started with the publication of Theodor Viehweg's *Topics and Law* in 1953. Since that time a number of scholars have explored Viehweg's insights and have expanded the theme. In particular, a small "school" of thought developed around Viehweg and later Ottmar Ballweg and Peter Schneider at the University of Mainz.

Rhetoric was practiced by the ancient Greek Sophists. It was analyzed philosophically by Aristotle in his *Rhetoric* and *Topics* and further adapted and simplified by the Roman jurist, Cicero. Rhetorical ideas were pursued by various medieval scholars and were again resurrected by Giambattista Vico in the early eighteenth century. Friedrich Nietsche's work at the end of the nineteenth century also reflects some similar notions. The current thinking has been influenced by semiotics, particularly the work of Charles William Morris, and the rhetorical theories advanced in the middle of this century by linguistic scholars Chaim Perelman and Noam Chomsky; early critiques that proved valuable to the debate in Germany were contributed by Franz Wieacker and Josef Esser. The discussion which follows is based primarily on the work of Ottmar Ballweg,[2] Wolfgang Gast,[3] and Viehweg himself.[4]

1. Otmar Ballweg, "Semiotik und Rhetorik" in *Rhetorische Rechtstheorie*, ed. Otmar Ballweg and Thomas Seibert (Freiburg: Alber, 1982), 31.

2. Ballweg, supra note 1.

3. Wolfgang Gast, *Juristische Rhetorik: Auslegung, Begründung, Subsumption*, 2d ed. (Heidelberg: Decker, 1992).

4. Theodor Viehweg, *Topics and Law* (translated by Cole Durham, Frankfurt: Peter Lang, 1993). Original German edition: *Topik und Jurisprudenz* (1953).

Aims

Rhetorical theory is essentially a skeptic's theory. This skeptic is one who refuses to accept the abstract arguments for the "ultimate grounding" of the law in immutable moral principles, or who denies that legal discourse can be proved "rational" through a consensus hammered out through debate, or who rejects the strict proof of the certainty of the law through the tricks of symbolic logic. In short, this skeptic is one who thinks that law cannot be turned into morality or geometry.[5] In support of such a position are all the failures to do just this that history has presented.

> The theory of legal rhetoric . . . suggests at first a skeptical basic attitude to every participant in the processes of legal argumentation. Such a skeptical basic attitude is encountered everywhere where the sense of the conditions of practical rhetoric is developed. But here skepticism does not mean . . . the renunciation altogether of influence on practice. Rather, it is thought that a skepticism proceeding from a converse impulse appears suited for a useful influence on practice.[6]

Our skeptic is thus not a complete skeptic. One can reject the various efforts to turn law into a system, or to make it scientific, or to "found" it on objective principles of justice, and yet still recognize that law exists in society, that a very real and teachable practice is carried on that requires intellectual skill, and that practitioners of law can use the assistance of theoreticians who can show them what they are doing and how they should do it. Rhetorical theory disavows the grander moral and scientific ambitions and seeks to accomplish the latter; its approach is to explain how legal debate, drawing on a storehouse of arguments and viewpoints, can bring about agreement and decision, that is, can actually create law. The basic foundations for legal rhetorical theory lie in the practice of law. It is a theory about a practice. Its aim is to inform the work of lawyers and judges.

It is therefore not the object of rhetorical theory to find a moral basis for law, nor indeed to explore the relationship between law and morality. Theories of natural law or of the ultimate grounding of law in morality are therefore irrelevant. Neither should we expect the exploration of the application of scientific method to the law. Rhetoricians are concerned only with rhetorical methods. This also excludes consideration of any behavioral aspects of law. While rhetorical theory is concerned with the analysis of legal language from its own point of view, it does not seek to analyze terms and concepts from the standpoint of positivism or

5. See Heino Garrn, "Zur rechtspraktischen Bedeutung einer Theorie der juristischen Rhetorik," *Archiv für Rechts- und Sozialphilosophie* Special Edition 44 (1991), 96, 102.

6. *Id.* at 101.

analytical jurisprudence, which rhetorical theory regards as fundamentally misguided.

Main Ideas

What, then, does rhetorical theory stand for? A first component is the idea of situational thinking. The situation centers around a problem, in the case of legal rhetorical theory, a legal problem. The starting point for rhetoric is always disagreement or doubt. That there is a problem means that there is or can be a difference of opinion about what the law is in the particular situation. The rhetoricians admit that there are undoubtedly situations in which there is no reasonable disagreement over what the law is.[7] By this is meant merely that everyone who gives thought to the matter holds the same opinion. If asked to explain what the law is on some point, one would give reasons, that is, some kind of argument, and others would agree that this argument is compelling. But in those situations in which the expertise of a lawyer is called upon to state what the law is, the matter is more or less in doubt. This, the concrete problem situation, is the starting point for the operation of rhetorical practice. "The most important point to bring out is that [rhetoric] is the specific art of thinking that always takes its orientation from a problem."[8]

A second component is the notion of topics, or catalogs of arguments that the rhetorician turns to in order to find the means of bringing the opinions of others into line with his. These catalogs may be at varying levels of generality; they may include moral, legal, or political norms and values; they may include procedural considerations or appeals to consistency, to history, or to justice. They furnish the premises for argument about the specific situation. Important here is the fact that there is no necessary logical connection between the different topics. The catalog may be a grab bag. Not everything, of course, can serve as the basis for a legal argument; however, there are a vast array of topics available for the lawyer's use besides the formally legal materials found in statutes and precedents.

This raises the question of the moral or legal "basis" of the law. How can the law, propped up by an interest-guided selection of pertinent arguments, be legitimate? The rhetorician will immediately point out that such a question implies the very type of thinking that rhetorical theory rejects. It assumes that there is some ultimate principle or procedure that justifies legal decisions. Such a line of thinking is rejected for many reasons, the most significant being the past failure of legal theorists to

7. See Gast, supra note 3 at 4.
8. Viehweg, supra note 4 at 9.

demonstrate the connection between such assumed (or speculatively constructed) ultimate principles and the daily operation of legal decisionmaking. However, rhetorical theory recognizes that the use of logic presumes some starting points and that the effectiveness of argument will depend in part on the persuasiveness of those original premises. What would make them persuasive? The answer is very simple, once one rejects the assumption of the necessity for ultimate principles.

The starting points for legal arguments, as Aristotle pointed out long ago, lie in the truths that a society regards as self-evident at any given time.[9] By "truths" here is meant both interpretations of what is the fact (ontological propositions) and of what should be (normative propositions). These truths may be historically contingent, but at any given time a large segment of society accepts them without question; hence they are suitable for use as the basis for argument. Of course, where appropriate for the resolution of a legal question, any such truth may itself be challenged and debated. The study of legal argumentation as it is practiced confirms this view. Ultimate justifications are never sought; solid bases for argument can be found everywhere.

A third closely related component is the idea that law is a matter of opinion, in particular the opinion of the legal community. The statute on the books (the "law" in the layman's eyes) does not enforce itself, nor does it impart an unambiguous and unvarying meaning for every context. That meaning is provided by the persons who must use the law; hence, the opinion of lawyers and judges as to what the law is takes priority over formal sources.[10] "The positive law is overall a fund of effectively potent viewpoints."[11] This view has some curious implications. It means that law in the abstract doesn't mean much of anything; and it further means that in a concrete situation the law may be unsettled, with competing arguments appearing to carry nearly equal persuasive power, and it may remain unsettled because there is no generally accepted opinion on the matter in the legal community.[12] A further consequence is

9. Garrn, supra note 5 at 106. Aristotle described these self- evident propositions as those "which appear to be true to all, or at most to the wise, and again of the wise either to all or to the most, or to the best known or to the most respected." Viehweg, supra note 4 at 9.

10. The reader will note the similarity of perspective to that of the American legal realists. This is not entirely accidental. See Bernd Oppermann, *Die Reception des nordamerikanischen Rechtsrealismus durch die deutsche Topikdiskussion*, doctoral dissertation, Frankfurt University (1985).

11. Gast, supra note 3 at 5.

12. In the common law the doctrine of *stare decisis* operates (as one more reason or argument) to finalize or give authority to one legal opinion in a concrete situation; however, students of the common law know that precedents often fail to constrain future court decisions.

that legal "reality" is not the same as the official formal law, nor is it equivalent to what "courts do."[13] The latter is closer, but is derivative from the more basic *opinion* of judges and lawyers.

At this point we should note the claim of rhetoricians that the rhetorical perspective clashes with some assumptions that are more or less built into the language we use in talking about the law. The first such assumption is that there is one true or correct version of the law, however difficult it might be to discern in some cases. This is the idea that "the law" must be found and applied impartially by courts in contrast to the imposition of subjective views or the use of incoherent political arguments or the injection of the morality of a particular group. For the rhetorician legal argument produces various alternative solutions for specific legal problems; these have varying degrees of plausibility. Some solutions will appear better than others, but none will come labeled as the correct version or be identifiable as such. That version is authoritative ("true," "real") that is accepted by the relevant audience. Another assumption is that one furnishing a legal opinion, a judge or legal expert, is expected to provide genuine enlightenment to his audience; he is expected to speak the truth. Such "truth," in the sense of statements that correspond to reality, or norms that are logically grounded in the axioms of the system, is not achievable because the reality of the legal world is the reality of opinion.[14] Opinion, to use a favorite German term, is not truth-capable [*wahrheitsfähig*]. The soundness of opinion is supported by argumentation.

With these factors in mind we can present in simplified form rhetorical theory's view of the legal process or that part of the process that is of special concern to lawyers. Where a problem of law, that is, a disagreement about the law, arises, various law-trained actors present arguments for the solution of the problem. Depending on their positions, they may argue for certain interests (as with advocates or negotiators for parties) or they may try to be impartial (as with judges or legal commentators); because of their training and the conventions of the society, they generally know what kind of reasons will be acceptable to listeners. They use what they believe to be the most effective arguments from their catalog. They attempt to bring the opinions of others on the matter in question (tied to the context, of course) into line with their own understanding. A congruence of opinion is sought. The arguments of one or another may be successful or not; if successful, agreement will be achieved. This agreement does not need to carry the force of sincere conviction; it may

13. See Katherina Sobota, *Sachlichkeit: Rhetorische Kunst der Juristen* (Frankfurt: Peter Lang, 1990), 20–21.

14. A related assumption is that the self-reflective language used in legal opinion ("the law provides . . . ") consists of or should consist of true statements. According to rhetoricians this also is false because the law is not found but constructed.

be achieved with considerable doubts. The emergent opinion that gains consensus (more or less) is not some form of objective truth, but a *construct* made from the arguments. The communicative process of argumentation does not produce knowledge [*Erkenntnis*], but agreement [*Einverständnis*].[15] Through this process the law itself is created. Legal reality is the product of the argumentation process.

Is there any reason to believe that the law so created is "right" or "just" or has any claim to legitimacy? Such a question might be answered by recourse to a general theory of justice or some theory of legal justification, but we have already noted that rhetoricians reject such approaches. A pragmatic argument is made, however, to the effect that the resulting prevailing opinion on any point (and therefore the law) is the result of weighing alternatives, and, of course, the best alternative is selected.[16] Thus, the winning argument represents the best thinking on the issue that the fund of common wisdom (found in the topoi or catalogs) can supply.[17] In this limited sense the legal outcome can be said to be right or just. This view of justification is, of course, a cousin to the Anglo-American notion that an adversarial legal process is well suited to bring out truth and fairness.

And so it turns out that argumentation and consensus are at the heart of rhetorical theory, just as they are at the heart of discourse theory. But the two part company in several respects. For discourse theory there is, in principle, one right answer; rhetorical theory admits of several plausible solutions. Discourse theory assumes unbiased, systematic, strictly logical argumentation in accordance with the rules of discourse; rhetorical theory admits flexibility of both starting points and methods in argumentation and allows arguments from interest to shape the ultimate agreement. Discourse theory sees argumentation starting from the top and moving down, that is, from the abstract to the concrete; rhetoric always starts from the specific problem situation. Perhaps most important, discourse theory insists on an overall rationality such that legal conclusions can be logically grounded on the higher norms of the system; rhetoric rejects the possibility of such grounding and sees such norms merely as potential bases for argument.

Within the general field of rhetorical theory there appear to be a number of variations. Some rhetoricians, aiming at providing intellectual help to the practice of law, are concerned with the analysis of actual argumentation as it is carried on in the profession. This may take traditional forms; for example, one highly regarded text for students and

15. Gast, supra note 3 at 9.

16. Rhetorical theory here shows an affinity to critical rationalism, but, of course, does not purport to be "scientific."

17. See Garrn, supra note 5 at 102.

practitioners explains, from a rhetorical point of view, the traditional methods of statutory interpretation, types of arguments (*ad hominem, ad absurdum*), analogy, subsumption, definitions, etc.[18] Other theorists have utilized the much more elaborate approach known as semiotics in which communication is analyzed in terms of sign-users, signs, and that which is signified and their corresponding relationships.[19] One author has suggested that a "law and literature" movement might be derived from rhetorical theory.[20] Another uses rhetorical theory to show that a "matter of factness" type of discourse is an essential art for jurists.[21]

It seems clear that many new questions are presented for jurisprudence when the rhetorical approach is adopted: how are topics used in the discourse of a democratic society? Can a more realistic (and humble) role be found for systematic rationality in legal discussion? How can topics be categorized and elaborated in helpful ways? How should legal education be structured and presented? What are the roles of abstraction, rationality, authority, analogy, tradition, the psychology of persuasion in legal argument? While the rhetorical approach accomodates a multiplicity of variations, it differs substantially from other approaches to law such as legal sociology, systems theory, legal positivism, natural law, and discourse theory; it is the theory most closely connected to the practice of law and arguably of most benefit to practitioners.

Critique and Reply

One obvious criticism of rhetorical theory is that it does not attempt to address many of the things that jurisprudence has historically worried about. It does not explain how legal validity is dependent on moral principles. It does not attempt to establish the autonomy of the law. It does not treat the matter of historical development, nor does it take up the question of the just legal system. In short, it does not ask the right questions. The rhetorician's answer to this kind of objection is twofold: some of those matters are left to be grappled with by other disciplines, and some of those questions assume a framework of thinking that cannot pass the skeptical perspective of rhetorical theory, that is, those questions are will-o-the-wisps that philosophers have chased for centuries without ever satisfactorily grasping.

Among the latter type of question is the problem of the legitimacy of

18. See, e.g., the book by Gast, supra note 3.

19. See Ballweg, supra note 1.

20. Peter Schneider, "Jurisprudenz, Utopie und Rhetorik," *Archiv für Rechts- und Sozialphilosophie* Special Edition 44 (1991), 337–338.

21. See Sobota, supra note 13.

law and of the ultimate grounding of the legal system. As we have noted, rhetoricians are skeptical of such undertakings:

These [neo-Kantian] attempts to show a universal validity of criteria of rectitude convince us no longer today. It is certainly no accident that in Kant's legal and moral philosophy are found again the conventional ideas of his time and the requirements of an ascending bourgeoisie. Neo-Kantianism may be regarded finally as a kind of academic religion of the bourgeois world.[22]

Further, rhetoricians have argued that such theories are a waste of time and effort because they are first, unneeded, and second, of no practical value.[23] Abstract justification is unneeded because there are sufficient bases for legal argument in the accepted wisdom of any society[24] and is of no value to the practice of law because it deals in abstractions too far removed from the real problems of the law. "It appears that legal or moral theories exert little direct influence on a society."[25] As one author notes, the actual problems of legal argumentation are not in the direction of substantiating the validity of norms, but in choosing between competing valid norms, fashioning effective justificatory arguments, and reaching conventionally acceptable results in the specific case context.

A second criticism of rhetorical theory is that it is anti-rational, antiscientific, and perhaps anti-intellectual. This argument takes two forms. First, it is claimed that rational argument presupposes a system, a framework or structure in which argument can take place. Since rhetorical theory rejects the idea of an overall system, it necessarily becomes irrational.[26] Both discourse theorists and more conventional analysts see the necessity for an integrated legal order in which the norms of the system cannot be contradictory to each other. In their view rationality means consistency with the provisions of the entire order. The rhetoricians' answer to this is that such system and order are products of the philosopher's mind, not some ontological reality. Rationality for the rhetorician is taken to mean the much simpler idea of using logic to go from premises to conclusions in a particular argument; of course, consistency is itself a basis for argument in the context of a particular case. The necessity

22. Waldemar Schreckenberger, "Notizen über die rhetorische Semiotik," *Archiv für Rechts- und Sozialphilosophie* Special Edition 44 (1991), 348.

23. *Id.* at 350–55.

24. *Id.* at 349; Garrn, supra note 5 at 105–106.

25. Schreckenberger, supra note 22 at 349. Basically the same argument is made by the American, Stanley Fish, "Dennis Martinez and the Uses of Theory," *Yale Law Journal* 96 (1987), 1773.

26. Rhetoricians agree that many discrete areas of the law may be regarded as systems, but deny that a comprehensive system is necessary or important. The strength of the rhetorical position lies in its antisystemic features. See Viehweg, supra note 4 at 20–23.

for overall system consistency is assumed by positivists and discourse theorists, an assumption that is not warranted by experience in the real world of legal argumentation.

Second, it is contended that the willingness of rhetorical theory to accept a logically unrelated multiplicity of bases for argument demonstrates that rhetoric is simply a game—that rhetoricians are interested only in winning cases or writing persuasive opinions to justify a political position, not in the justice or correctness of the law. Without a system designating the rational priorities of the law, argumentation becomes arbitrary. Since good technique of argument can serve bad causes, some critics would add that the endorsement of argumentation for its own sake is an endorsement of the abuse of argument. The rhetorician's reply makes three points. First, the criticism assumes that there is a just or correct law in some absolute sense. For reasons already mentioned, the rhetoricians reject this assumption. Second, the law created through legal argument is not arbitrary because it has come out of a process of rational argumentation that draws on the accepted wisdom of the society; these constraints make it difficult to abuse the process.[27] Third, the rhetorician's view of the legal process more accurately accounts for what actually happens than does any competing theory; the competitor's theories are utopian and therefore essentially valueless.

Does rhetorical theory have any future? It is far from the dominant jurisprudence in Germany today; it has had rough sledding in a legal culture where systemization and abstraction are held in high esteem. However, the theory or something like it is just beginning to become widespread in the land of the common law where it should find a more sympathetic audience.[28] It is perhaps worth noting here why a rhetorical approach should have an appeal to Anglo-American thinking.

First, the history of the common law shows that it did in fact develop along topical lines. Case law was created in an ad hoc and unsystematic fashion, relying on specific arguments appropriate to compartmentalized areas of the law. Common lawyers, typified by Edward Coke, have been traditionally distrustful of generalization and abstract theory. The English law was taught primarily at the Inns of Court from the fourteenth through the seventeenth centuries. These venerable institutions were largely free of the "scientific" doctrines of the universities. Later, both in England and the United States, law was learned by most lawyers in the

27. See Gast, supra note 3 at 275–283.

28. See, e.g., the work of James Boyd White and Stanley Fish. James White, *Heracles' Bow: Essays on the Rhetoric and Poetics of the Law* (Madison: Univ. of Wisconsin Press 1985); Stanley Fish, *Doing What Comes Naturally* (Oxford: Clarendon Press, 1989). See also, Austin Sarat and Thomas Kearns, eds., *The Rhetoric of Law* (Ann Arbor: Univ. of Michigan Press, 1994).

law office. Lawyers and judges were not exposed to the fancy thinking of theorists.

It is significant that in the whole period from Thomas Aquinas through the Spanish natural law thinkers, through Grotius and Pufendorf, there was no common lawyer who attempted to systematize or theorize about the English law.[29] At the turn of the nineteenth century when Jeremy Bentham and John Austin offered scientific-theoretical theories about the law, those theories bore little resemblance to the English practice, and their authors proved to be critical enemies of the common law.[30] Bentham in particular ridiculed the unorganized mass of precedents and procedures that had grown into the English legal "system." What did the common lawyers think they were doing all of this time? It is clear now with hindsight that they were engaging successfully in a rhetorical problem-oriented practice based on topics or discrete areas of judicial doctrine. This tradition of distrust of theory and corresponding high respect for experience has survived down to the present time. Holmes' famous statement that "the life of the law has not been logic; it has been experience" still evokes as much sympathy with today's common lawyers as it did a hundred years ago. The practice of the common law has indeed been, and to a large extent remains, a rhetorical enterprise.

One has only to look at contemporary legal practice in Anglo-American jurisdictions today to see the rhetorical method flourishing. There is little in the way of system in the legislative realm. Statutes, like the early case law, are sporadic, irregular, and ad hoc. Systematic treatment of the body of legislation has seldom materialized.[31] The emphasis on the adversary system also shows a faith in the power of interest to find and fashion adequate legal argument in contrast to reliance on systematic professorial theory. The practice of legal research, the finding and constructing of the valid law, is perhaps most indicative of the rhetorical nature of common law practice. Relying on digests, on annotations, and, especially in the contemporary United States, on word searches in the

29. Thomas Hobbes and John Locke were important political theorists, but they were not trained as lawyers and they did not attempt to give theoretical explanations or guidance to actual English legal practice, although Hobbes attacked the common law from a philosophical standpoint. In the late eighteenth century William Blackstone gave some degree of system to the common law in his *Commentaries*. However, a comparison of Blackstone's work with civilian (Roman) scholarship shows that Blackstone was only superficially systematic. He essentially collected the various topics and lumped them under general headings.

30. Both Bentham and Austin had training and limited experience in English law. Austin had also been influenced by German scholars.

31. The Uniform Commercial Code and the Internal Revenue Code would probably be noted as important exceptions.

great computer data bases, legal research is literally a search of topics for effective legal arguments.

It would appear, then, that the developers of rhetorical theory in Germany should have something significant to say to the Anglo-American legal world. They have been explaining, mainly to an inhospitable audience, how the actual practice of law can be rationalized and guided with the help of rhetorical theory. This is perhaps one of the few areas where German legal philosophy could have a direct and immediate impact on jurisprudential activity in America today.

Chapter 6
Systems Theory

> [The] works [of European jurists] abound with theoretical discussions, which serve little other purpose than to provoke idle discussions, and with metaphysical subtleties, which perplex, if they do not confound the inquirer.
>
> —Joseph Story[1]

Background

Perhaps the best historical example of "systems" thinking was Adam Smith's eighteenth-century view of the economy in which he envisaged individual human beings separately pursuing their personal economic goals in a way that gave rise to a "system" in which the distribution of goods and services was arranged for everyone's benefit. Other modest beginnings in the nineteenth century advanced the idea of "evolved law," that is, that law developed according to factors independent of individual personal will. Marxism advanced the idea that law was determined by economic factors. Other evolutionary theories of law contained similar ideas, and sociology was ultimately forced to take impersonal evolution into account.

A recurring problem with most evolutionary theories was a determinism that ran counter to the everyday experience that individuals make choices, including the choice of whether to comply with norms. Outside the evolutionary tradition the leading theoretical thinkers in sociology, Max Weber and Emile Durkheim, pursuing a kind of methodological individualism, also found no need for a conceptual orientation toward systems theory. The first significant thinking about systems occurred outside the area of law and society, primarily in connection with the

1. Joseph Story, *Commentaries on the Conflict of Laws* (Boston: Little Brown, 1834), 10.

development of certain military weapons in World War II and the development of computers in the immediate post war period.

The theory of social systems has been most fully developed in Germany by Niklas Luhmann, both generally as a sociological theory and specifically as a way of explaining law.[2] Luhmann was originally trained in law and served as a government lawyer before pursuing a scholarly career in sociology. He studied under Talcott Parsons at Harvard in 1960 and 1961, where he was introduced to systems theory. He pursued sociological studies at the University of Münster under Helmut Schelsky and was habilitated in 1966. He joined the faculty at the University of Bielefeld in 1968, where he has remained. In addition to building on the work of Parsons and Ludwig von Bertalanffy, Luhmann has read very widely, and his thinking has been influenced by many scholars in various disciplines, especially Norbert Wiener, George Spencer Brown, Heinz von Foerster, and biologists Humberto Maturana and Francisco Varela. A critical stimulus for perfecting and refining his theory was the intellectual debate with Jürgen Habermas in the 1970s and 1980s.[3]

Although Luhmann's work is spoken of as sociological, it is concerned only with the theory of sociology, or, as it is often called in Germany, social theory. As such, Luhmann's work is not empirical, although he occasionally refers to empirical work done by other sociologists, anthropologists, and historians. As a theoretician, he provides a philosophy of sociology, or of the social sciences generally (the larger, German meaning of sociology), in much the same way that Karl Popper and Hans Albert have provided a philosophy of science in general.

Luhmann's work can be divided into a sequence of steps that have developed from the 1970s to the present. He initially accepted Parsons' adaptation of general systems theory as a way of explaining social behavior. At this time systems were viewed as "open," with inputs and outputs, and with the elements of the system viewed as individual human actions. Later, however, he came to accept the idea that systems could explain society better if they were viewed as closed, that is, as self-operating or self-sustaining processes built around certain structures; he then combined this with the idea developed in biological theory that systems could be self-reproducing, or autopoietic. At the same time, he found it necessary to make a major modification of social systems theory by positing that the basic elements of social systems were not human actions, but communications. Finally, he asserted that because society as a whole was

2. Others who have contributed significantly to the application of systems theory to law are Gunther Teubner and Helmut Willke. Limitations of space do not allow an exposition of their views. It should be noted that these two scholars do not always agree with Luhmann. See the bibliography.

3. See chapter one.

such an autopoietic system, the legal system, the economic system, the educational system, and others could also best be conceptualized as autopoietic subsystems of that overall system.

Aims

After building a radically new multi-disciplinary theory of society, Luhmann extended his approach into the sociology of economics, of education, of science, and of law. While addressing the subject of law from the standpoint of social science, he remains the philosopher of science, aiming to supply a conceptual framework that will, with appropriate empirical and historical study, provide enlightenment. Luhmann does not offer particular suggestions for achieving justice or for justifying or criticizing existing legal arrangements. He explicitly does not try to help judges, legislators, or practitioners in their legal work.[4] In his view, the concept and role of law perceived by these persons operating within the system is an internal one, perhaps suitable for their purposes but not suitable for a scientific understanding of the law.

Luhmann does not undertake to explain all legal phenomena in terms of cause and effect, or even of social "understanding" as that concept was developed by Max Weber. In this respect he departs significantly from the more traditional scientific philosophy of Popper and Albert. Luhmann's systems theory leaves room for causal explanation and empirical science within its contours, but the theory itself is essentially tautological or definitive. It proposes new ways to look at the social world. As Luhmann himself puts it:

> Directly or indirectly the entire investigation that follows has to do with the question [of the specific characteristics of legal operations]. . . . Its starting point is a purely tautological, formal, content-empty answer that says only that all further analyses will appear as the "unfolding" of a tautology, and not as logical conclusions from axioms.[5]

Main Ideas

Luhmann defines law in terms of its function. It is a social system of communication that serves to secure normative expectations. As such, it is an autopoietic subsystem of the social system.

> We maintain that the differentiation of an operatively closed legal system unfolds through recursive relationships of legal operations on legal operations.

4. See Niklas Luhmann, *Das Recht der Gesellschaft* (Frankfurt: Suhrkamp, 1993), 24, 48.

5. *Id.* at 56. Although Luhmann has discussed the law in many publications, this book is his latest and most comprehensive work on this subject, and much of the discussion in the text is drawn from it.

The system operates, like every autopoietic system, in continuous self-contact. In order to be able to qualify its own operations as legal, it must find out what it has already done previously and what it will continue to do in order to qualify its own operations as legal.[6]

To explain this idea, we can start with the notion of several books on a library shelf. One is a law book. Another is a book on economics. Another deals with politics. The texts in the respective books contain discussions about their respective subjects. Discussions of economics are not found in the law book unless they have some particular legal significance, and vice versa. Now suppose that the books are very big and contain *all* the communications about their respective subjects. Further suppose that the books are not inert texts, but data being processed by a dynamic system of computers. New communications are regularly produced by the system, but the system is programmed to steer legal communications to the legal circuit, economic communications to the economic circuit, etc. Which communications belong to which circuit is a question determined by each circuit itself according to its own code. This metaphor roughly suggests Luhmann's idea of a legal system.

Just as the subject matter of the books in our metaphor is divided into categories appropriate for some use, other subsystems of the social system are analogously differentiated. The legal system has become differentiated from the more general system through a historical process of sociocultural evolution, denoting that it performs a certain function for society. Traditionally, among sociological theorists who have considered it necessary for law to have a function, one or the other of two functions have been suggested: social control or conflict resolution. Recently other thinkers have attributed a multitude of functions to the law. Autopoietic theory requires that a functionally differentiated system have only a single function, although the system may perform other functions in a secondary or derivative way. For Luhmann, the function of law, in layman's terms the "reason" for its existence, is to secure normative expectations.

In explaining what is meant by normative expectations, Luhmann suggests a model of human action geared to the expectation of future experience. Human action is directed toward what the human being expects to experience, that is, when one inserts a key in the door and turns it, it is expected the door will unlock. Of course, there are more possibilities of future experience than can actually occur. Luhmann calls this the complexity of the world. We know that the possibilities of further experience may turn out differently than expected, that is, the door remains locked. Luhmann calls this contingency. Contingency is that area of pos-

6. *Id.* at 196.

sibilities that lies between what necessarily must happen and what cannot possibly happen.

We also have expectations with respect to the behavior of other people. Human beings interact in many different ways and develop expectations of how others will react to their own actions, that is, they develop expectations of expectations. Sometimes these are disappointed. An individual who reacts to this disappointment by changing his or her expectations can be said to react cognitively, to learn from the experience. If, however, expectation is maintained in the face of disappointment, one is reacting normatively, claiming that one's expectation of the behavior of others is right. In this way norms are created by individuals.

Humans cannot consciously construe all possible expectations of expectations of others in daily life, so we begin to rely on norms, or rules of thumb, to avoid this strain or difficulty in interaction created by complexity. We further assume that others will act (and react to our own action) according to social rules. To function as a system, such rules must not be idiosyncratic but must be institutionalized by society so that our assumptions about others' behavior are generally reliable. Our norms must be congruent with those of others. This congruence is achieved through a process of institutionalization.

Stabilization of expectations of expectations through the structure of norms is essential to reduce the complexity of life. The norm structure thus becomes a support or a social guarantee of how others will behave. Life would be entirely too complicated, and cooperation toward common ends impossible, if all norms of behavior (possibly including contradictory norms) fluctuated unpredictably. The social mechanism that guarantees, or perhaps more accurately exerts pressure toward, observance of the most important norms, is the legal system.

This institutionalization of certain expectations could accomplish what has been called "social control," and, of course, institutionalized norms are also commonly applied through legal processes to resolve conflicts. These two functions (or performances, accomplishments) of the law are, however, secondary. They are, in Luhmann's view, special cases of the more general function. This is true because law often produces conflict as well as resolving it. Moreover, law often enables people to do things if they want to, but in so enabling does not "control." Nor does law control in the sense that it is primarily an instrument through which certain persons exercise power over others, although in some circumstances it may have that effect.

As an autopoietic system, the law internally processes legal communications. Like analogous processes in a living cell which reconstitute and reproduce the cell, the operation of the legal system continuously produces and reproduces the system itself (it reproduces meaningful legal communications). Law comes out of law. Hans Kelsen had this insight years ago in a non-system form. In his "Pure Theory," laws are norms that derive their validity (their legal existence) from other norms. To Kelsen, only through judicial decision or legislative enactment could more law be created or older law be abolished. However, Kelsen's scheme was static and hierarchical. It required a hypothetical Grundnorm as the basis of all legal validity. When viewed as a dynamic autopoietic system, (valid) law continuously produces (valid) law through its communicative operations. There is no starting point and no ending point (unless the system disintegrates). One communication leads to another, which leads to another, and so forth.

In Kelsen's theory the content of law could change through legislation or judicial application. So, too, in systems theory. Law absorbs change, sometimes abruptly, sometimes gradually, as the system receives stimuli from its environment and as the law reflects upon itself. Far from being static, the system is constantly remaking the law.

> In a sense the law is an historical machine, namely insofar as every autopoietic operation changes the system, displaces the machine into another condition, and thereby creates changed starting conditions for further operations. In the terminology of Heinz von Foerster it is not a matter of a trivial machine that continuously transforms inputs and outputs in the same repetitive way (if it doesn't make a mistake or collapse), but a machine that brings its own condition into play with every operation and therefore constructs a new machine through every operation.[7]

In reducing complexity, the legal system limits itself to certain kinds of communications, that is, only certain kinds of communications generate further communication and thereby continue operation of the system. Somewhat like a digital computer, law does this by selecting communications according to a binary code, the code of "lawful/unlawful" (*Recht/Unrecht*).[8] The legal system does not recognize discourse that does not relate to this distinction. It is not concerned with stupid/clever, true/false, wealth/poverty, or good/bad. Communications involving these or other distinctions are processed by the general social system or by other differentiated subsystems. In Luhmann's theory the true/false distinction, for instance, is the code for scientific discourse, and payment/nonpayment is the code for the economic system.

A particular communication may possess meaning for more than one social subsystem. For example, the statement that "X has paid back a

7. *Id.* at 58.

8. This code could be translated as: law/non-law, right/wrong, legally valid/legally invalid, just/unjust, legal/illegal. It might make a difference in certain contexts which term is used.

loan from the bank" has economic significance (transfer of funds from X to bank) and therefore is a communication within the economic system. However, the statement also has legal significance (fulfillment of a contract, extinguishment of a legal debt) and therefore is also a legal communication. Obviously, in today's society many communications can have legal, political, economic, moral, and other meanings. Because of the binary coding of each system, however, the communication will have only one meaning within each system. This sheds light on our frequent usage of such terms as "In contemplation of law, X is . . . "; or "The legal significance of X is . . . "; or "In the eyes of the law, X is . . . ".

The coding is what gives communication within the legal system its legal meaning and excludes from the system other meanings. Through self-reflection the system constructs a legal world that mirrors or duplicates its environment (including other systems in its enviroment), but the duplication is incomplete. Only legally relevant communications are operative. In this internal world, what is correct or true or required or permitted is only that which is legally correct, legally true, legally required, and legally permitted. Thus, a system of legal meaning is created.

Luhmann explains that the operations of the legal system are programmed. The programs are characterized as conditional, that is, they take the form of "if . . . , then . . . ". For example, if one negligently injures another, then one must pay damages. Viewed from a static perspective, these programs are legal norms or norm complexes. Viewed from a dynamic perspective, they are guides to system operations. Contrasted with conditional programs are purposeful programs that are phrased in terms of accomplishing some goal. Conditional programs look backward and are oriented to past events; purposeful programs aim for future results. While purposeful programs may be useful for making decisions in areas like economic planning or project engineering, they cannot be used by the legal system. They leave too many loose ends. The legal system must operate in a more certain and predictable manner; otherwise it would not secure normative expectations.

> The form of the conditional program is one of the greatest evolutionary accomplishments of social development. They are found soon after the introduction of writing in Mesopotamia, and certainly in the divinatory texts of wisdom theory, in medical texts, and legal texts. In a rapidly changing world they offer the possibility of introducing order in the form of secure connections, and this likewise in areas in which it depends (according to present day concepts) on knowledge, or rather normative regulation.[9]

With this rough idea of Luhmann's notion of law and the legal system in mind, it will be helpful to examine his general systems theory. This is

9. Luhmann, supra note 4 at 196.

not easy, because the theory is very abstract, and Luhmann uses terms in specific ways that depart from normal word usage. Hence, it is easy to become confused.[10] In this respect we have a interesting parallel to a development that took place in the United States in the 1940s and 1950s when Myres McDougal and Harold Lasswell developed an approach to understanding politics and law that was called "Law, Science, and Policy" (or LSP). They developed their own jargon and used common words as special terms of art. The result was that most of those in the audience to which they appealed did not understand them. On the other hand, most of those who did understand their new system thought it a wonderful intellectual advance.[11] The same can be said of Luhmann at this point. Many of his critics seem unable to penetrate his message, but his followers are enthusiastic, perpetuating the Luhmannese.

We may take as a starting point the complexity of human experience as mentioned above. The world is complex in the sense that human beings must simplify it, reduce the contingency in their expectations in various ways in order to deal with it. This reduction in complexity can be accomplished by social systems. The way in which a system reduces complexity can be illustrated by a very simple example. A thermostat in a home is attached electrically to a furnace. When the furnace runs, hot air is produced and funnelled into the room where the thermostat is located. The thermostat is set so that it turns on the furnace when the temperature in the room drops below 70 degrees Fahrenheit and turns it off when the temperature reaches that figure. The system in a sense "knows" when it should produce heat and when not. It is built so as to select information (the temperature) that is relevant to its function and to ignore all other information. That the walls of the room are painted green, or that the humidity is 90%, or that a chess game is being played in the room, all mean nothing to the heating system. The only thing that has meaning is the temperature. The complexity of the enviroment is thus reduced to a simple binary relationship: over 70 degrees/under 70 degrees, or, within the system itself, run/do not run.

This example also illustrates how Luhmann intends to use the term "meaning." The crude heating system "knows" only two possibilities. At any given time it is selecting from between those two; it determines the actual temperature from the possible. In simplified terms, meaning is the continuous rearrangement of the difference between possibility and

10. At least two books have been written that attempt to simplify systems theory and make Luhmann's work more understandable. See Georg Kneer and Armin Nassehi, *Niklas Luhmanns Theorie sozialer Systeme* (Munich: W. Fink, 1993); Peter Fuchs, *Niklas Luhmann—beobachtet: Eine Einführung in die Systemtheorie* (Opladen: Westdeutscher, 1992).

11. See the discussion of this movement in James Herget, *American Jurisprudence 1870–1970: A History* (Houston: Rice Univ. Press, 1990), 220.

actuality. This is not a psychological or logical use of the term; meaning in the systems sense does not refer to any kind of mental process. The heating system does not "think," however, the reader will note that in describing the operation of the heating system, we have used terms that are normally reserved for descriptions of mental activity.[12] Luhmann also uses such anthropomorphic terms, perhaps necessarily, throughout his work. In the case of the simple heating system, we need not worry about confusing its operation with the mental activity of a thinking being. But this is not always so clear as we move to more abstract and complicated ideas in Luhmann's discussion. We will return to this problem below.

The thermostat illustration can also serve to demonstrate the fundamental idea of a system. A system is an operating entity that functions through its own structures and processes. In our example the system consists of the totality of components that systematically perform the function of heating (the thermostat, the furnace, the electrical wiring, etc.) plus their dynamic operations. Everything else is the environment of the system.[13] This distinction between system and environment is an important basic concept in Luhmann's thinking.

Let us now turn to the idea of social systems. How are they constituted? In most classical sociological theory the basic element of society was the individual human being, or the Weberian "human action," or the Habermasian variant, "communicative action." Using one of these ideas as basic, sociologists could describe patterns of behavior, social structures, and relationships of various kinds. Luhmann rejects these traditional concepts. For him the basic component of a social system is "communication." Social systems process communications through their operations and structures.

At this point the reader will see that Luhmann's approach is radical, indeed. Not only are human beings and human actions not the basic elements of a social system, they are not part of the system at all. Human beings, from the viewpoint of systems theory, are a part of the world, and they are themselves a complex of systems. They consist of various physiological systems, including neurological systems, as well as psychic systems, and perhaps others. Each system processes its own basic elements. What Luhmann calls the psychic system, or system of consciousness, comes closest to what would more traditionally be called "mind." The mind, or consciousness system, processes thoughts. These human systems are independent of social systems, that is, they are part of the environment of social systems, and in turn social systems are a part of

12. This tendency seems inevitable when talking about social systems; hence the title of one of Gunther Teubner's works: "How the Law Thinks," *Law and Society Review* 23 (1989), 727.

13. The heating system is not an autopoietic system, however.

their environment. This is not to say, of course, that social systems could exist without human beings. Social systems, as others, are dependent on their environments, including the existence of human beings.

Human beings, or their psychic systems, clearly have some impact on the social system of communication. Luhmann calls the connection between these two systems a "structural coupling," apparently meaning that the communicative system is necessarily and permanently linked together with individual psychic systems (minds). The thoughts that operate within a system of consciousness can lead to expression in speech or writing. That expression will become communication within the social system or one of its subsystems. There is no communication within the psychic system, only the production of ideas and trains of thought; but there are no thoughts within the social system, only communication. The relationship between the psychic system and the social system is not causal. One system can only excite, irritate, or stimulate the other.

In Luhmann's view communication itself has three components: information, utterance (or articulation, transmission), and understanding. Information refers to the content or substance of the communication, utterance to the mode of expression (written, spoken, poetic, humorous), and understanding to the way in which the communication is interpreted and therefore potentially leads to the next communication. Since these three components require at least two persons (psychic systems) to operate, communication can only take place in a situation involving at least two persons. Accordingly, Luhmann rejects the idea of a "communicative act" that could be performed by one person. In Luhmann's world of communication, human beings (their psychic systems) become points of reference, addresses, semantic artifacts, which exert perturbations or stimuli on the communicative system, or may be influenced by it, but are not a part of it.

Luhmann pictures society as a great buzzing network of communication. The social system is one vast network that processes communications with a resulting reduction of complexity. The world itself, of course, consists of much more than communication, but all the rest becomes the system's environment. Part of that envirolment consists of physical things, and part of it consists of other systems, such as the psychic (consciousness) systems of human individuals. Within the social system there are also subsystems (of communication) which include, among others, the economic system, the educational system, the political system, the religious system, the system of science, and the legal system. Just as the general social system has the function of generally reducing the complexity of the world, each subsystem reduces complexity in a special way within its particular field. This can be conceived in terms of meaning. The various communicative systems are systems of meaning—legal meaning, economic meaning, scientific meaning, and so forth. Each system screens communication for the meaning connected with its function and thereby reduces its complexity.

Where did all these systems come from? According to Luhmann, they evolved historically through functional differentiation. The Durkheimian idea of the differentiation of society through the division of labor furnishes the model. Through time, societies develop different ways of doing things; some of these ways work better than others in serving the functions that keep society going, and they are preserved. Where there is a division of labor, that is, where workers do different jobs compared with simpler societies where individuals or families do everything themselves, various advantages are achieved for the society with the division of labor. As modern societies have developed, Luhmann notes that certain communicative functions have been taken over by subsystems. The differentiation of the legal system from a more traditional and amorphous moral-political-religious-legal system occurred in the eighteenth century when positive law lost its traditional and religious moorings. Such subsystems were not invented by anyone; rather, they are the product of sociocultural evolution. Thus, the idea of evolution becomes important for Luhmann's theory; indeed, the presence of functional systems presumes a kind of evolutionary origin. In turn, Luhmann's theory sheds some new light on the phenomenon of sociocultural evolution.

But how can this evolutionary differentiation come about? Luhmann suggests that the increasing complexity of the world (in the sense described above) drives the formation of social subsystems. In the case of law, the need to stabilize normative expectations became more intense with the increase in kinds and numbers of potential social relationships brought about by relatively radical changes in society. The old mushy mix of religion, morality, and law became inadequate to meet expectations of expectations. A system with a more definite norm structure that could be changed to meet new circumstances was needed. A dynamic system that could define itself was called for.

Such a communicative system is conceived to be self-referential, self-maintaining, and self-reproducing. The system itself produces and reproduces all of its own components; it is autopoietic. Thus it is closed in one sense and open in another. It is closed because the environment can have no effect on its internal operations; those operations are determined only by the system itself, that is, there is no input or output. However, it is open in the sense that the system can learn about its environment and react to it. It is said that autopoietic systems are "operationally closed and cognitively open."

The notion of autopoiesis was borrowed from biological theory, and an illustrative model can be presented from that field. A living cell is autopoietic. It absorbs nutriments and energy from its environment and transfers wastes back to the environment. Through its own operations it consitutes itself and reproduces itself. While the cell is dependent on the environment, the environment cannot alter or determine the operations of the cell; these are entirely controlled by the cell itself. In the course of its operations the cell makes its own structures and biochemical processes. The limits of the cell, its boundaries, its unity, are also defined and produced by the cell itself. Of course, the cell fulfills a function in a larger lifesystem.

Luhmann says that autopoietic social systems are capable of observation. Since these systems are not thinking (conscious) systems, and we usually think of observation as a capacity of the conscious mind, a modified concept of observation is required. Luhmann proposes that observation be tied to the idea of distinction. When we make an observation, we distinguish something from something else (cold/hot, man/woman, plain/fancy) by designating one or the other. "The coffee is hot." Although both sides of the distinction are logically given at the same time, we can only designate one side of the dichotomy at one time (in one operation). We can, of course, designate the other side—"The coffee is cold"—at another time (in another operation). For Luhmann, this is the essence of observation: it is the designation of one side in the framework of a distinction.

This apparently peculiar characterization of the idea of observation is general enough that it can be used in relation to any kind of system; it is not limited to psychic systems. To take our earlier example of the simple heating system, the thermostat operates on the basis of the distinction between temperature above/temperature below. It distinguishes low temperature, and the system turns on; later, it distinguishes higher temperature and the system turns off. We can say that the system observes the temperature. Such an observation can only be made on the basis of the distinction that is chosen. The thermostat cannot observe red/green, smooth/rough, citizen/alien. Consequently a system cannot observe itself at the same time that it is observing in accordance with its original distinction. However, another system can observe the observation made by the first system; or, the first system, in another operation using a different distinction, can observe its own primary observance. Luhmann calls this "observation of the second order." Autopoietic systems observe their own operations in this way.

In the case of operatively closed social (communicative) systems, all communications are internal. Therefore, the observation of a system operation by the same system is an operatively produced construction of the system. This capacity for self-organization results in an ability of the system to describe itself. For example, since the legal system's communications deal with all facets of life that are relevant to the law, the system constructs internally a reproduction of all of those facets, but only to the extent that they have meaning for the law. Thus, a construct such as a "legal person" is created that has some attributes of human beings, but not all; only those attributes that have legal significance are reflected (capacity to sue, inherit, marry, divorce, contract, vote).

The reader will now see that Luhmann's model of the legal system resembles a sort of dynamic positivism. As in traditional positivist theories, Luhmann's world contains a clear and unbridgeable separation of law from religion, morality, and politics. This is accomplished through the closure of the autopoietic legal system. Only legal communication can come from legal communication. The binary code lawful/unlawful screens out other kinds of discourse. At the same time the system continuously adjusts its internal operations to remain consistent.

> We understand as "system" not, like many jurists, an interconnection of coordinated rules, but an interconnection of factually executed operations that as social operations must be communications, however they may additionally be distinguished as legal communications. That means that the original distinction must be sought not in a norm or value typology, but in the distinction between system and environment. . . . Normally legal theories are related to structures (rules, norms, text) that are classified as law. That is especially true for theories of positive law; it is explicitly true, for example, for the "rules of recognition" in Hart's legal theory. The question what is and is not law is thereby asked only with respect to the specifically determined rules. If one would follow the encouragement that has been given by the newer systems theory, then one must change over from structures to operations.[14]

Luhmann has also apparently solved two difficulties that traditional positivist theories have encountered. The first is the question of how positive law becomes "valid." Conventional positivist theory proposes a hierarchy of norms. A particular judgment is valid because it follows from the application of a valid rule; the rule is valid because it is duly enacted by the legislature; the legislative enactment is valid because done in accordance with the valid constitution; the constitution is valid because it corresponds to the Grundnorm or the Ultimate Rule of Recognition. The justification of the Grundnorm, however, is a traditional puzzle.[15] Luhmann provides the merry-go-round solution to this problem.[16] The legal system is a continuing operation; it has been operating

14. Luhmann, supra note 4 at 40–41.

15. For Hans Kelsen the Grundnorm must be "presupposed" as the condition for the existence of a legal system. For H.L.A. Hart the Ultimate Rule of Recognition is either "accepted" or not by a particular society, a matter of empirical fact.

16. The reader will recall that this is the third option in Hans Albert's Münchhausen Trilemma. See chapter three.

in modern Western societies at least since the eighteenth century. Law is validated by law which is validated by law which is . . . etc.

> Validity is a product of the system worked out from moment to moment. It is therefore to be secured only through recursive networking of operations with the least possible expenditure of information. . . . The changeover from hierarachy to time allows us to give up a normative grounding of validity in "higher" norms.[17]

There is no hierarchy; everything is contemporaneous. Luhmann says that validity is the symbol of the unity of the legal system. It is the meaning of "legal."

The second difficulty to which the positivist perspective can give rise is its statist orientation. The hierarchy of legal norms is often interpreted to imply a hierarchy of governmental organization and the idea that law can come only from the top down. As we have noted in chapter one, this implication produced much soul-searching on the part of German jurists after World War II in response to allegations that a climate of positivism had enabled the Hitler regime to impose an evil order. Luhmann avoids this problem entirely. With the merry-go-round solution, no hierarchy is necessary or suggested, and, indeed, the legal system as a system operates itself. For instance, the autopoietic legal system provides a new and insightful account of how common law judges make case law from other case law.

Luhmann's solution to the problem of validity gives rise, however, to another question. When and how did this buzzing perpetual motion system come into existence? When was the first norm legally "valid?" The question in Luhmann's terms, of course, is how and when did the legal system become differentiated from the general social system and become closed. Autopoietic systems either exist (are closed) or they do not. It is difficult to see how evolution can accomplish this jump. Luhmann's response to this problem is less than crystal clear:

> The evolution of the law as an autopoietic system is no problem. The time necessary for that is always a construction in the middle of time, in the respective present. And, in any case, with the objectifying perspective of an historian one can ask about the conditions under which such a construction can be offered as plausible. There must have been, for example, conflicts in which the winner can assert his victory as law and therefore binding for the future.[18]

Luhmann's position on natural law follows the positivist tradition. He sees natural law as a theory or ideology that justifies the law, when the law needed to be justified, by combining the concepts of moral and legal

17. Luhmann, supra note 4 at 109–110.
18. *Id.* at 57–58.

validity; it provides an ultimate grounding in religion, or the nature of humanity as created by God, or something similar. This theory suited an "early European" society where positive law had not yet been differentiated, and the idea of law was bound up with moral and religious notions. In today's society moral discourse is excluded from legal communication by the binary code of the legal system. We have a positive law. Luhmann recognizes, of course, that many legal norms have the same substantive content as moral norms and that morality has undoubtedly greatly influenced legal thinking.

Critique and Reply

A number of objections to Luhmann's theory have been raised by both legal philosophers and sociologists. We can consider here only a few of the main ones, both to systems theory generally, and to Luhmann's legal theory.

The first critique is an overall objection to the application of systems theory to society. This kind of theory obviously has a place when the subject is computers, games, electronic processing of data, and the like. Its application in biology may still be controversial, but there at least it has intuitive plausibility. Applying it to society, however, requires us to reject all of our old notions and to accept an especially odd concept of "communication," one that seems to have no necessary connection with human thinking. The fact that this new idea of communication is difficult for mere mortals to grasp does not, of course, mean that it is wrong or lacks utility. It may be the great paradigm breakthrough for social theory, or it may be another "phlogiston" or electromagnetic "aether." Luhmann has written fifty books and over 300 articles and book chapters (not counting translations), yet he has only a relative handful of followers among legal theorists. The case of McDougal and Lasswell and their system of LSP, mentioned above, comes to mind. In addition, leading proponents of systems theory in other areas, in particular Maturana, Varela, and Heinz von Foerster, insist that social systems cannot be autopoietic. Although one can gradually absorb a social systems orientation by reading about it, an intuitive grasp of it is elusive. Luhmann may have taken some long steps down a road so mysterious and paradoxical that few will follow.

Luhmann counters this objection by pointing out that new paradigms both are hard to come by and require a complete rethinking of the subject. He also points out, correctly, that many critics who feel uncomfortable with systems theory have failed to make the effort to understand it. As to the charge of nonadaptability of the idea of autopoiesis to social systems, Luhmann says that these critics fail to understand that the basic element of social systems is communication, not human action. With respect to empirically oriented American critics, Luhmann suggests that their traditional social theory has not reflected the level of abstraction and degree of rigorousness that European social theory has. They should try harder.

A second problem with Luhmann's theory is its own status as a theory. It is not clear whether the legal system, as an autopoietic subsystem of communications, is supposed to "exist" as a matter of fact, or whether it is a concept, an intellectual tool that can be used to organize our thinking about law, or whether it is a sort of mental construct that only leads to interesting insights (which it does).[19] Is a social system an analytical construct or an ontological entity? At times Luhmann talks about the system as though it arose, came into being, at a point in European history just like the Black Plague or the Industrial Revolution. Or, similarly, he talks about its operation in the context of contemporary German constitutional rights. At other points Luhmann suggests that law as an autopoietic system is a matter of definition, an explicit tautology. Putting the question another way, some critics have said that Luhmann's theory is a belief system not empirically verifiable. The response seems to be that such an objection assumes a Popperian type of paradigm of natural science where empirical research is designed to verify or falsify general laws hypothesized by theory. The theory of social systems does not belong to that paradigm (or, in Luhmann's own terms, to the subsystem of natural science with its code of true/false). Social systems theory is an overarching theory that has itself as one of its subjects. Just what Luhmann's theory is, as a threshold question, nevertheless, remains problematic in the eyes of many critics.

Another problem related to the question of definition may be stated as follows. Accepting Luhmann's approach, how do we know what systems there are? The standard ones mentioned by Luhmann are the political, legal, scientific, religious, educational, and moral. Are there others? What about medical, welfare, transportation, philosophical, agricultural, military, or entertainment systems? Or, more controversially, how do we know that the legal system and the political system are not one political-legal system?[20] How do we determine whether any of these

19. It may be that Luhmann's systems theory offers a new and helpful way to analyze laws or legal problems, without providing any program for empirical research. For work done along these lines, see Michael King and Christine Piper, *How the Law Thinks About Children* (Aldershot: Avebury, 1990); Gunther Teubner, "Unitas Multiplex: Corporate Governance in Group Enterprises" in *Regulating Corporate Groups in Europe*, ed. David Sugarman and Gunther Teubner (Baden-Baden: Nomos, 1990).

20. Such a characterization would be well received by many legal theorists like the American legal realists, the German *Freirechtler*, and the proponents of sociological juris-

have "differentiated out" from the general social system? Is the answer empirical or definitional? Are the systems created by God, by Nature, or by Luhmann? Is it possible that Luhmann has confused what are contingent and historically particular ideas about conceptualizing social processes or ways of organizing decisionmaking with some sort of evolutionary universality? Again, in trying to answer these questions, we face the same ambiguity about the status of the theory mentioned above.

A further objection is raised in this general vein. Luhmann's concept of communication is also a creature of his definition. He presents us with the idea of a screening process or operation that reduces the complexity of the world. But isn't the complexity of the world something created by the human mind? Intuitively, at least for adults, the world is complex in some ways and simple in others; there is no a priori complexity. The idea of complexity itself includes the notion of difficulty of comprehension or prediction, a notion related to our mental processes. Yet Luhmann's ingenious way of defining communication is a clear attempt to avoid any necessary connection with thinking or mental processes. Otherwise systems couldn't communicate unless they could think. It would appear that Luhmann's use of the term "communication" may obscure more than it explains.

This leads to a more general objection along the same lines. To describe social systems or their operations Luhmann constantly uses terms imported from the realm of discourse about the mind. Does this not at the very least lead to confusion? For example, legal norms, as programs, are an important part of Luhmann's theory, and they are a part of the operations of a "mindless" legal system of communication. But Luhmann forms his concept of a legal norm from the more elementary idea of disappointed expectations. Can expectations be defined or characterized in a way that avoids reliance on mental processes, emotions, or ideas?[21] Recognizing this difficulty, Luhmann recently has cleverly provided an explanation of expectations in terms of "time bonds" or time commitments, but this explanation is obscure and consequently unpersuasive.

Another example of the borrowing of terms from traditional discourse about mind is Luhmann's concept of understanding. Understanding is apparently made a necessary component of communication in order to account for the interpretive aspect of it. But can understanding be

---

prudence who have gone to great efforts to prove that law and politics are inseparable. Luhmann's insistence that these are two distinct systems possibly reflects his legal educational background built around German positivism. See chapter eight.

21. Expectations, and norms as well, can be observed as "facts" under more conventional sociological theory (usually characterized by methodological individualism), but such observation usually implies the Weberian notions of meaning (*Sinn*) and understanding (*Verstehen*) that Luhmann is seeking to get away from.

understood apart from thinking or mental activity? Luhmann seems to say that understanding occurs when a communication leads to further communication. This avoids attributing thinking skills to the system, but it seems to have nothing to do with what could possibly be understood as "understanding." The use of a term or concept in an exceptionally unique way may hide an important fallacy.

One further example can illustrate the point. Luhmann makes a convincing argument by defining simple observation in terms of distinction and designation. We can understand how a heating system "observes" the temperature in its environment, although we recognize that this somewhat stretches the ordinary meaning of the word "observation." However, from this simple notion of observation Luhmann moves to more complex observations of a system by itself and even to the capacity of a system to describe itself. How this capacity is based on simple observation remains obscure. It certainly appears that thinking capabilites are being attributed to the system.

Our final criticism of the general systems theory relates to Luhmann's concept of structural coupling—the connection that one system makes with another. The most important such connection is that between the psychic system of human beings and the social system of communication. Both systems are said to be autopoietic, and so their operations are completely self-determined. Although Luhmann says there can be no communication without consciousness (the functioning of psychic systems), he also maintains that one system cannot communicate with the other; there are no communicative and no causal connections between the operations of one system and the other. One can influence the other only as a source of "irritation, stimulation, or disturbance" (irritation is a "system condition").[22] Does this explain anything? Ideas seem to originate in the mind, but find their way into Luhmann's nonhuman communication in some mysterious way. It is clear why Luhmann wants to keep thought and communication separate; without this distinction the whole theory of social systems would go down the drain. But the price paid for the separation is that there seems to be no way to put the two back together again.

Let us now turn our attention more specifically to some criticisms of Luhmann's idea of law. It might at first be objected that systems theory does not answer many of the traditional questions of jurisprudence; it does not give any guidance to lawyers or judges. We must remember, however, that this is not the purpose of systems theory. We cannot criticize Luhmann for failing to do something that he has not tried to do.

22. The German terms here are *Irritation, Reizung,* and *Störung.* These terms sound as if they have been borrowed from a biological context.

Theorizing about law from the internal point of view (the view of teachers and scholars of law) belongs to the legal system itself.

More questionable is Luhmann's idea of the function of law. It might be argued that Luhmann's definition of the function of law seems designed to meet the requirements of the rest of systems theory, rather than describing any intuitive or empirical concept of function. Expectations are often secured by means other than law. Ongoing relationships such as those in the family, at the workplace, or in continuing business dealings often secure expectations simply because of their more or less permanent nature. Legal obligations incurred in such relationships usually come into play only when the relationship breaks down. Parents will normally support their children, employers will normally pay their employees, and sellers will meet their obligations to their regular customers. All these expectations will be met, not because of the threat of legal enforcement but because they are necessary to facilitate the ongoing relationship. Insistence on the observance of legal norms in such relationships can be counterproductive and will often be deliberately avoided. Conceivably an empirical study might show that more expectations are secured in this way than by the legal system. If so, this puts in doubt the importance or necessity for a special societal subsystem aimed solely at securing normative expectations. It also suggests that law, if it must have a sole function, actually serves the more modest purpose of cleaning up social messes (resolving conflicts?) after relationships have broken down.

The principal criticism of Luhmann's legal system is, however, the same criticism that has been leveled at positivists for a long time. In conventional terms, we would say that there is a failure to establish the autonomy of the law. With reference to Luhmann's theory we would say that the system is not closed. The binary code of lawful/unlawful does not work. Law cannot produce law by itself because the operational network is full of breaks. The legal system is not an airtight construction of rules and concepts that can be employed with rational rigor (or should we say mechanically or electronically?) to determine the outcome of cases. It is a loose assemblage of rules, doctrines, principles, concepts, and interpretations floating on a bed of changing social conventions and beliefs (including morality and politics). Ronald Dworkin has probably made the best case for this in recent years.[23] Luhmann's theory bears too close a resemblance to Kelsen's classic Pure Theory in this respect. Both are too pure to reflect the realities of the legal process with any degree of adequacy. Both give exaggerated significance to the role of official

23. See Ronald Dworkin, *Law's Empire* (Cambridge, Mass.: Harvard Univ. Press, 1986); *Taking Rights Seriously* (Cambridge, Mass.: Harvard Univ. Press, 1977).

norms, a flaw, from an Anglo-American perspective, common to much of the German jurisprudential tradition.

Luhmann's reply presumably would echo the position of more traditional positivists. The skeptics mistake the exceptional case for the normal one. Most legal norms are clear and can be applied easily to the situations they are intended to cover. The "hard" case will come up from time to time and must be resolved with creative interpretation; but the legal system provides for this as a part of its operations. If there were no operating system using the code lawful/unlawful and programming clear and sharp norms, the activity of the judge would be a sham, and the activity of the legislator would be futile. When one moves away from the hard case, the system itself appears solid, functional, indispensable.

Chapter 7
Institutional Legal Positivism

> The author . . . makes observations concerning human affairs, when of a sudden I am surprised to find that instead of the usual copulations of propositions, *is*, and *is not*, I meet with no proposition that is not connected with an *ought*, or an *ought not*. . . . For as the *ought*, or *ought not*, expresses some new relation or affirmation, it is necessary that it should be observed and explained; and at the same time that a reason should be given, for what seems altogether inconceivable, how this new relation can be a deduction from the others which are entirely different from it.
>
> —David Hume[1]

Background

Institutional legal positivism, also called the institutional theory of law, is associated primarily with the Czech-Austrian scholar, Ota Weinberger, who studied under Frantisek Weyr at Charles University in Prague. Weyr was a disciple of Hans Kelsen, but Weinberger was uncomfortable with the "pure" theory of law, although it led him to do innovative work in the logic of norms and of teleology. Sometime in the 1970s he was attracted to the sociological theories of Helmut Schelsky (who was also a mentor to Niklas Luhmann). Weinberger perceived defects, on the one hand, in the Kelsenian tradition of positivism which focused on the purely normative aspect of law to the exclusion of empirical reality and, on the other hand, in behaviorist legal sociology which focused on the purely behavioral aspects of law to the exclusion of its normative side.

For Weinberger this bifurcation of the science of law was intolerable. He thought the solution to the problem of providing a complete explanation of law could be found in the idea of the "institution." For Wein-

1. David Hume, *A Treatise of Human Nature* (Oxford: Clarendon Press, 1958) vol. II, book 3, pt. 1, sec. 1. Original published in 1739.

berger the institution became the means by which the normative and descriptive aspects of law could be fused into a comprehensive legal theory. While led in the direction of an institutional explanation by Schelsky's work, Weinberger found a more secure philosophical foundation for his theory in the writings of the English scholar, John R. Searle, and his concepts of "speech acts" and "institutional facts."[2] The idea of an institutional theory of law is not new. Earlier scholars, principally Maurice Hauriou in France and Santi Romano in Italy, developed theories in which the idea of an "institution" was prominent.[3] However, there seems to be no direct link between those theories and the work of Weinberger. The contemporary Scottish scholar, Neil MacCormick, has also developed independently an institutional theory that comes close to Weinberger's at many points. In recent years these two scholars have collaborated, although they do not agree in all respects.[4] Aspects of Weinberger's theory have also been endorsed by Werner Krawietz, Franz Bydlinski, Peter Koller, and Massimo La Torre.

Aims

Weinberger seeks to provide the philosophical basis for a science of law that will comprehend and integrate the more traditional analytic jurisprudence of legal scholars, including inquiry into legal argumentation, with sociological study of legal phenomena. At the same time he attempts to provide a basis for critique of the law and for a better understanding of justice. In Weinberger's view the study of law from a purely normative point of view, usually called "legal dogmatics" in German, is inadequate to provide a full understanding, although it is valuable as a part of a greater enterprise, particularly for professional practitioners. On the other hand, behavioral studies of legal phenomena are also regarded as inadequate because they fail to account for the important normative and logical aspects of law by relegating them to the realm of the psychological. Traditionally the normative analyses of law have been

2. See John Searle, *Speech Acts: An Essay in the Philosophy of Language* (London: Cambridge Univ. Press, 1969).

3. See Santi Romano, *L'Ordinamento Giuridico,* 2d ed. (Florence: Sansoni, 1951); Santi Romano, *Principii di diritto constitutionale generale,* 2d ed. (Milan: Giuffré, 1947); Maurice Hauriou, *Aux sources du droit: Le pouvoir, l'ordre et la liberté* (Paris: Bloud and Gay, 1933); Maurice Hauriou, "La théorie de l'institution et de la fondation," *Cahiers de la Nouvelle Journée* 23 (1933), 89.

4. Neil MacCormick and Ota Weinberger, *An Institutional Theory of Law* (German chapters translated by Ruth Adler and Neil MacCormick, Dordrecht: Reidel, 1986). Original German edition: *Grundlagen des Institutionalistischen Rechtspositivismus* (1985). This work is not strictly a collaboration because it contains a collection of essays written by the authors separately, except for the introduction, which is co-authored.

philosophically based on a faulty understanding of what norms are, while behavioral studies have relied on a crude empiricism. Weinberger seeks to provide a new philosophical underpinning for both kinds of study that will allow each to complement the other.

It may be profitable to note what Weinberger does *not* attempt to do with his theory. He does not try to give an explanation of the relationship between law and morality, or answer the question why law should be obeyed, except perhaps incidentally. Nor does he try to establish a final grounding for the legal (or moral) validity of the law. He rejects the assumptions and approach of traditional natural law. And, although the evolution of cultural institutions is compatible with his approach, Weinberger does not attempt to explain such evolutionary process.

Main Ideas

The theory of institutional legal positivism can be viewed as composed of four components: a theory of human action, a logical (and teleological) theory of practical reasoning, a positivist view of law, and a normativist concept of institutions. All of these components are, of course, tied together in the theory and are interrelated.

In his theory of human action Weinberger deals with the same basic problem addressed by Max Weber in his attempt to explain human action through *Verstehen* and *Sinn* and addressed by Jürgen Habemas in terms of communicative action. It assumes that society is the result of individual human beings interacting in various ways so as to produce social phenomena. The explanation of these social phenomena begins with the activity of the individual human being. The "unit," so to speak, of sociological (or legal) theory is the individual, just as the unit of chemical theory is the atom. It is therefore philosophically necessary to clarify just what human action is.

Weinberger subscribes to the principle of the "primacy of praxis,"[5] that action is more fundamental than theory or language. The latter are instrumental for action and have significance only because they serve action. Thus, information and logical operations, including ways of thinking about what should be done and what the factual situation is, are the tools of practical decisionmaking.

> The systems of knowledge are independent thought complexes—statement and rule systems—that are isolated from objective orientation on account of the relationship of application in action, but in two directions show a primary connection with practice: the placing of questions arises often directly or indirectly from

5. See the discussion in chapter two of the work of Thomas Rentsch, who also subscribes to the primacy of practice.

practical interests, and the structure of knowledge is of the kind that in principle is practically (i.e., in actions) applicable.[6]

Weinberger defines action as behavior governed by information. He conceives the human being as capable of making choices or decisions; action is not causally determined by physical laws like the direction of a rolling billiard ball. However, action is constrained to limited alternatives by certain factors. The first of these is the information or knowledge available to the individual. The term "information" has a particular meaning in Weinberger's thinking. There are two types. The first is what might be called descriptive information, or knowledge of what *is*. Included here would be our understanding of how the world is constituted, how it generally works, and how certain causes generate certain effects. The second is practical information (practical in the Kantian sense of practical reason), or knowledge of what ought to be done and of what is better or worse. For example, if I decide to go outside my office, I utilize both kinds of information: I know the physical characteristics of the walls and the door, and I know that I must turn the knob to open the door. The latter "information" is an ought proposition, a norm. Practical information is made up of normative propositions and includes preferences, rules, principles, goals, and values. The information, both descriptive and practical, that one processes in making a decision comes from learning (formal and informal) through experience in one's cultural environment. Therefore, culture is to some extent a determinant of action.

The second major determinant of human action is the scope of action permitted by institutions. Just what is meant by institutions will be explored further below. Here we can point out that human beings operate within frameworks or structures of rules that both enable them to achieve certain ends and limit them from achieving others. One may be "free" to pursue a degree in biology at most universities but not in astrology or card tricks. In Europe and America one may marry one spouse but not two. One may move the bishop diagonally in chess but not the rook. Human action is thus channeled into limited alternatives. Institutions provide the scope for action. Familiarity with various human institutions also becomes a part of the information that an actor processes in taking action.

Weinberger further characterizes the nature of the "information" that governs human action. Descriptive information consists of "thought objects," or ideas which can be but need not be, articulated as descriptive propositions. Following a correspondence theory of truth, Weinberger asserts that such thought objects expressed as propositions are truth-

6. Ota Weinberger, "Grundlagenprobleme des Institutionalistischen Rechtspositivismus und der Gerechtigkeitstheorie," *Rechtstheorie* Special Edition 14 (1994), 178.

capable. If they correspond to reality, they are true. They are also subject to the usual propositional logic, Aristotelian or modern. These propositions may also reflect varying degrees of abstraction from "grass is green" to "in a given volume of gas the temperature is directly proportional to the pressure."

Practical information consists of norms, or of value statements that can be reduced to the form of a norm, which are also understood as thought objects. These can also be articulated as normative propositions of varying degrees of abstraction. They do not, however, correspond to reality in the way that descriptive statements do; there is no Platonic world of ought. Of course, normative propositions can be valid or invalid with reference to a particular system of norms. According to Weinberger, however, norms can also be "real." What this means will be explained below in our discussion of institutions.

Weinberger's theory of action raises a general question about the way in which norms, preferences, and values operate in human decisionmaking (action). What is the "processing" that leads to action? He is careful to avoid furnishing a psychological answer to this question; such an answer, or answers, would presumably be based on empirical studies or perhaps on some kind of introspection. An important reason for avoiding psychological explanation is that Weinberger expects his theory of action to explain the actions of collectivities of persons (corporations, legislatures, etc.) and of agents acting on behalf of other persons or collectivities. In these contexts psychological explanation would be inappropriate since we are not necessarily dealing with a single human mind.

Instead, Weinberger seeks to provide a logical foundation for analysis of action, or, in other words, to formalize decisional procedures in terms of logical rules. Traditional logic has been applied in the realm of cognition, that is, to descriptive propositions.[7] Without considerable modification this logic is not suitable for justifying inferences in the field of normative propositions. It is therefore necessary to develop a system or systems of logic that can operate with norms and values. Weinberger sees a need for a logic of preferences, a logic of values, and a formal teleology. The latter in particular has been an object of his scholarship.[8]

This concept of teleology is characterized as formalist and finalist. It is formal in that it is an abstract framework for practical thinking independent of any particular goals or values. It is finalist in that it deals with

7. The work of Georg von Wright in the field of deontic logic should be noted here. See Georg von Wright, *Norm and Action: A Logical Inquiry* (New York: Humanities, 1963); Georg von Wright, *An Essay in Deontic Logic and the General Theory of Action* (Amsterdam: North Holland, 1968)

8. In the scope of this book we will not be able to go into the details of Weinberger's logic.

ends which are not actual states of being. Such a logical system must deal with the problem of ends and means, of contradictory ends, and of a plurality of means and ends. This kind of theory cannot furnish an algorithmic or mathematical solution to decisionmaking, of course, because there always remains the nonrational element of decision on the part of the actor. However, a framework for teleogical deliberation can provide a sort of regulative idea for the enterprise of practical thinking in the same way that philosophies of natural science provide an explanation for scientific thinking.

> In my view formal teleology is a rationally based theory of relations and operations of practical thinking which does not offer an alternative to the causal explanation of the world, no more than it is a theory for certain phenomena of consciousness. Neither does it constitute a theory of idealized (rational) action in the sense that it might describe the correct way of deciding and acting which man's real actions ought to aspire to as to an ideal; instead, it provides a schematisation founded on causal relations which finds application in the theory of action. In the context of a series of further reflections it is not to be regarded merely as a system of postulates for rational decisions and actions, but as a fundamental schematisation of the analysis of action in general.[9]

We noted above that Weinberger maintains that norms can be real. This does not mean that they can be logically inferred from descriptive propositions; this would violate what Weinberger calls the "postulate of non-inferability" and seems to be equivalent to what is more commonly regarded as avoiding the naturalist fallacy. To determine what is meant by suggesting that norms can be real,[10] we must turn to the idea of institutional facts.

Following G. E. M. Anscombe and John Searle, Weinberger distinguishes between "brute facts" and "institutional facts." The former are determined directly through sensory perception: "the ball is red"; "the water is hot." However, human beings experience reality in more complex ways than this simple correspondence. For example, I know that I am working in the law school. This does not mean only (or even primarily) that I am situated in a particular physical location. The "law school" is not a building; its activity can be moved to another building. It is an organization of persons, all of them having certain roles. It is an operating system that follows certain conventions and rules in a particular real

9. Ota Weinberger, *Law, Institution, and Legal Politics: Fundamental Problems of Legal Theory and Social Philosophy* (translated by Ruth Adler et al., Kluwer: Dordrecht, 1991), 14. Original German edition: *Recht, Institution und Rechtspolitik* (1987).

10. Weinberger distinguishes between the ontological status of the *objects* of propositional and normative statements (both are potentially real) and the semantic requirement that the two kinds of statements cannot be confused, i.e., that "ought" statements cannot be derived from "is" statements and vice versa.

time frame. It has a purpose.[11] It is an institution, and it exists as a matter of fact. The statement, "I am working in the law school" is truth-capable.

We notice, of course, that an institution like a law school is constituted of such things as norms, roles, and purposes. Institutions are patterns of action and frameworks for possible action; people organize their interactions with others within the framework of institutions. What individuals are supposed to do within these frameworks is dictated by rules and purposes. Indeed, the institution itself is constructed of norms. Do these norms really exist? They do not refer to anything that could be verified through sensory perception, but they are a part of our reality. They determine the scope of what is done, by whom, and how. They actually have an operational effect in a particular time and place in our world. Weinberger says that norms "exist" in this institutional sense.

> "Ought" is reality when it is an element of the system determining action. As far as the individual is concerned, this means that norms, whether autonomous [self-determined] or heteronomous [socially determined], are elements of the deliberation determining action; as far as the community is concerned norms establish the forms of behavior in society, the social structures (e.g. legal persons) and human interaction.[12]

Thus, by recognizing that norms have a reality in the world of *Is* because they partially determine human action, the connection is made between the world of Ought and the world of Is. Institutions are real, and therefore the norms that constitute and regulate institutions are also real.

Weinberger's favorite example of an institution is the game of chess. The game is entirely constituted by rules, although the physical pieces and board are needed. It is not possible to play chess without following the rules, although the rules do not dictate each actual move. When two people sit down to play chess, is the game real? We know that where the pieces end up after each move is partially dictated by the rules of the game. The game of chess "exists" as a part of our reality even though its rules cannot be validated through sensory experience. This is a broader view of reality than a strict empiricist would allow; however, it corresponds more closely with our intuitive understanding of reality. Since what constitutes reality is a matter of convention anyway, why not recognize "institutional reality?"

Institutional legal positivism combines the specific theory of action outlined above with the concept of institution to provide a framework for legal science that can accommodate normative inquiry (analytic jurisprudence and doctrinal analysis, or legal dogmatics) and sociological

11. Cf. Phillip Nonet, "The Legitimation of Purposive Decisions," *California Law Review* 68 (1980), 263.

12. Weinberger, supra note 9 at 101.

inquiry. What actually happens in society can be related to the norms of a positivist legal system. The legal system can be subjected to criticism from an internal or hermeneutic standpoint and from an external or functional standpoint. The contribution of institutional legal positivism is described by Weinberger as follows:

> The contribution . . . lies at four levels: (1) in the complex conception of the content of law whereby an appropriate basis is created for argumentation and interpretation of law and legal dogmatics; (2) in the institutional conception of meaning, meaningful acts, and of processes of development of meaningful elements in the institutions; (3) in such a positivist view that rejects the arbitrary positivism that holds that the law can have any content if it is implemented through power, and that connects non-cognitivism with rational argumentation in the area of legal politics; (4) in offering a pragmatics of argumentation that connects logical analysis with societal processes of discourse.[13]

Weinberger's view of the legal system does not depart in major respects from more traditional positivist views such as those of Hart or Kelsen. In fact, he appears to accept Hart's view of the legal system as a structure of primary and secondary (power conferring) rules. Further, morality is viewed as a separate system of norms that cannot determine the content of the law, but can influence the law through legislation and perhaps other ways. Ordinary cases in the courts are to be resolved by the traditional subsumption of their facts under the appropriate legal rules. We have already pointed out that Weinberger rejects the natural law thesis that law must have some inherent moral value, that is, is in some way morally "valid."

In response to Ronald Dworkin's critique of positivism[14] as failing to account for the operation of "principles" in adjudication, Weinberger employs a typical positivist strategy. He agrees that principles do enter into the process, but he insists that they can be captured in the official system of norms. He maintains that the principles used in judicial argumentation can be found in three authoritative sources: from customary law (which for Weinberger includes judge-made law and judicial opinions), by abstracting from the general system of authoritative rules (general principles of the legal system), and by finding abstract norms or determinations of purpose in legal texts. Assuming they can be found, just how these principles are to be used in connection with the more conventional rules which may conflict with them "can be problematical" according to Weinberger.[15] However, he implies that a system of priorities can be devised with proper legal analysis.

13. Weinberger, supra note 6 at 246.

14. Ronald Dworkin, *Taking Rights Seriously* (Cambridge, Mass.: Harvard Univ. Press, 1977), 14–45.

15. Weinberger does not respond to the problem of "discretion" as posed by Dworkin.

Weinberger recognizes the role of interpretation in law. He draws a distinction between formal and instrumental interpretation. The former, typical of Austrian jurisprudence, seeks to derive the meaning of legal provisions strictly from their language and the historical context of their enactment (intent of lawmakers). On the other hand instrumental interpretation relies on purpose and involves teleological analysis. Weinberger contends that such analysis is unavoidable, but cautions against its overuse because multiple purposes can be attributed to the law, and the determination of purpose is not always free from subjectivity. He says that institutional legal positivism tries to steer a path between the extremes of literalism and purposeful interpretation.

Weinberger has some observations on morality and justice that are, if not typical, common to the positivist perspective. He recognizes that morality plays an important part in human life and that moral norms "exist" in an institutional way. However, he believes that these moral norms are subjective in the sense that no one can demonstrate their objectivity and that morality differs from person to person, from culture to culture, and from time to time. Justice is a particular aspect of morality that relates to the relations between people in a society, particularly legal relations. While subjective, it is nevertheless an ideal that provides a basis for critical reflection of human institutions. Principles of justice can be determinants of human action, and progress in ways of doing things (from a utilitarian standpoint at least) has probably been made under the banner of a call for justice. Justice is not equated, of course, with the precepts of the legal system.

Weinberger's institutional view does depart in some ways from traditional positivist jurisprudence. First, the legal system itself is conceived as an institution; it is constituted by rules, roles, and purposes. The institution in turn creates legal norms. There is a rough resemblance here between Weinberger's law as institution and Luhmann's law as self-producing system.[16] This means that the existence of the social institution of law is intrinsically connected with its norms, particularly the power-conferring norms. Like the game of chess, law is constituted by its own rules. A further corollary is that law is a dynamic normative system. The operation of the system is an interaction of social processes and legal acts; it relies on normative understanding and deduction as well as on information drawn from observations of social reality. This approach resolves the problem of the *Grundnorm* as the basis of validity in Kelsenian theory. For Weinberger the validity of particular laws can be traced back to fundamental norms in "genealogical" fashion, but the validity of these norms depends on whether they are elements of an actually exist-

16. See the discussion in chapter six.

ing institution, that is, whether they are in fact determinative of the scope of action in the empirically observable world.[17] Thus, in Weinberger's view the dual task of legal theory, or legal science, is both to analyze the normative structure of law and to investigate its functioning in the social context. It can be critical in both respects.

Critique and Reply

Weinberger's theory of action gives rise to a number of questions. First, he pursues a methodological individualism which rules out explanation of human behavior in non-intentional terms. For instance, Luhmann's approach to sociology and some areas of economic theory or evolutionary theory[18] is incompatible with an individualistic method. Nevertheless, this approach is consistent with much of the work done in sociology and anthropology. Arguably it improves upon the explanation given by Weber in terms of *Verstehen* and upon the obscurely complex notion of communicative action offered by Habermas.

It is also unclear in Weinberger's theory of action how information "governs" behavior. The relationship is not causal, and Weinberger recognizes that there is a nonrational element of decision in addition to the "information." This element of will or volition, or "attitude," makes it possible for individuals to make irrational decisions, or partially rational decisions, or perhaps something else. How does the information, both cognitive-descriptive and normative, operate on this volition? Is this volition a matter of emotion? These matters remain unclear.

A related question is whether Weinberger has succeeded in eliminating psychological explanation in this scheme. What he talks about in terms of teleology, means-ends assessments, seem to be mental processes. The capacity to engage in teleological reasoning may assume the presence and operation of such human characteristics as intelligence, learning, comprehension, and emotion, all of which appear to belong to the realm of the psychologist. If psychology has not been avoided, what damage (or possible good) does this do to the theory?

The notion of institution that Weinberger advances is a real contribution to legal philosophy. He presents convincingly a relationship between norms and social reality that is novel in modern jurisprudence. In doing so he appears to bridge a gap between normative discourse and scientific discourse. The world of Ought exerts an impact on and plays a part in the world of Is. We seem to have known this as a matter of com-

17. Cf. Karl Llewellyn, "The Constitution as an Institution," *Columbia Law Review* 34 (1934), 1.

18. See, e.g., Paul Rubin, "Why Is the Common Law Efficient?" *Jour. Legal Studies* 6 (1977), 51.

mon sense, but a persuasive theory was lacking. Nevertheless, the theory is far from irresistable. The exact relationship between the norm and social reality is still somewhat puzzling. Also puzzling is the way in which we perceive institutional facts. How do we "know" the norms that constitute an institution? In what sense are they real? Perhaps further development of this idea will provide clarification.

Institutional legal positivism is subject to most of the criticisms leveled at positivism generally. Dworkin's famous critique based on the distinction between rules and principles is not adequately answered, although the direction in which a positivist response could be developed is indicated. The answer to the problem of the Grundnorm is at first glance ingenious. However, it is not entirely clear that Weinberger's explanation, when cleared of its peculiar terminology, is essentially different from Hart's, that is, that the Grundnorm or Rule of Recognition is "accepted" by a particular society. Again, further discussion might clarify this matter.

The most fundamental criticism of institutional legal positivism is that it does not seem to do anything practical for us. It is a striking work of philosophical speculation. It purports to provide a philosophical basis for a science broad enough to encompass the subject matter of traditional jurisprudence and of the sociology of law. Yet, if we accept the entirety of the theory, we are still left with the same two types of practical inquiry that we had before. We end up analyzing the validity of legal norms and explaining the internal relationships between legal concepts and rules in the same way analytical jurisprudence has always done. Likewise, on the other side sociological study proceeds no differently with or without the benefit of the institutional theory. True, a conceptual connection has been made between the two realms of discourse, and this is a substantial philosophical achievement; but the discourses themselves have not been integrated in any way. Perhaps it is philosophically more satisfying to know that one theory can account for both realms of inquiry. Beyond this, it is not clear what has been accomplished.

Chapter 8
An Assessment of German Legal Philosophy

> The two legal cultures of the civilized world are so different from one another that even the adequate translation of the legal words of one into the language of the other is almost impossible.
>
> —Gustav Radbruch [1]

Exciting things are, indeed, happening in German legal philosophy. As the foregoing chapters have shown, many interesting ideas have been formulated, and new solutions to old problems have been advanced that have no counterparts in current American jurisprudential scholarship. Whether any of these new ideas will take hold within the American discussion remains to be seen. This may depend partly on the degree to which they can be "translated" into the American legal culture.[2] In this concluding chapter we will assess the German work from the point of view of the American traditions in law and philosophy. We will also try to explain some of the underlying differences in how the enterprise of legal philosophy is carried on in the two countries.

The Tasks of Legal Philosophy in Germany

Throughout history legal philosophy has devoted itself to two main tasks: explaining law and evaluating law. A theory may offer a framework of thinking to explain what the law is, how it relates to other social phenomena (morality, custom, political power), or both. Alternatively, a

1. Gustav Radbruch, *Der Geist des englischen Rechts* (Heidelberg: Rausch, 1946), 8.

2. On the concept of legal culture, see Lawrence Friedman, *The Legal System: A Social Science Perspective* (New York: Russell Sage Foundation, 1975). To Friedman's idea of a legal culture we would add the notion of an academic or intellectual culture as well.

theory may offer a justification for law or a critique of law showing that it is unjustified (unjust). It is not uncommon for a single theory to attempt both to explain and evaluate. These same goals, with variations, are pursued today in both the United States and Germany. The more specific aims of contemporary German legal philosophers—their own ideas of what they are doing—can be classified in a few categories. A handful, notably Jürgen Habermas, Robert Alexy, the Kantians, and the Aristotelians, have a political or moral aim; they seek to establish a *Letztbegründung*—an ultimate justification—for the law. Starting from the observation that law is coercive and prohibits people from doing what they want, or sometimes requires them to do what they do not want, it is concluded that law is oppressive and unjust unless some basis can be established proving that the law is morally right. These theorists seek to explain how legal legitimacy can be achieved or demonstrated, or at the least what the conditions are for a legitimate legal system.[3] Well-known American counterparts to the justificatory enterprise are the works of John Rawls, Robert Nozick, and the proponents of law and economics.[4] On the negative critical side the remaining German Marxist theorists seek to critique the (bourgeois, capitalist?) law and show its biases and injustices within the edifice of the Marxist ideology. The negative critics in America would include the critical legal scholars and their offshoots, the proponents of critical race theory and feminism.[5]

A second and perhaps more common goal of German legal philosophy is to characterize and explain what is embraced by the idea of a legal system or legal order—what law is. Scholars like Hans-Joachim Koch, Helmut Rüßmann, Delf Buchwald, Robert Walter, Ota Weinberger, and also Robert Alexy seek to provide a philosophical map that will explain the relationships between rules, principles, and valid argumentation

3. Even Luhmann, whether incidentally or purposefully, gives a peculiar evolutionary explanation for what might be regarded as the ultimate legitimacy of law through his merry-go-round functional solution.

4. See John Rawls, *A Theory of Justice* (Cambridge, Mass.: Harvard Univ. Press, 1971); John Rawls, *Political Liberalism* (New York: Columbia Univ. Press, 1994); Robert Nozick, *Anarchy, State, and Utopia* (New York: Basic Books, 1974); Robert Cooter and Thomas Ulen, *Law and Economics* (New York: Harper-Collins, 1988). Other American scholars are also pursuing the justificatory goal. See R. George Wright, *Reason and Obligation: A Contemporary Approach to Law and Political Morality* (Lanham, Md.: Univ. Press of America, 1994); Rex Martin, *A System of Rights* (Oxford: Clarendon Press, 1993); Eric Rakowski, *Equal Justice* (Oxford: Clarendon Press, 1991); Bruce Ackermann, *Social Justice in the Liberal State* (New Haven, Conn.: Yale Univ. Press, 1980); Charles Fried, *Right and Wrong* (Cambridge, Mass.: Harvard Univ. Press, 1978).

5. See Mark Kelman, *A Guide to Critical Legal Studies* (Cambridge, Mass.: Harvard Univ. Press, 1987); Patricia Smith, ed., *Feminist Jurisprudence* (Oxford: Oxford Univ. Press, 1993); Richard Delgado, "Legal Scholarship: Insiders, Outsiders, Editors," *Colorado Law Review* 63 (1992), 717.

within a system of legislation and adjudication. Armed with a satisfactory map provided by the philosophers, the legal analyst can project and teach the law as an organized system, and perhaps judges will be guided to clear thinking in deciding difficult cases. While this type of analytic jurisprudence is also dominant in Britain, it does not have much support in the United States.[6]

Related to legal analysis and rational argumentation is the more modest approach of the proponents of rhetorical theory. They seek to provide guidance to practitioners and judges in resolving legal disputes by showing how rhetoric, including both substantive arguments and technique, is central to judicial decisionmaking. This is, of course, closer to the activity of many American legal philosophers like James Boyd White, Ronald Dworkin, Stanley Fish, Melvin Eisenberg, and others.[7]

Finally, some legal philosophers seek to establish an intelligible framework for relating the legal order to other social phenomena and also for providing a critique of law from that standpoint. Sociologists like Hans Albert and Niklas Luhmann try to bring the law within the framework of a larger scientific system. Ota Weinberger presents his own way of explaining the relationship between the normative legal system and the factual reality of life.

While the four aims suggested above—determining legitimacy, providing an analytic framework for law, analysis of legal argument, and conceptual integration with other fields of knowledge—account for most of the work being done in legal philosophy, they are usually not exclusive aims for any one theorist. Each thinker has his own concept of what legal philosophy should entail, so often more than one of these goals is pursued. The Germans are generally much more focused on the logical analysis of the legal order, the structure and substance of the law, whereas the Americans are mainly concerned, as they have been since the time of Holmes, with process, especially the explanation of appellate court decisionmaking. It seems clear that, in a rough way, scholars in both countries are wrestling with the same problems. There nevertheless remain significant differences; in particular, assumptions and starting points in the analysis undertaken by scholars in the two countries often

6. See, however, Steven Burton, *An Introduction to Law and Legal Reasoning*, 2d ed. (Boston: Little Brown, 1995).

7. See Ronald Dworkin, *Law's Empire* (Cambridge, Mass.: Harvard Univ. Press, 1986); Stanley Fish, *Doing What Comes Naturally* (Oxford: Clarendon Press, 1989); Melvin Eisenberg, *The Nature of the Common Law* (Cambridge, Mass.: Harvard Univ. Press, 1988). The German rhetorical movement also has its closest counterpart in the work of James Boyd White. See James White, *Heracles' Bow: Essays on the Rhetoric and Poetics of the Law* (Madison: Univ. of Wisconsin Press, 1985); James White, *When Words Lose Their Meaning: Constitutions and Reconstitutions of Language, Character, and Community* (Chicago: Univ. of Chicago Press, 1984).

diverge. We will examine these differences below under the heading of "Comparative Analysis."

Some Common Grounds

First, it will be helpful to highlight some of the common themes found in contemporary German theory. In spite of considerable variation, some common grounds do emerge among the current thinkers. One feature that appears in different guises in the various philosophies is the idea of *agreement as the basis for right decision.* In discourse theory ultimate justification is achieved in the ideal speech situation through debate leading to consensus-agreement. In the real world less than ideal debate leading to agreement is still the justifying feature. In Hans Albert's critical rationalism, agreement also surfaces as a justifying feature for legislative and judicial decisions. In Albert's social technology performance characteristics must be hypothesized. These performance characteristics incorporate values. In order to proceed rationally to determine what decision should be made, there must first be agreement on the hypothesized goals. From this standpoint Albert's scheme is not that different from discourse theory in the real world. The rhetoricians also offer agreement as the basis for decision. Here the agreement is characterized in terms of the pursuit of argumentation on a given topic to reach a common opinion; common opinion is, of course, opinion agreed to. It may even be argued that the Kantians rely on a moral agreement implied in the notion of the categorical imperative and universalizability. Requiring oneself as well as all others to act on maxims that can be universalized suggests that everyone can understand his or her own need for universalizability and hence can agree to act morally.

A second common ground among many of the German thinkers is *the centrality of language* or communications to their theories. For Habermas and Alexy communication is crucial at two levels. In discourse theory the ultimate justification of the consensus reached through ideal argumentation is said to rest upon the presuppositions of communications, an idea related to John R. Searle's speech acts. Secondarily, particular legislative and judicial decisions themselves can be justified only through the appropriate argumentation carried out according to the rules of legal discourse. Reliance is also placed on the notion of speech acts in Weinberger's institutional positivism. The idea of the speech act leads to the concept of institutional facts which serves as the basis for Weinberger's demonstration of the connection between the real world of descriptive propositions and the equally real world of normative propositions. In Luhmann's world, communication becomes the pivotal feature; society is defined as a system of communication. Of course, for the rhetoricians communication in the form of argumentation is also central; law is constructed through argumentation.

Finally a common feature that might be characterized as a form of *pragmatism* runs through some of the discussion.[8] For the rhetoricians "valid" law is constructed through argumentation; it emerges when a common opinion is formed. The argumentation leading to the common opinion is based on experience and the unquestioned verities of the culture. This "truth" of the common opinion is, of course, subject to change with new circumstances and new argumentative premises. Critical rationalism also bears a close resemblances to pragmatism. In that view all knowledge is tentative; scientific laws are hypotheses; everything is subject to criticism and evaluation. What is currently truth are those hypotheses with the most support from experts who have a critical attitude. In the normative realm those hypothesized "performance characteristics" that guide decisionmaking are tentatively accepted as morally or politically right based on our experience, subject, of course, to further critique. Although in many ways Ota Weinberger's neo-Kelsenian approach seems about as far from pragmatism as possible, he nevertheless subscribes to the notion of the "primacy of praxis" which shares some common ground with pragmatism, viz., that theory (and truth) are subordinate to action and serve to facilitate action. Even discourse theory has its pragmatic aspect. Pragmatism, at least in the Peircean tradition, holds that a judgment is true if it would be agreed upon at the end of an inquiry duly pursued. This bears considerable likeness to Habermas' truth through consensus.

Historical Reasons for Divergence in Thinking

Both the perceived tasks and the common grounds among the German scholars have counterparts in American jurisprudence. Nevertheless, the vocabulary of the two traditions differs, the focus of discussion differs, attitudes toward what is important differ, and the jurisprudential discussions in the two countries seem to run on different tracks. It may therefore be helpful to review the history that has led to this divergence.

One divergence has long been recognized; it is in the two general philosophical traditions—continental and Anglo-American.[9] This classic division, each tradition using its own concepts and terminology, has

8. By pragmatism here is meant a philosophy associated with Charles S. Peirce, William James, and John Dewey, and more recently Richard Rorty and Donald Davidson. In this view reliable knowledge is determined by inquiry based on experience and tested by experiment or further experience. There is no transcendental or ultimate truth.

9. See Roger Scruton, *A Short History of Modern Philosophy: From Descartes to Wittgenstein*, rev. ed. (London: Routledge, 1995).

continued down to the present time, although each has often cross-pollinated the other. Of course, American philosophers have absorbed ideas from a wide variety of sources, including German philosophers, but the mainstream scholarly activity still appears to follow an empiricist Anglo-American tradition. In twentieth-century America, pragmatism in particular seems the most vital perspective with seminal contributions from Charles S. Peirce, William James, and John Dewey at the turn of the century down to the work of scholars like Willard Quine, Donald Davidson, or Richard Rorty in recent years. In contrast, the Germans are more likely to pursue inquiry in the tradition of Dilthey, Husserl, and Heidegger, or, as noted in earlier chapters, to attempt to rework the thinking of Kant and Hegel. The Marxist heritage and the linguistic heritage associated with Wittgenstein have had influence in both countries.[10] However, not too much should be made of this divergence in the general philosophical tradition because legal philosophy has to a great extent led a life of its own. Consequently, having noted this factor, we will not pursue it further.

A more significant historical divergence relates directly to the law and the different ways in which law evolved in Germany and America. The particular concept of law (with all its connotations and assumptions) that has marked the German tradition goes back at least as far as the eleventh century, when the earliest universities were founded in Italy and Justinian's great compilation was rediscovered and subjected to intensive study.[11] The notion of law formed at that time has essentially been transmitted through the academic tradition with minor modification to the present day. In contrast, the basic Anglo-American notion, while much influenced by Roman models, is derived from different origins, has been transmitted through different academic institutions, and has resulted in a concept that contains different assumptions and implications.

In Germany and continental Europe generally, law has been the object of study in the universities, but initially the law studied was the ancient Roman law and its newer cousin, canon law.[12] Scholars did not observe or consider the actual administration of justice that was carried on in their own societies. The folk law and feudal law were regarded as crude

10. Interestingly, since the demise of the German Democratic Republic, Marxist scholarship has rapidly declined in Germany, while it has increased in the United States in the modified form of critical legal studies and some feminist legal scholarship.

11. For an interesting examination of the historical reasons why this particular concept of law was worked out, see Peter Goodrich, "Historical Aspects of Legal Interpretation," *Indiana Law Journal* 61 (1986): 315. More generally, see Harold Berman, *Law and Revolution: The Formation of the Western Legal Tradition* (Cambridge, Mass.: Harvard Univ. Press, 1983).

12. Law, theology, philosophy, and medicine were the first university disciplines. They were all originally pursued through the study of ancient texts.

and unworthy of scientific treatment. The magnificent structure of the Roman law as found in Justinian's Code and Institutes was considered the embodiment of reason and hence worthy of serious investigation. Over the years the study of this law was given various emphases. In one phase scholars wanted to subject the texts to analysis and to synthesize principles, in another phase scholars wanted to bring the Roman law to bear on contemporary institutions and make it useful, and in still another phase they wanted to return to the historical roots of the Roman law and learn what it originally meant. However, in all of this scholarly activity, extending over several centuries, a three part academic tradition persisted: (1) the law was to be understood through exegesis—the logical analysis, comparison, and rationalization of norms and concepts contained in the authoritative text; (2) the law was regarded as a consistent whole emanating from one lawgiver (as it did in fact); and (3) the law was complete in the sense that it contained an answer for every question.

In the sixteenth century the reception of Roman law occurred in most of the German-speaking countries. It became a "common law" throughout much of the continent and was no longer the private property of the professors. Although sometimes modified, it replaced much of the local law. Courts and administrative offices, often staffed by law-trained university graduates, cooperated with law faculties. Courts sometimes submitted difficult cases to a law faculty for an authoritative opinion (the practice of *Aktenversendung*). As the Roman law penetrated the practice, the academics began to pay more attention to the actual operation of existing legal systems.

Legal philosophy down to the end of the eighteenth century was dominated by the idea of natural law, first in the comprehensive scheme designed by Thomas Aquinas, then by rationalist legal philosophers like Grotius, Locke, Pufendorf, and Wolff. In the thinking of these theorists the concept of *human* law (later to be called positive law) remained essentially the same as it was in the eleventh and twelfth centuries.

An apparent change of great significance occured when Savigny advanced his historical theory. Natural law was rejected; the law was now thought to be culturally created from the spirit of the people.[13] The task of the scholar was to examine the historical record, to extract those rules and principles that represented the true genius of the nation, discarding accidental accretions, and to build these principles into an abstract and comprehensive body of knowledge—the scientific knowledge of the legal order. The historical aspect of the theory was largely ignored by Savigny's followers, especially Puchta and Windscheid. Instead, the pursuit

13. See Mathias Reimann, "Nineteenth-Century German Legal Science," *Boston College Law Review* 31 (1990), 837.

of legal knowledge became a system-building exercise known as *Begriffsjurisprudenz*. This was in some respects the same kind of academic activity that had occupied the medieval scholars, but it was taken to extremes of abstraction by the nineteenth century German scholars.

Begriffsjurisprudenz came under attack by the Free Law movement at the turn of the century.[14] The *Freirechtler* maintained that abstract doctrine did not determine cases, that law could not be understood in a vacuum, that judges had to take into account social, psychological, and economic factors in making their decisions, and that Begriffsjurisprudenz was not modern science at all but merely warmed-over scholasticism. These criticisms created quite a stir among the German academic establishment, and the more extreme aspects of *Begriffsjurisprudenz* were toned down. However, the *Freirechtler* did not win this intellectual battle. The old ways of thinking had been battered and cracked, but they were pieced together by the mainstream scholars. The scholastic tradition persisted, but in new form. Now it centered around the modern codes rather than the historical learning. While legal philosophers toyed with ideas like "natural law with a changing content"[15] and "the antinomies of the concept of law,"[16] they nevertheless continued to assume that law had a logical, systematic, authoritative character. Hans Kelsen set the tone for the twentieth century, not the Free Law movement.

We noted in chapter one that positivism came under a dark cloud after 1945 due to the experience with the Hitler regime. While the argument that positivism aided Hitler's cause is dubious, the fact that it made legal scholars rethink their legal philosophy was indeed a good thing. German legal philosophy since 1945 has probably been more open to new ideas than in previous eras. Foreign influences have been very significant. One of the most pronounced of these is the influence of Ludwig Wittgenstein and the British language-philosophy theorists. The work of these philosophers has given new impetus and direction to almost all of the current scholarship in Germany. The work of H.L.A. Hart, which is related to the language-philosophy school, has also had considerable impact. Among Americans, works of John Rawls and Ronald Dworkin have been translated into German, and their ideas have stirred some debate. Finnish scholars, including Aulis Aarnio, Alexsander Peczenik, and Georg Hendryk von Wright, have also had some influence, perhaps in part because they often publish in the German legal literature in the German language. Somewhat surprisingly, comparatively few citations are found

14. See James Herget and Stephen Wallace, "The Free Law Movement as the Source of American Legal Realism," *Virginia Law Review* 73 (1987), 399.

15. Rudolf Stammler, *The Theory of Justice* (translated by Hastie, New York: Macmillan, 1925). Original German edition: *Die Lehre von dem richtigen Rechte* (1902).

16. Gustav Radbruch, *Rechtsphilosophie*, 8th ed. (Stuttgart: Koehler, 1973).

in recent years to works of French and Italian scholars, and there seems to be little input coming from other countries not mentioned above. In spite of these external influences, however, German legal philosophy still has an identifiable character of its own; this will be analyzed below. But first we will point out how the American jurisprudential history diverges from the German.

The beginning of this divergence can be found in the assumption of legal jurisdiction by the King's Courts in England in the twelfth and thirteenth centuries.[17] Due to centralization of power after the Norman conquest, the law of crime and property (feudal tenures) became the province of the king. A sophisticated legal profession grew up around the institution of the Inns of Court. Originally intended only to furnish lodging and food for the lawyers and judges during terms of court at Westminster, these guild-like organizations became real educational institutions. The law studied was not the Roman law, however, but the peculiar practices of the English king's judges. Study of law was not text centered, but court centered. Apprentices would attend court, hear the arguments of lawyers and judges, make notes and summaries of the proceedings, and develop a type of learning centering around the writs (later, forms of action) used to carry on the legal process. After the evening meal readers might discuss various points of law, or moot courts (hypothetical debates) might be conducted for the benefit of the apprentices. The only textual materials generally available were the student notes about what went on in court. As time went on, the best summaries of these were collected from each term of court and were placed in a "yearbook." The yearbooks eventually became the record of what the courts had done in past cases, including what arguments were successful and unsuccessful.

The concept of law that this train of events fostered was far from that promoted by the scholastic study of Justinian's code. For the early English barristers the law consisted of discrete sets of rules and arguments related to specific procedural devices. This procedural orientation, so strange to German thinking, has continued to influence Anglo-American lawyers throughout history. The early English law had as its source the thinking of the king's judges who sat on three different courts. Such law was always articulated in the context of specific cases. The king's law was consequently neither comprehensive nor complete. The barristers were fully aware that other jurisdictions had their own law (church courts, manorial courts, merchant courts, county and hundred courts) and that the sources of those laws varied considerably. The barrister also viewed

17. For an overview, see Theodore Plucknett, *A Concise History of the Common Law*, 5th ed. (London: Butterworth, 1956).

the law as a practical matter, aimed at resolving disputes in a settled and reliable way. The barristers were not theoreticians, but (hopefully) clever practioners. Theory counted for nothing, results for everything. This perspective on the law was strongly reinforced by the practice of appointing the king's judges from the ranks of the barristers. The doctors of civil and canon law were entirely excluded.

In the course of the first five centuries of the English common law a few texts were written attempting to explain the law.[18] These dealt primarily with property law because that subject was most important economically and was also the most complicated. These texts did not resemble the more sophisticated tomes authored by doctors of the civil law at the universities (including the English universities). Rather, they were essentially commentaries on the various writs available in the king's courts. As time went by and the law became more complicated, the texts also increased in sophistication. The exemplary treatise, and an excellent example of how the classic common law mind worked, is Edward Coke's excellent *Institutes* (Coke on Littleton) published between 1628 and 1641.

After printing was introduced in England in the sixteenth century, the educational role of the Inns of Court declined. Would-be lawyers began to apprentice in the office of established barristers where law was learned by imitation and by trial and error. The apprenticeship system also became the standard method by which lawyers were trained in the American colonies for a century after independence as well. Except for occasional chairs established at a few universities through which a semester or year's series of lectures were offered, law was learned in the law office and the courtroom. Some lawyers did not even apprentice, since the qualifications for the practice of law were virtually nonexistent in some parts of the United States.

Needless to say, with this practical orientation to law there was nothing that could pass in America as legal philosophy until near the end of the nineteenth century. Beginning with Langdell's Harvard in the 1870s, attempts were made to introduce the "science" of law on the continental (chiefly German) model.[19] Treatises were written in the scientific mode, and eventually in the twentieth century the *Restatements of the Law* were published in an effort to forge clarity and system out of case law. These efforts were only partially successful; the common law mind-set of the American lawyers was difficult to dislodge.

18. See the compilation of texts on the common law collected in Max Radin, *Handbook of Anglo-American Legal History* (St. Paul, Minn.: West, 1936), x–xxii.

19. See generally James Herget, *American Jurisprudence 1870–1970: A History* (Houston: Rice Univ. Press, 1990), 63–116.

The attempts to be scientific and systematic eventually met with a strong reaction from legal academia. First led by Roscoe Pound and his sociological jurisprudence, then by the American legal realists, a skeptical critique was launched against conceptual jurisprudence.[20] These movements were highly successful in reinforcing the earlier practitioner's view of law as a pragmatic technique with learning centered on court decisions. The disposition to see law in these terms is still very strong in the United States. This in turn has had a forceful impact on how the enterprise of legal philosophy is carried on.

Comparative Analysis of the German and American Perspectives

From a reading of contemporary scholarship, we can identify some assumptions about the enterprise of legal philosophy that may explain why American and German efforts in this field are not congruent. Our first focus will be on the presuppositions surrounding the German concept of law.[21] Of course, the concept of law itself is a subject of jurisprudential inquiry, and the preceding chapters have demonstrated that there is a great variety of thinking on this matter.[22] However, it is the connotations of the term "law" that are referred to here. These are basic, almost unconsciously held notions. They consist of a system of meanings or implications that are ordinarily accepted without question. Of course, it is possible to modify our concepts rationally when we decide to examine them; however, basic notions often go unexamined, and it is a common human weakness to resist rethinking when such rethinking threatens to upset the way we have rationalized a certain subject matter.

We obtain our basic concept of law when we learn to use language and the word law, and, of course, our general experiences relating to law also shape the concept. Thus, every adult who can use the word has some notion of law.[23] The lawyer, however, and to a lesser extent the philoso-

20. *Id.* at 147–227.

21. These assumptions are not necessarily limited to the Germans. Most of them are probably consistent with continental thinking in general. It has also been said that the Italians are more German than the Germans.

22. For some general reflections on this subject by German scholars, see Ralf Dreier, "Some Remarks on the Concept of Law," in Werner Krawietz et al., eds., *Prescriptive Formality and Normative Rationality in Modern Legal Systems* (Berlin: Duncker and Humblot, 1994), 109; Robert Alexy and Ralf Dreier, "The Concept of Jurisprudence," *Ratio Juris* 3 (1990), 1; Arthur Kaufmann and Winfried Hassemer, "Enacted Law and Judicial Decision in German Jurisprudential Thought," *Toronto Law Journal* 19 (1969), 461. The latter article is dated but insightful.

23. This observation needs to be limited to western societies, however, since law is a cultural artifact of the Graeco-Roman, judeo-christian tradition.

pher, have a more definite idea of the subject that has been shaped and determined by formal educational processes. In the following we will point out some of the connotations or unarticulated meanings to be found in the German notion of law where those notions depart to any significant degree from those of American scholars.[24]

Perhaps the first assumption about law in the German tradition is the idea that law must emanate from a central authority. A norm of law is an "ought" proposition established by appropriate authority that controls or is intended to control human behavior. It must originate in the source that has legitimate power to govern.[25] In modern democracies like Germany and Austria this power lies in the duly elected legislatures which derive power themselves from a legitimately constituted basic law or constitution. Lawmaking power can be delegated to inferior legislative bodies, but the authority of these bodies is derivative from and limited by the higher authority. Courts are not inferior legislative bodies in this sense because they are conceived to have a different function. This is one reason that the doctrine of *stare decisis* has never been adopted or even seriously considered as possible in Germany.[26] While it is true that court opinions are published, and courts tend to follow the reasoning set out in prior cases, the opinions themselves are never looked on as the source of the law but as expositions of how the law (stemming from the legislature) should be applied and interpreted with respect to specific fact situations. The term *Rechtsfindung* (literally, law-finding) is often used to describe the process in which the courts doctrinally supplement the statutory authority in order to reach conclusions in particular factual situations. They "find" the law implicit in the statute because they lack authority to make law.[27]

24. British scholarship is not included in this comparison. The British appear to represent somewhat of a hybrid or compromise between the German and American perspectives in the areas discussed here.

25. It is not accidental that this notion of law might be called "Austinian." John Austin was greatly influenced by German scholarship when he studied at Bonn and Heidelberg. Arguably the great progenitor of English jurisprudence provided a German model for the legal system, one completely unrelated to the common law of England. See the comment in the preceding footnote. See also Gerald Postema, *Bentham and the Common Law Tradition* (Oxford: Clarendon Press, 1986).

26. Some concession must be made here to the decisions of the German Constitutional Court whose decisionmaking is considered by the Germans to be partly "political" as opposed to strictly "legal."

27. There is a resemblance here to the old claim of common law judges that they "find" the law. Of course, some contemporary German scholars have rejected this attitude and have pointed out specifically how judges make law. See Friedrich Müller, *Juristische Methodik*, 5th ed. (Berlin: Duncker and Humblot, 1993). The earlier works of Esser and Kriele mentioned in chapter one also emphasize judicial creativity. It would appear that German thinking on the question of how courts operate is moving in an "American" direction. Perhaps

This view of the law as necessarily emanating from higher authority precludes the possibility that a court could judge a case by resorting to what seems "fair," or by "inventing" a rule solely for the purpose of deciding a case. The authority requirement modifies the concept of a court's function in a way that is different from the American tradition which regards the main function as resolving disputes. In the German view the first duty of the court is to implement the policy of the state as contained in the law. A court is viewed primarily as an enforcer of public policy. Of course, in carrying out this function, the court will also dispose of the case. This attitude is reflected in a widespread practice in which trial courts give oral opinions explaining their decisions at the conclusion of a trial. These opinions are supposed to show the logical connection between the will of the legislator and the behavior of the parties. The same attitude is also reflected in the broad power of the German judge to shape the issues in a case, to determine what witnesses will appear, to do most of the questioning of witnesses, and generally to "conduct" the proceedings. It is further reflected in the principle that prosecutors must prosecute all criminal cases even when the defendant admits guilt and is willing to take the appropriate punishment. The public policy of the state must be vindicated and demonstrated; the outcome of a case must conform to this policy and therefore cannot be left entirely in the hands of private parties.

A feature of the German meaning of law that is related to the authority requirement, and is lacking in the American perspective, is the unity, or univocality, of the system. By unity is meant that law is normally conceived as a whole; it is a single body of norms that are necessarily interrelated because they cannot contradict one another either logically or in terms of policy; human conduct can be regulated this way or that way, but not such that the same act is prohibited and permitted. For this reason, legal norms are viewed as constituting a single structure, an integrated whole; multiple clusters of law would present the possibility of contradiction or mutual nullification.[28] Of course, laws should not be contradictory in the American view either. What is essentially different between the two perspectives is that the German lawyer sees all of human conduct as comprehensively regulated (including conduct "permitted"), whereas the American sees only certain areas of life regulated, and these discrete areas of regulation need not be compatible in

the *Freirechtler* will ultimately win the day (see the discussion in the text above accompanying footnote 14).

28. Of course each area of law has its own vocabulary and concepts; these are, however, complementary, not competing, even where a concept in one area of the law or in one context carries a meaning different from the apparently similar concept in another area or context.

terms of their aims, their concepts, the techniques of law employed, or their terminology, although they cannot contradict laws in other areas of regulation.

This concept of unity in German jurisprudence is illustrated by the frequent use of the term "Legal Order." The Legal Order is the sum total of all legal relationships subsisting between entities recognized by the law. Where Americans are likely to visualize the "legal system" either as a procedural apparatus or as an organization of persons (courts, legislatures, lawyers, etc.) who enact, apply, administer, and otherwise deal with the rules of law, the German would ordinarily visualize an unpeopled abstract entity (the Legal Order) that has comprehensively determined all legal rights, duties, and powers within a society.[29] An implication of this unitary concept of law is a strong emphasis (almost an obsession) on the need for rationality. Since the law cannot require persons to do contradictory things, a premium is placed on the logic of the law. A specific norm must fit within the overall Order in its proper place. This results in a demand for careful structure and systemization; the language of German jurisprudence is peppered with concerns about "validity." From this perspective the great enemy of law is ambiguity or indeterminacy; its ally is rationality and certainty. Thus, an important, if not primary, task of the legal philosopher is to devise the proper plan for the logical analysis of a tight, closed system of norms, or for the tightening and closing of such a system. Robert Alexy, Ota Weinberger, Delf Buchwald, and other modern analysts devote their principal energies to this task. Niklas Luhmann, while not a legal analyst, must assume a rigid positivist model of the autopoietic legal system; otherwise, the system would not be differentiated from politics and morals. Of course, rationality in law has a practical aim; it purports to reduce the chance of discretionary or arbitrary decisions. However, the Germans appear to have more faith in the constraining power of words and logic than do the Americans.

The importance of the unity of the Legal Order is illustrated in the area of legal education. Courses in General Legal Theory (*Allgemeine Rechtslehre*) are taught at some German universities, and books are written on this subject.[30] Texts of this type will have as their content such things as the concept of law, the basis of legal scientific theory, classification of legal norms, the distinction between subjective and objective

29. This is not to say, of course, that German lawyers cannot talk about specific laws. They obviously do so all the time. Particular laws are, however, always a part of the overall Legal Order, and this can have consequences for how the specific laws are interpreted, applied, evaluated, etc.

30. A recent example of such work is Klaus Röhl, *Allgemeine Rechtslehre: Ein Lehrbuch* (Cologne: Heymanns, 1994).

law, sources of law,[31] legal method, and the relationship between law and justice. Such an exposition is premised on the unity and rationality of the Legal Order. Also, the term "legal dogmatics" is often used to describe the contents of traditional law courses. The implication of this term is that each area of the law (e.g., civil law, administrative law, commercial law) is constituted by a highly structured system of norms and concepts based in legislation and that this doctrine constitutes the sole subject matter to be studied. Textbooks present this doctrine in dogmatic form.[32]

The connotations of authority, unity, and rationality that surround the German idea of law also lead to another notion often found in legal scholarship—the belief that, in principle, there is one right answer to every legal problem.[33] Or, to use the more common term found in the discourse, a court (or a professor) should be able to find "the solution" to every case. It is thought that in routine cases the solution is found simply by subsuming the facts of the case (or hypothetical case) under the appropriate legal norm and deducing the conclusion from these premises. The Germans will, of course, admit the occurrence of the "hard" case; in such instances opinions may differ over which is the right solution, but in theory one exists.[34] The traditional German prohibition on dissenting opinions mirrors this view,[35] since a dissenting opinion would imply that the court did not reach "the" solution. American scholars of the law also strive for the "right" answer, and sometimes courts write their opinions in a way that suggests that no other answer would have been possible. Nevertheless, in the American view one right answer is regarded at best as an ideal, and one not expected to be achieved in very many cases.[36] In fact, it is probably fair to say that the optimistic

31. The ultimate single source of law is the constitution. However, the constitution allocates lawmaking power to various governmental entities. In this sense laws can be made by state legislatures, the national parliament, administrative agencies, etc., but they all derive their authority from the power-conferring norms of the constitution.

32. In the last few years casebooks have been introduced at the German universities in the areas of constitutional law, administrative law, labor law, and perhaps others. These books bear a resemblance to American casebooks, but they usually provide approved "solutions" to the cases as well as presenting various alternative arguments. This is perhaps another area where German academics are moving in an American direction.

33. Of course, the advocates of rhetorical theory entirely reject this view, as do the exacting followers of the hermeneutics of Hans-Georg Gadamer. See chapter five.

34. Robert Alexy realistically takes the position that more than one right answer is "discursively possible" within his approach to legal decisionmaking. Of course, real discourse only approximates ideal discourse. See chapter four.

35. The German Constitutional Court does permit dissenting opinions. The reader will recall, however, that the decisions of this court are regarded as partly "political."

36. Ronald Dworkin deals with this thorny problem through the hypothetical perfect judge, "Hercules." See Ronald Dworkin, *Law's Empire,* supra note 7.

expectation in the United States is that a judicial decision be grounded in well-founded arguments, even though a number of well-founded arguments may lead in different directions in a particular case.

In addition to the assumptions connected with the concept of law in Germany, there is also a tradition of the study of law that differs significantly from the American. The discipline of law in the university is known as *Rechtswissenschaft*—legal science. This is not just a quirk of terminology; legal scholars in Germany regard their work as truly scientific. This reflects a difference in academic culture between the two countries.

Since the nineteenth century Germans have conventionally divided academic disciplines into *Naturwissenschaften* and *Geisteswissenschaften*—roughly translated as natural sciences and cultural sciences—whereas in America the conventional classifications are natural sciences, social sciences, and humanities.[37] Social sciences include sociology, anthropology, psychology, economics, and related disciplines that rely basically on empirical methods. Humanities would include history, literature, philosophy, languages, government (politics), and perhaps a few other subjects. Law is sometimes considered one of the humanities and sometimes simply as professional training; either way it is not a science. In Germany law is one of the cultural sciences. What does this mean?

First, legal science provides scientific knowledge. This kind of knowledge is of a higher order than ordinary information or technical expertise. It deals systematically with principles and processes; it is methodical, abstract, and reliable. Legal science strives for Truth, the particular truth about its subject—the Legal Order. In this respect it is no different than physics or economics. It does differ, however, in method, and what this method is or should be is, of course, one of the controversial topics of legal philosophy. Sociologists like Hans Albert and Niklas Luhmann would apply their respective sociological methods to the law, while legal scholars like Robert Alexy, Ota Weinberger, and the Kelsenian Robert Walter would utilize their own versions of legal method. Whichever way it is done, the scholarly enterprise is regarded as a scientific search for truth. One of the practical implications of this view is that university instruction in law is regarded primarily as the exposition of legal principles rather than training for law practice.

We may summarize the foregoing discussion by listing a set of characteristics (exaggerated, of course) that illustrate the differences between German and American approaches to legal philosophy:

37. The use of the term "science" in the late nineteenth century in the United States was much like the use of that term today in Germany. Law was treated as a science by Langdell and most of the jurisprudential scholars of the time. See Mathias Reimann, *Historische Schule und Common Law* (Berlin: Duncker and Humblot, 1993).

GERMAN	AMERICAN
Theories of high abstraction	Low level of abstraction
Focus on the Legal Order	Focus on legal process
Rationality demanded	Skepticism of rationality
Necessity for system	System unimportant
"The Solution" sought	Good arguments sought
Courts apply law	Courts make law
Legal science	Legal technique, analysis
Academic (scientific) orientation	Practice orientation
Enforcement of state policy as primary court function	Resolution of the case as primary court function

Having made the foregoing distinctions, it is appropriate to emphasize that things are changing. American influence in recent years among German legal academics has been substantial. Many Germans have earned LL.M. degrees at American universities, and others have visited American law schools as lecturers or researchers. American attitudes and perspectives are more and more frequently surfacing in the German literature. On the other side, in the past ten or fifteen years a fair number of German articles and books have been translated into English. Many works of Habermas and Luhmann in particular have become available to American scholars in translation. A few Americans have also studied or taught in Germany. There can be no doubt that a convergence in thinking is taking place.

Some Conclusions

The differences in attitude toward the law between American and German thinkers are gradually being eroded. More exchange of ideas and more translation of materials will continue to facilitate better understanding. The Germans have already absorbed many important ideas from the British and Americans in the post-war period. It would appear that more transmission in the other direction is now in order.

The Americans can also benefit by learning from the Germans the importance of relating jurisprudential theory to broader philosophical theory. Epistemological and ontological underpinnings for legal theory are important, and Americans have been lax in making these connections.

American legal philosophy has usually been informed by empirical work in the social sciences. The German scholars have largely ignored this kind of empirical information, probably to their detriment. Looking at reality from time to time is a healthy practice.

Finally, from the American point of view, much of the German work in legal analysis, especially the application of formal logic to legal argumentation, is likely to be regarded skeptically. Stated in a more forceful way, this ultra-rationalism serves no useful purpose. From the perspective of many American scholars who follow the realist tradition, it is founded on an illusion: that law is an autonomous body of norms and concepts that determine the outcome of cases. In spite of the work of the Mainz school of rhetoricians, it will take some doing, however, to convince the mainstream German legal philosophers of the truth of this proposition. If the American view is correct, then Americans must make much more convincing arguments and explanations than have thus far been offered.

The scholarly activity and ferment in contemporary German legal philosophy, undertaken in a grand academic tradition, offers a great opportunity to American theorists. Promising ideas and insights are there for the picking. We can enrich our own jurisprudential enterprise by being open to these foreign ways of thinking.

Appendix: Biographical Information

The scholars listed below were selected (1) because of the number and significance of their contributions to the current discussion in legal philosophy, or (2) because their works are presently the subject of attention in the scholarly community, or (3) because they have made a landmark or seminal contribution to the literature.

Adomeit, Klaus
b. 1935; studied law in Göttingen; doctorate 1959 Heidelberg; habilitation 1969 Köln; since 1975 Professor of legal theory, labor law, and civil law at Free University of Berlin.

Albert, Hans
b. 1921; studied economics, sociology, and business theory in Köln; Diploma, Business 1950; Dr. Social Science 1952; habilitation 1957 Köln; 1958–1963 Professor of economics and social science at Köln; 1963–1989 Professor of sociology and theory of science at Mannheim.

Alexy, Robert
b. 1945; studied law and philosophy in Göttingen; doctorate 1976 Göttingen; habilitation 1984 Göttingen; since 1986 Professor of public law and legal philosophy at Kiel.

Ballweg, Otmar
b. 1928; studied law, philosophy, and literature in Freiburg and Basel; doctorate 1960 Basel; habilitation 1968 Mainz; since 1973 Professor of legal philosophy, rhetoric, and legal sociology at Mainz; visiting scholar UC Berkeley, 1991–92.

Baruzzi, Arno
b. 1935; studied philosophy at Freiburg, Bonn, and Munich; doctorate 1965 Munich; habilitation (philosophy and political theory) 1972 Munich; since 1972 Professor of philosophy at Augsburg.

Brugger, Winfried
b. 1950; studied law, psychology, philosophy, history, and sociology in Munich and Tübingen; 1976–83 assistant at Tübingen; doctorate 1980 Tübingen; UC Berkeley 1981; habilitation 1986 Tübingen; 1985 adjunct professor of law Georgetown University; 1986–87 Professor of law at Tübingen; 1987–92 Professor of law at Mannheim; 1991–92 visiting Professor at Georgetown University; 1995 visiting Professor at Houston; since 1992 Professor of law at Heidelberg.

Buchwald, Delf
b. 1957; studied law and philosophy in Göttingen; M.A. 1984, doctorate 1987 Göttingen; since 1991 assistant at Göttingen.

Dreier, Ralf
b. 1931; studied law in Hamburg, Freiburg, and Münster; doctorate 1963 Münster; habilitation 1970 Münster; since 1973 Professor of general legal theory at Göttingen.

Frommel, Monika
b. 1946; studied law in Tübingen and Munich; doctorate 1979 Munich; habilitation 1986 Munich; since 1987 Professor of legal philosophy and criminal law at Frankfurt.

Garrn, Heino
b. 1939; studied law and philosophy in Mainz and Hamburg; doctorate 1968 Mainz; 1970–78 assistant in law at Bielefeld; habilitation 1978 Bielefeld; since 1982 Professor of law at Bielefeld.

Gast, Wolfgang
b. 1940; adjunct professor of law Mannheim; attorney at law, Heidelberg; book publisher.

Günther, Klaus
b. 1957; studied philosophy and law in Frankfurt; 1983–86 assistant in law Frankfurt; doctorate 1987 Frankfurt; since 1987 assistant in law and researcher in legal philosophy at Frankfurt.

Habermas, Jürgen
b. 1929; studied philosophy in Frankfurt; doctorate 1954 Frankfurt; 1954–59 assistant, Institute for Social Research in Frankfurt; habilitation 1961 Marburg; 1961–64 Professor of philosophy in Heidelberg; since 1964 Professor of philosophy at Frankfurt.

Haney, Gerhard
b. 1926; studied law in Jena; doctorate 1961 Jena; habilitation 1964 Jena; since 1968 Professor of law at Jena.

Hassemer, Winfried
b. 1940; studied law in Heidelberg, Geneva, and Saarland; 1964–69 assistant, Institute for Social Philosophy, Saarbrücken; doctorate 1967 Saarbrücken; 1970–72 assistant, Institute for Legal Philosophy Munich; habilitation 1972 Munich; since 1972 Professor of legal theory, legal sociology, and criminal procedure at Frankfurt.

Hilgendorf, Eric
b. 1960; studied law and philosophy at Tübingen; M.A. (philosophy and history) 1987 Tübingen; doctorate 1990 (philosophy) Tübingen; doctorate 1992 (law) Tübingen; habilitation 1994 Tübingen; since 1994 Professor of criminal law and legal philosophy at Tübingen.

Hoerster, Norbert
b. 1937; studied law at Munich and Münster; M.A. (philosophy) from University of Michigan 1963; doctorate (law) 1964 Münster; doctorate (philosophy) 1967 Bochum; habilitation 1972 Munich; 1972–74 lecturer in philosophy Munich; since 1974 Professor of jurisprudence at Mainz.

Höffe, Otfried
b. 1943; studied philosophy in Münster, Tübingen, Saarbrücken, and Munich; doctorate 1970 Munich; habilitation 1975 Munich; visiting scholar Columbia University 1970–71; 1971–76 assistant Munich; 1976–78 Professor of philosophy Duisberg; 1978–92 Professor of ethics and social philosophy Fribourg (Switzerland); since 1993 Professor of practical philosophy at Tübingen.

Kaufmann, Arthur
b. 1923; studied law in Heidelberg; doctorate 1949 Heidelberg; 1952–57 Judge in Karlsruhe; 1960 assistant at Heidelberg; 1960–1969 Professor of criminal law, criminal procedure, and legal philosophy at Saarbrücken; 1969–89 Professor of criminal law, criminal procedure, and legal philosophy at Munich.

Klenner, Hermann
b. 1926; studied law in Halle; 1951–56 assistant in law Humboldt University, Berlin; 1958–60 Professor of law at Humboldt; 1960–66 Professor at the College of Economics, Berlin; Professor at the Academy of Science, Berlin 1967–1991.

Klug, Ulrich
b. 1913; studied law and philosophy in Berlin; doctorate 1938 Berlin; habilitation 1950 Berlin; 1950–56 assistant in Heidelberg; 1956–60 Professor at Mainz; 1960–77 Professor of law at Köln; member, Federal Senate 1974–77; 1965 visiting professor, University of Cordoba, Argentina.

Koch, Hans-Joachim
b. 1944; studied law in Frankfurt; doctorate 1971 Frankfurt; habilitation 1978 Frankfurt; since 1978 Professor of public law and legal philosophy at Hamburg; judge of the state court of appeals in Hamburg.

Koller, Peter
b. 1947; studied law and philosophy in Graz; doctorate (law) 1971 Graz; doctorate (philosophy) 1981 Graz; habilitation 1981 Graz; 1988 visiting professor at University of Minnesota; 1990 visiting professor at Rutgers University; 1991 visiting professor at Munich; since 1985 professor of law and philosophy, University of Graz.

Krawietz, Werner
b. 1923; studied law and political science in Münster; doctorate (political science) 1960 Münster; doctorate (law) 1965 Münster; habilitation 1974 Münster; personal assistant to the Rector, Münster, 1964–66; since 1974 Professor of public law, legal theory, legal sociology and political philosophy at Münster.

Kriele, Martin
b. 1931; studied law and philosophy in Freiburg, Münster, and Bonn; LL.M. Yale, doctorate 1963 Münster; habilitation 1966 Münster; 1966–88 Judge of the Constitutional Court of the State of Nordrhein-Westfalen; since 1967 Professor of political theory and public law at Köln.

Kühl, Kristian
b. 1943; studied law 1964–68 in Würzburg, Berlin, and Heidelberg; studied philosophy 1968–72 in Heidelberg; doctorate (law) 1972 Heidelberg; 1975–81 assistant in law at Bielefield; promotion Dr. Phil. 1983 Heidelberg; since 1984 Professor of criminal law, criminal procedure, and legal philosophy at Gießen.

Kuhlmann, Wolfgang
b. 1939; studied philosophy in Kiel, Paris, Saarbrücken, and Frankfurt; doctorate 1975 Frankfurt; habilitation 1983 Frankfurt; director, Forum for Philosophy at Bad Homburg; Professor at Erfurt; Professor at Frankfurt; Professor of philosophy, Philosophical Institute, Rhein-Westfalische technische Hochschule Aachen.

Lampe, Ernst-Joachim
b. 1933; studied law in Frankfurt, Mainz, and Free University of Berlin, studied music in Musikhochschule Berlin; doctorate 1957 Mainz; habilitation 1966 Mainz, since 1971 Professor of legal philosophy and criminal law at Bielefeld.

Luhmann, Niklas
b. 1927; habilitation 1966 Münster; since 1968 Professor of sociology at Bielefeld.

NEUMANN, ULFRID
b. 1947; studied law in Tübingen and Munich; doctorate 1977 Munich; habilitation 1983 Munich; 1983–87 Professor of legal philosophy at Frankfurt; since 1987 Professor of criminal law, criminal procedure, legal philosophy and legal sociology at Saarbrücken.

OTT, WALTER
b. 1942; studied law in Zürich; doctorate (law) 1966 Zürich; doctorate (JUD) 1971 Zürich; habilitation 1978 Zürich; since 1979 professor of law at Zürich.

PAWLOWSKI, HANS-MARTIN
b. 1931; studied law in Münster, Freiburg, and Munich; doctorate 1960 Göttingen; habilitation 1964 Göttingen; since 1966 Professor of civil law and civil procedure in Mannheim; 1969–70 Rector of the University of Mannheim.

RENTSCH, THOMAS
b. 1954; studied philosophy, literature, and theology in Münster, Zürich, Tübingen and Konstanz; habilitation 1988 Konstanz; since 1989 Professor of philosophy, Technical University of Dresden.

ROELLECKE, GERD
b. 1927; studied law in Würzburg and Freiburg; doctorate 1960 Freiburg; habilitation 1967 Mainz; Professor of public law and legal philosophy at Mannheim.

ROTTLEUTHNER, HUBERT
b. 1944; studied law, sociology and philosophy; doctorate 1972 Frankfurt; since 1975 Professor of legal sociology at the Free University, Berlin.

RÜßMANN, HELMUT
b. 1943; studied law at Frankfurt; doctorate 1967 Frankfurt; assistant at Frankfurt 1971–75; Professor at Bremen 1975–87 and judge of the state court of appeals; since 1987 Professor of civil law, civil procedure, and legal philosophy at Saarbrücken; Judge of the State Court of Appeals, Saarland.

SCHILD, WOLFGANG
b. 1946; studied law and philosophy in Vienna; doctorate 1968; habilitation 1977 Munich; since 1977 Professor of criminal law, history of criminal law, and legal philosophy at Bielefeld.

SCHNEIDER, PETER
b. 1920; studied law in Zürich and Geneva; habilitation 1955 Bonn; since 1956 Professor of public law and legal philosophy at Mainz; 1969–80 Rector and President of the University of Mainz.

Schreckenberger, Waldemar
b. 1929; habilitation 1976 Mainz; since 1978 Professor of legal philosophy, legal politics, and legal sociology at College of Administrative Sciences, Speyer.

Spaemann, Robert
b. 1922; studied philosophy in Munich, Fribourg (Switzerland), Münster, and Paris; doctorate Münster; habilitation 1962 Münster; Professor at Stuttgart, Heidelberg, Salzburg, and Munich; visiting Professor at Rio de Janeiro and Paris; now Professor emeritus, Munich.

Starck, Christian
b. 1937; habilitation 1969 Würzburg; since 1971 Professor of public law at Göttingen.

Teubner, Gunther
b. 1944; studied law at Tübingen; doctorate 1970; judge in Stuttgart 1971; M.A. sociology of law, UC Berkeley 1974; habilitation 1977 Tübingen; assistant in law Frankfurt 1977; 1977–92 Professor of law at Bremen; visiting professor, UC Berkeley 1980–81; visiting professor, Michigan and Stanford 1987–88; Professor of law, European University Institute, Florence, since 1981; since 1993 Professor of law, London School of Economics.

Seibert, Thomas-Michael
b. 1949; studied law at Mainz; doctorate 1975; 1975–82 justice department, Wiesbaden; since 1982 judge, Landgericht Frankfurt; guest lecturer Frankfurt University.

Siep, Ludwig
b. 1942; studied law at Köln and Freiburg; doctorate 1969; habilitation 1976 Freiburg; Professor Duisburg 1979–86; Director of the Philosophical Seminar at Münster since 1986.

Thienel, Rudolf
b. 1960; studied law in Vienna; doctorate 1982 Vienna; habilitation 1989 Vienna; since 1989 Professor of law at the Institute for Constitutional and Administrative Law, University of Vienna.

Walter, Robert
b. 1931; studied law at Vienna; doctorate (law) 1953 Vienna; doctorate (political science) 1956 Vienna; habilitation 1960 Vienna; 1960–62 lecturer Vienna; 1962–66 Professor at Graz; 1966–75 Professor, School of Economics, Vienna; since 1975 Professor of law at Vienna.

Weinberger, Ota
b. 1919; studied law and philosophy at Masaryk University and Charles University (Prague); doctorate (law) 1947 Masaryk; doctorate (philoso-

phy) 1961 Charles; habilitation 1964 Charles; Professor, Institute for Legal Philosophy, University of Graz.

WILLKE, HELMUT
b. 1945; studied law in Tübingen and Köln; doctorate 1974 Tübingen; habilitation 1982 Köln; since 1983 Professor of Planning and Decision Theory at Bielefeld.

ZIPPELIUS, REINHOLD
b. 1928; studied law in Würzburg, Erlangen, and Munich; government service, State of Bavaria 1956–63; habilitation 1961 Munich; since 1963 Professor at Erlangen-Nürnberg.

Bibliography

The following materials are provided for the reader who wishes to pursue particular topics in the field of German legal philosophy. The order in which they are arranged is indicated below under organization. The topic headings parallel the discussion of topics in the text.

Organization

HISTORICAL MATERIALS (TO 1975)

I. Secondary Sources

II. Primary Sources

- Critical Theory and Marxism
- Existentialism
- Hermeneutics
- Language and Law
- Logic and Law
- Natural Law
- Rhetorical Theory
- Social Science of Law
- Systems Theory

CONTEMPORARY MATERIALS (SINCE 1975)

- Analytic Jurisprudence
- Anthropological Jurisprudence
- Aristotelian Theory
- Communitarianism
- Critical Rationalism
- Discourse Theory
- Feminist Jurisprudence
- Hegelian Theory
- Hermeneutics
- Institutional Positivism
- Integrative Jurisprudence
- Kantian Theory
- Law and Economics
- Marxist Theory

Neo-Kelsenism
Rhetorical Theory
Systems Theory

Historical Materials (to 1975)

I. Secondary Sources

Adorno, Theodor et al., eds. *The Positivist Dispute in German Sociology*. Translated by Glyn Adey and David Frisby. New York: Harper Torchbooks, 1976. Original German edition: *Der Positivismusstreit in der deutschen Soziologie* (1969).

Dreier, Ralf, ed. "Rechtspositivismus und Wertbezug des Rechts." *Archiv für Rechts- und Sozialphilosophie* Special Edition 37 (1990).

Haft, Fritjof, and Eric Hilgendorf. "Juristische Argumentation und Dialektik." In *Strafgerechtigkeit: Festschrift für Arthur Kaufmann*, edited by Fritjof Haft, 93. Heidelberg: C. F. Müller, 1993.

Haller, Rudolf. *Neopositivismus: Eine historische Einführung in die Philosophie des Wiener Kreises.* Darmstadt: Wissenschaftliche Buchgesellschaft, 1993.

Huke-Didier, Eckart. *Die Wissensoziologie Karl Mannheims in der Interpretation durch die kritische Theorie: Kritik einer Kritik.* New York: Peter Lang, 1985.

Kaufmann, Arthur. "Durch Naturrecht und Rechtspositivismus zur juristischen Hermeneutik." *Juristenzeitung* 30 (1975): 337.

———, ed. *Rechtsphilosophie im Wandel: Stationen eines Weges.* 2d ed. Köln: Heymanns, 1984.

Langner, Albrecht. *Der Gedanke des Naturrechts seit Weimar und in der Rechtssprechung der Bundesrepublik.* Bonn: H. Bouvier, 1959.

Maschke, Andreas. *Gerechtigkeit durch Methode: zu Karl Engischs Theorie des juristischen Denkens.* Heidelberg: Winter, 1993.

Raiser, Thomas. *Einführung in die Rechtssoziologie.* 4th ed. Berlin: J. Schweitzer, 1985.

Rosenbaum, Wolf. *Naturrecht und positives Recht: Rechtssoziologische Untersuchungen zum Einfluß der Naturrechtslehre auf die Rechtspraxis in Deutschland siet Beginn des 19. Jahrhunderts.* Neuwied: Luchterhand, 1972.

Rottleutner, Herbert, ed. *Recht, Rechtsphilosophie und Nazionalsozialismus.* Stuttgart: Steiner, 1983.

Schelauske, Hans. *Naturrechtsdiskussion in Deutschland: Ein Überblick über zwei Jahrzehnte 1945–1965.* Köln: J. P. Bachem, 1968.

II. Primary Sources

Critical Theory and Marxism

Adorno, Theodor. *Einleitung in der Positivismusstreit in der deutschen Soziologie.* Neuwied: Luchterhand, 1969.

———. *Negative Dialectics.* Translated by E. B. Ashton. New York: Seabury Press, 1973. Original German edition: *Negative Dialektik* (1973).

———. "Soziologie und empirische Forschung." In *Wesen und Wirklichkeit des Menschen: Festschrift für Helmut Plessner.* edited by Klaus Ziegler, 245. Göttingen: Vanderhoeck and Ruprecht, 1957.

Bloch, Ernst. *Naturrecht und Menschliche Würde.* Frankfurt: Suhrkamp, 1961.

Habermas, Jürgen. *Knowledge and Human Interests.* Translated by Jeremy J. Shapiro. Boston: Beacon Press, 1972. Original German edition: *Erkenntnis und Interesse* (1968).

———. *Kultur und Kritik.* Frankfurt: Suhrkamp, 1973.

———. *Legitimation Crisis.* Translated by Thomas McCarthy. Boston: Beacon Press, 1975. Original German edition: *Legitimationsprobleme in Spätkapitalismus* (1973).

———. *The Structural Transformation of the Public Sphere.* Translated by Thomas Burger. Cambridge, Mass.: MIT Press, 1991. Original German edition: *Strukturwandel der Öffentlichkeit* (1962).

———. *Technik und Wissenschaft als "Ideologie".* Frankfurt: Suhrkamp, 1968.

———. *Theorie der Gesellschaft oder Sozialtechnologie.* Frankfurt: Suhrkamp, 1971.

———. *Theory and Practice.* Translated by John Viertel. Boston: Beacon Press, 1973. Original German edition: *Theorie und Praxis: Sozialphilosophische Studien* (1963).

———. "Wahrheitstheorien." In *Wirklichkeit und Reflexion,* edited by Helmut Fahrenbach, 259. Pfulligen: Neske, 1973.

———. *Zur Rekonstruktion des historischen Materialismus.* Frankfurt: Suhrkamp, 1976.

Horkheimer, Max. *Critical Theory: Selected Essays.* Translated by Matthew J. O'Connell et al. New York: Herder and Herder, 1973. Original German edition: *Kritische Theorie* (2 vols. 1968).

———. *The Eclipse of Reason.* New York: Oxford Univ. Press, 1947.

Paul, Wolf. *Marxistische Rechtstheorie als Kritik des Rechts.* Frankfurt: Athenäum, 1974.

Schüßler, Gerhard et al., eds. *Einführung in die marxistisch- leninistische Staats- und Rechtslehre.* 2d ed. Berlin: Dietz, 1986.

Wiethölter, Rudolf. *Rechtswissenschaft.* Frankfurt: Fischer, 1968.

Existentialism

Maihofer, Werner. *Naturrecht als Existenzrecht.* Frankfurt: V. Klostermann, 1963

———. *Recht und Sein.* Frankfurt: V. Klostermann, 1954.

Philipps, Lothar. *Zur Ontologie der sozialen Rolle.* Frankfurt: V. Klostermann, 1963.

Hermeneutics

Esser, Josef. *Vorverständnis und Methodenwahl in der Rechtsfindung: Rationalitätsgrundlagen richterlichen Entscheidungspraxis.* Frankfurt: Athenäum, 1970.

Hassemer, Winfried. *Tatbestand und Typus: Untersuchungen zur strafrechtlichen Hermeneutik.* Köln: Heymann, 1968.

Larenz, Karl. *Methodenlehre der Rechtswissenschaft.* Berlin: Springer, 1960.

Language and Law

Eckmann, Heinrich. *Rechtspositivismus und Sprachanalytische Philosophie: Der Begriff des Rechts in der Rechtstheorie H.L.A. Harts.* Berlin: Duncker and Humblot, 1969.

Horn, Dieter. *Rechtssprache und Kommunikation.* Berlin: Duncker and Humblot, 1966.

Rave, Dieter et al., eds. *Analyse der Juristischen Sprache.* 4 vols. Darmstadt: Wissenschaftliche Buchgesellschaft, 1971–74.

Logic and Law

Engisch, Karl. *Logische Studien zur Gesetzesanwendung.* Heidelberg: Winter, 1943.
Esser, Josef. *Grundsatz und Norm in der richterlichen Fortbildung des Privatsrechts.* Tübingen: Mohr, 1956.
Klug, Ulrich. *Juristische Logik.* Berlin: Springer, 1951.
Lenk, Hans, ed. *Normenlogik.* München: Pullach, 1974.
Rödig, Jürgen. *Die Denkform der Alternative in der Jurisprudenz.* Berlin: Springer, 1969.
Stegmüller, Wolfgang. *Probleme und Resultate der Wissenschaftstheorie und analytischen Philosophie.* Berlin: Springer, 1973.
Weinberger, Ota. *Rechtslogik.* Berlin: Duncker and Humblot, 1970.

Natural Law

Coing, Helmut. *Grundzüge der Rechtsphilosophie.* Berlin: de Gruyter, 1950.
———. *Die obersten Grundsätze des Rechts: Ein Versuch zur Neubegründung des Naturrechts.* Heidelberg: L. Schneider, 1947.
Fuchs, Josef. *Lex Naturae: Zur Theologie des Naturrechts.* Düsseldorf: Patmos, 1955.
Funk, Josef. *Primat des Naturrechts: Die Transzendenz des Naturrechts gegenüber dem positiven Recht.* Modling bei Wien, St. Gabriel-Verlag, 1952.
Hartmann, Nicolai. *Das Problem des geistigen Seins.* 3d ed. Berlin: de Gruyter, 1962.
Kaufmann, Arthur. *Naturrecht und Geschichtlichkeit.* Tübingen: Mohr, 1957.
Messner, Johannes. *Das Naturrecht: Handbuch der Gesellschaftsethik, Staatsethik und Wirtschaftsethik.* Innsbruck: Tyrolia, 1950.
Radbruch, Gustav. "Die Erneuerung des Rechts." *Die Wandlung* 2 (1947): 9.
———. "Gesetzliches Unrecht und Übergesetzliches Recht." *Süddeutsche Juristische Zeitung* 1 (1946): 105.
———. *Der Innere Weg.* Stuttgart: Koehler, 1951.
———. *Rechtsphilosophie.* 4th ed. Stuttgart: Koehler, 1950.
———. *Vorschule der Rechtsphilosophie.* Göttingen: Vanderhoeck and Ruprecht, 1948.
Rommen, Heinrich. *Die ewige Wiederkehr des Naturrechts.* Leipzig: Hegner, 1936.
Welzel, Hans. *Naturrecht und materiale Gerechtigkeit.* Göttingen: Vanderhoeck and Ruprecht, 1951.

Rhetorical Theory

Ballweg, Otmar. *Rechtswissenschaft und Jurisprudenz.* Basel: Helbing and Lichtenhahn, 1970.
Ballweg, Otmar, and Thomas Seibert. *Rhetorische Rechtstheorie.* Freiburg: Alber, 1972.
Struck, Gerhard. *Topische Jurisprudenz.* Frankfurt: Athenäum, 1971.
Viehweg, Theodor. "Historische Perspektiven der juristischen Argumentation: II. Neuzeit." *Archiv für Rechts- und Sozialphilosophie* 7 (1972): 63.
———. "Notizen zu einer rhetorischen Argumentationstheorie der Rechtsdisziplin." *Jahrbuch für Rechtssoziologie und Rechtstheorie* 2 (1972): 439.
———. "Positivismus und Jurisprudenz." In *Positivismus im 19. Jahrhundert,* edited by Jürgen Blühdorn and Joachim Ritter, 105. Frankfurt: Kostermann, 1971.

———. "Systemprobleme in Rechtsdogmatik und Rechtsforschung." *Studien zur Wissenschaftstheorie* 2 (1968): 96.

———. *Topics and Law.* Translated by Cole Durham. Frankfurt: Peter Lang, 1993. Original German edition: *Topik und Jurisprudenz* (1953).

Wieacker, Franz. *Gesetz und Richterkunst: Zum Problem der außergesetzlichen Rechtsordnung.* Karlsruhe: C.F. Müller, 1958.

Social Science of Law

Albert, Hans. *Konstruktion und Kritik.* Hamburg: Hoffmann and Campe, 1972.

———. *Marktsoziologie und Entscheidungslogik.* Neuwied: Luchterhand, 1967.

———. *Plädoyer für kritischen Rationalismus.* München: Piper, 1971.

———. *Traktat über kritische Vernunft.* Tübingen: Mohr, 1968.

Dreier, Ralf. "Zum Selbstverständnis der Jurisprudenz als Wissenschaft." *Rechtstheorie* 2 (1971): 37.

Ebeling, Gerhard. *Kritischer Rationalismus?* Tübingen: Mohr, 1973.

Gehlen, Arnold, ed. *Studien zur Anthropologie und Soziologie.* Berlin: Luchterhand, 1963.

Geiger, Theodor. *Arbeiten zur Soziologie, Methode, Großgesellschaft, Rechtssoziologie, Ideologiekritik.* Enlarged ed. Neuwied: Luchterhand, 1962.

———. *Vorstudien zu einer Soziologie des Rechts.* Neuwied: Luchterhand, 1964.

Henke, Wilhelm. *Kritik des kritischen Rationalismus.* Tübingen: Mohr, 1974.

Hirsch, Ernst, and Manfred Rehbinder, eds. *Studien und Materialen zur Rechtssoziologie.* Opladen: Westdeutscher, 1967.

Janich, Peter et al., eds. *Wissenschaftstheorie als Wissenschaftskritik.* Frankfurt: Aspekte, 1974.

Kambartel, Friedrich, ed. *Praktische Philosophie und kronstruktive Wissenschaftstheorie.* Frankfurt: Suhrkamp, 1974.

———. *Theorie und Begründung.* Frankfurt: Suhrkamp, 1974.

Kambartel, Friedrich, and Jürgen Mittelstrass, eds. *Zum normativen Fundament der Wissenschaft.* Frankfurt: Athenäum, 1973.

Lorenzen, Paul. *Methodisches Denken.* Frankfurt: Suhrkamp, 1968.

Lorenzen, Paul, and Otto Schwemmer. *Konstruktive Logik, Ethik und Wissenschaftstheorie.* Mannheim: Bibliographisches Institut, 1973.

Mittelstrass, Jürgen. *Die Möglichkeit von Wissenschaft.* Frankfurt: Suhrkamp, 1974.

Nauke, Wolfgang. *Über die juristische Relevanz der Sozialwissenschaften.* Frankfurt: A. Metzner, 1972.

Popper, Karl. *Conjectures and Refutations: The Growth of Scientific Knowledge.* New York: Basic Books, 1963.

———. *The Logic of Scientific Discovery.* New York: Basic Books, 1959. Original German edition: *Logik der Forschung* (1935).

———. *Objective Knowledge: An Evolutionary Approach.* Oxford: Clarendon Press, 1972.

———. *The Open Society and Its Enemies.* Princeton, N.J.: Princeton Univ. Press, 1950.

———. *The Poverty of Historicism.* Boston: Beacon Press, 1957.

Savigny, Eike von. *Die Überprüfbarkeit der Strafrechtssätze.* Freiburg: Alber, 1967.

Schelsky, Helmut, ed. *Zur Theorie der Institution.* Düsseldorf: Bartelsmann, 1973.

Schnur, Roman, ed. *Institution und Recht.* Darmstadt: Wissenschaftliche Buchgesellschaft, 1968.

Schwerdtner, Peter. "Rechtswissenschaft und kritischer Rationalismus." *Rechtstheorie* 2 (1971): 67.

Spinner, Helmut. *Pluralismus als Erkenntnismodell.* Frankfurt: Suhrkamp, 1974.

Rottleutner, Hubert. *Rechtswissenschaft als Sozialwissenschaft.* Frankfurt: Fischer, 1973.

Systems Theory

Habermas, Jürgen, and Niklas Luhmann, eds. *Theorie der Gesellschaft oder Sozialtechnologie: Was leistet die Systemforschung?.* Frankfurt: Suhrkamp, 1971.

Luhmann, Niklas. *Legitimation durch Verfahren.* Frankfurt: Suhrkamp, 1969.

———. *A Sociological Theory of Law.* Translated by Elizabeth King and Martin Albrow. London: Routledge and Kegan Paul, 1985. Original German edition: *Rechtssoziologie* (1972).

———. *Soziologische Aufklärung: Aufsätze zur Theorie sozialer Systeme.* Opladen: Westdeutscher, 1970.

———. *Trust and Power: Two Works.* Translated by Howard Davis, John Raffan, and Kathryn Rooney. Chichester: Wiley, 1979. Original German edition: *Vertrauen: Ein Mechanismus der Reduktion sozialer Komplexität* (1968).

———. *Zweckbegriff und Systemrationalität: Über die Funktion von Zwecken in sozialen Systemen.* Frankfurt: Suhrkamp, 1968.

Parsons, Talcott. *The Social System.* New York: Free Press, 1952.

———. *The Structure of Social Action.* New York: Free Press, 1949.

———. *Zur Theorie sozialer Systeme.* Opladen: Westdeutscher, 1976.

Teubner, Gunther. "Folgenkontrolle und responsive Dogmatik." *Rechtstheorie* 6 (1975): 179.

Wiener, Norbert. *Cybernetics: or, Control and Communication in the Animal and the Machine.* Cambridge, Mass.: MIT Press, 1949. German edition: *Kybernetik: Regelung der Nachrichtenübertragung im Lebewesen und in der Maschine* (1963).

Contemporary Materials (Since 1975)

Analytical Jurisprudence

Alexy, Robert, and Aleksander Peczenik. "Coherence and Discursive Rationality." *Ratio Juris* 3 (1990): 130.

Arnaud, Andre et. al. eds. *Juristische Logik, Rationalität und Irrationalität im Recht.* Berlin: Duncker and Humblot, 1985.

Buchwald, Delf. *Der Begriff der rationalen juristischen Begründung: Zur Theorie der juridischen Vernunft.* Baden-Baden: Nomos, 1990.

———. "Die canones der Auslegung und rationale juristische Begründung." *Archiv für Recht- und Sozialphilosophie* 79 (1993): 16.

———. "Rational Legal Justification: Coherence and Concretness." *Archiv für Rechts- und Sozialphilosophie* Special Edition #53 (1994) 86.

———. "Statutory Interpretation in the Focus of Legal Justification: An Essay in Coherentist Hermeneutics." *Univ. Toledo Law Review* 25 (1994): 735.

Gethmann, Carl, ed. *Logik und Pragmatik: Zum Rechtfertigungsproblem logischer Sprachregeln.* Frankfurt: Suhrkamp, 1982.

Hassemer, Winfried et al., eds. *Argumentation und Recht.* Berlin: Duncker and Humblot, 1980.

Hilgendorf, Eric. *Argumentation in der Jurisprudenz.* Berlin: Duncker and Humblot, 1991.

Hoerster, Norbert. *Recht und Moral.* 2d ed. Munich: Deutscher Taschenbuch, 1980.

———. "Richtigstellung über den Rechtspositivismus." *Archiv für Rechts- und Sozialphilosophie* 9 (1993): 416

———. *Utilitarische Ethik und Verallgemeinerung.* 2d ed. Freiburg: Alber, 1977.

Hruschka, Joachim. "Recht und Unrecht bei Norbert Hoerster." *Archiv für Rechts- und Sozialphilosophie* 79 (1993): 421.

Koch, Hans-Joachim. *Juristische Methodenlehre und analytische Philosophie.* Kronberg: Athenäum, 1976.

Koch, Hans-Joachim, and Helmut Rüßmann. *Juristische Begründungslehre.* Munich: Beck, 1982.

Krawietz, Werner. "Juridisch-institutionelle Rationalität des Rechts versus Rationalität der Wissenschaften?" *Rechtstheorie* 15 (1984): 423.

———. "Neues Naturrecht oder Rechtspositivismus? Eine kritische Auseinandersetzung mit dem Begriff des Rechts bei Ralf Dreier und Norbert Hoerster." *Rechtstheorie* 18 (1987): 209.

———. *Recht als Regelsystem.* Wiesbaden: F. Steiner, 1984.

Krawietz, Werner, and Robert Alexy, eds. *Metatheorie juristischer Argumentation.* Berlin: Duncker and Humblot, 1983.

Mettenheim, Christoph. *Recht und Rationalität.* Tübingen: Mohr, 1984.

Müller, Friedrich. *Juristische Methodik.* 5th ed. Berlin: Duncker and Humblot, 1993.

———, ed. *Untersuchungen zur Rechtslinguistik.* Berlin: Duncker and Humblot, 1989.

Neumann, Ulfrid. *Juristische Argumentationslehre.* Darmstadt: Wissenschaftliche Buchgesellschaft, 1986.

Ott, Walter. *Der Rechtspositivismus: Kritische Würdigung auf der Grundlage eines juristischen Pragmatismus.* 2d ed. Berlin: Duncker and Humblot, 1992.

Pawlowski, Hans-Martin. *Einführung in die juristische Methodenlehre.* Heidelberg: C. F. Müller, 1986.

Peczenik, Aleksander. *Grundlagen der juristischen Argumentation.* Vienna: Springer, 1983.

———. "Legal Rationality and Its Limits." *Rechtstheorie* 15 (1984): 415.

———. "Moral and Ontological Justification of Legal Reasoning." *Law and Philosophy* 4 (1985): 289.

Rodingen, Hubert. *Pragmatik der Argumentation: Was Gesetze anrichten und was rechtens ist.* Freiburg: Alber, 1977.

Viehweg, Theodor, and Franz Rotter, eds. *Recht und Sprache.* Berlin: Duncker and Humblot, 1977.

Anthropological Jurisprudence

Höffe, Otfried. "Ein transzendentaler Tausch: Zur Anthropologie der Menschenrechte." *Philosophisches Jahrbuch* 7 (1992): 1.

Lampe, Ernst-Joachim. "Anthropologische Struktur und Geschichtlichkeit des Rechts." In *Strafgerechtigkeit: Festschrift für Arthur Kaufmann,* edited by Fritjof Haft, et al., 199. Heidelberg: C.F. Müller, 1993.

———. "The Concept and Development of Law." *Archiv für Rechts- und Sozialphilosophie* 77 (1992): 1.

———. "Entwicklungslinien in der rechtsanthropologischen Forschung." *Archiv für Rechts- und Sozialphilosophie* Special Edition 50 (1992): 232.
———. *Genetische Rechtstheorie: Recht, Evolution und Geschichte.* Freiburg: Alber, 1987.
———. *Grenzen des Rechtspositivismus: Eine rechtsanthropologische Untersuchung.* Berlin: Duncker and Humblot, 1988.
———. "Rechtsanthropologie heute." *Archiv für Rechts- und Sozialphilosophie* Special Edition 44 (1991): 222.
Rentsch, Thomas. *Heidegger und Wittgenstein: Existential- und Sprachanalysen zu den Grundlagen philosophischer Anthropologie.* Stuttgart: Klett-Cotta, 1985.
———. "Kommunikative Interexistentiale und praktische Weltkonstitution." In *Schöpferisches Handeln,* edited by Dietfried Gerhardus et al., 35. Frankfurt: Peter Lang, 1991.
———. *Die Konstitution der Moralität: Transzendentale Anthropologie und praktische Philosophie.* Frankfurt: Suhrkamp, 1990.

Aristotelian Theory

Baruzzi, Arno. *Einführung in die politische Philosophie der Neuzeit.* Expanded ed. Darmstadt: Wissenschaftliche Buchgesellschaft, 1993.
———. *Freiheit, Recht und Gemeinwohl: Grundlage einer Rechstphilosophie.* Darmstadt: Wissenschaftliche Buchgesellschaft, 1990
———. *Die Zukunft der Freiheit.* Darmstadt: Wissenschaftliche Buchgesellschaft, 1993.
Spaemann, Robert. *Die Frage Wozu? Geschichte und Entdeckung des teleologischen Denkens.* Munich: Piper, 1981.
———. *Moralische Grundbegriffe.* 2d ed. Munich: Beck, 1991.
———. *Das Natürliche und das Vernunftige.* Munich: Piper, 1987.
———. *Philosophische Essays.* Stuttgart: Reclam, 1983.

Communitarianism

Honneth, Axel, "Grenzen des Liberalismus: Zur politisch-ethischen Diskussion um den Kommunitarismus." *Philosophische Rundschau* 38 (1991): 83.
———. *Pathologien des Sozialen.* Frankfurt: Fischer, 1994.
Kallscheuer, Otto. "Michael Walzers kommunitärer Liberalismus oder die Kraft der inneren Opposition." In *Kritik und Gemeinsinn,* edited by Michael Walzer, 126. Berlin: Rotbuch, 1990.
Reese-Schäfer, Walter. *Was ist Kommunitarismus?* Frankfurt: Campus, 1994.

Critical Rationalism

Albert, Hans. *Aufklärung und Steurung.* Hamburg: Hoffmann and Campe, 1976.
———. "Critical Rationalism: The Problem of Method in Social Sciences and Law." *Ratio Juris* 1 (1988): 1.
———. "Dialektische Denkwege: Jürgen Habermas und der kritische Rationalismus." In *Mensch und Gesellschaft aus der Sicht des kritischen Rationalismus,* edited by Hans Albert and Kurt Salamun, 11. Amsterdam: Rodopi, 1993.
———. *Das Elend der Theologie.* Hamburg: Hoffman and Campe, 1979.

———. "Erkenntnis, Recht und soziale Ordnung: Zur Rechts- und Sozialphilosophie des kritischen Rationalismus." *Archiv für Rechts- und Sozialphilosophie* Special Edition 44 (1991): 16.

———. *Freiheit und Ordnung.* Tübingen: Mohr, 1986.

———. "Das Gewißheitsbedurfnis und die Suche nach Wahrheit." In *Pragmatismus versus Fundamentalismus,* edited by Hans Albert et al., 11. Vienna: Orlach, 1993.

———. "Hermeneutik als Heilmittel? Der ökonomische Ansatz und das Problem des Verstehens." *Zeitschrift für Soziologie* 18 (1989): 1.

———. "Ein hermeneutischer Rückfall: Jürgen Habermas und der kritische Rationalismus." *Logos (neue Folge)* 1 (1993): 3.

———. *Kritik der reinen Erkenntnislehre.* Tübingen: Mohr, 1987.

———. *Kritik der reinen Hermeneutik: Der Antirealismus und das Problem des Verstehens.* Tübingen: Mohr, 1994.

———. "Zur Kritik der reinen Jurisprudenz: Recht und Rechtswissenschaft in der Sicht des kritischen Rationalismus." *Intern. Jahrbuch Rechtsphilosophie und Gesetzgebung* (1992): 343.

———. *Kritische Vernunft und menschliche Praxis.* 2d ed. Stuttgart: Reclam, 1984.

———. "Law as an Instrument of Rational Practice." In *Contract and Organization,* edited by Terence Daintith and Gunther Teubner, 25. Berlin: de Gruyter, 1986.

———. "Methodologischer Individualismus und historische Analyse." In *Teil und Ganzes: Zum Verhältnis von Einzel- und Gesamtanalyse in Geschichts- und Sozialwissenschaften,* edited by Karl Acham and Wolfgang Schulze, 85. München: Deutsches Taschenbuch, 1990.

———. "Der Mythos des Rahmens am Pranger." *Zeitschrift für philosophische Forschung* 44 (1990): 85.

———. "Philosophie als Engagement für kritische Vernunft." In *Was ist Philosophie?* edited by Kurt Salamun, 237. Tübingen: Mohr, 1986.

———. *Plädoyer für kritischen Rationalismus.* 4th ed. Munich: Piper, 1975.

———. *Rechtswissenschaft als Realwissenschaft: Das Recht als soziale Tatsache und die Aufgabe der Jurisprudenz.* Baden- Baden: Nomos, 1993.

———. "Some Remarks on Reasons in Explaining Human Action." *Intern. Studies in Philosophy of Science* 7 (1993): 25.

———. *Traktat über kritische Vernunft.* 5th expanded ed. Tübingen: Mohr, 1991.

———. *Traktat über rationale Praxis.* Tübingen: Mohr, 1978.

———. *Transzendental Träumereien: Karl-Otto Apels Sprachspiele und sein hermeneutischer Gott.* Hamburg: Hoffmann and Campe, 1975.

———. *Treatise on Critical Reason.* Translated by Mary Varney Rorty. Princeton, N.J.: Princeton Univ. Press, 1985. Original German edition: *Traktat über kritische Vernunft* (1968).

———. "Die Wertfreiheitsproblematik und der normative Hintergrund der Wissenschaften." In *Wirtschaft und Ethik,* edited by Hans Lenk and Matthias Maring, 82. Stuttgart: Reclam, 1992.

———. "Der Wiener Kreis und die Problematik der Rationalität." In *Jour fixe der Vernunft: Der Wiener Kreis und die Folgen,* edited by Paul Kruntorad, 56. Vienna: Hölder-Pichler-Tempsky, 1991.

———. *Die Wissenschaft und die Fehlbarkeit der Vernunft.* Tübingen: Mohr, 1982.

Andersson, Gunnar. *Criticism and the History of Science.* Leiden: E. J. Brill, 1994.

Eikemma-Hommes, Hendrik. "The Relevance of Popper's Scientific Method for Legal Theory." *Rechtstheorie* 14 (1983): 459.

Fusfield, William. "Can Jürgen Habermas' 'Begründungsprogram' Escape Hans Albert's *Münchhausen Trilemma*?" *Rhetorik* 8 (1989): 73.
Haller, Rudolf. "Über das sogenannte Münchhausen Trilemma." *Ratio* 16 (1974) 121.
Hegselmann, Rainer. *Normativität und Rationalität.* Frankfurt: Campus, 1979.
Kellmann, Christof. *Kritischer Rationalismus in der Rechtswissenschaft?* 1975.
Keuth, Herbert. *Erkenntnis oder Entscheidung: Zur Kritik der kritischen Theorie.* Tübingen: Mohr, 1993.
———. *Wissenschaft und Urteil: Zu Werturteilsdiskussion und Positivismusstreit.* Tübingen: Mohr, 1989.
Musgrave, Alan. "Constructive Empiricism and Scientific Realism." *Philosophical Quarterly* 32 (1982): 262.
Neumann, Ulfrid et al., eds. *Juristische Dogmatik und Wissenschaftstheorie.* Munich: Beck, 1976.
Spaemann, Robert. "Überzeugung in einer hypothetischen Zivilisation." In *Abschied von Utopia?* edited by Otto Schatz, 311. Graz: Styria, 1977.
Thienel, Rudolf. *Kritischer Rationalismus und Jurisprudenz: Zugleich eine Kritik an Hans Alberts Konzept einer sozialtechnishcen Jurisprudenz.* Vienna: Österreichische Staatsdruckerei, 1991.
Walter, Robert. "Bemerkungen zur Albert: Zur Kritik der reinen Jurisprudenz." *Intern. Jahrbuch für Rechtsphilosophie und Gesetzgebung* (1992): 359.

Discourse Theory

Albert, Hans. "Ein hermeneutischer Rückfall: Jürgen Habermas und der kritische Rationalismus." *Logos (neue Folge)* 1 (1993): 3.
———. *Transzendentale Träumereien: Karl-Otto Apels Sprachspiele und sein hermeneutischer Gott.* Hamburg: Hoffman and Campe, 1975.
Alexy, Robert. *Begriff und Geltung des Rechts.* Freiburg: Alber 1992.
——— (with Aleksander Peczenik). "The Concept of Coherence and Its Significance for Discursive Rationality." *Ratio Juris* 3 (1990): 130.
——— (with Ralf Dreier). "The Concept of Jurisprudence." *Ratio Juris* 3 (1990): 1.
———. "A Discourse-Theoretical Conception of Practical Reason." *Ratio Juris* 5 (1992): 210.
———. "Human Rights and Popular Sovereignty: The Liberal and Republican Versions." *Ratio Juris* 7 (1994):1
———. "Idee und Struktur eines vernünftigen Rechtssystems." *Archiv für Rechts- und Sozialphilosophie* Special Edition #44 (1991): 30.
———. "Justification and Application of Norms." *Ratio Juris* 6 (1993): 157.
———. "Zur Kritik des Rechtspositivismus." *Archiv für Rechts- und Sozialphilosophie* 37 (1990): 9.
———. "On Necessary Relations between Law and Morality." *Ratio Juris* 2 (1989): 168.
———. "Problems of Discourse Theory." *Critica* 20 (1988): 43.
———. "Problems of Discursive Rationality in Law." *Archiv für Rechts- und Sozialphilosophie* 42 (1990): 174.
———, *Recht, Vernunft, Diskurs.* Frankfurt: Suhrkamp, 1995.
———. "Rechtssystem und Praktische Vernunft." *Rechtstheorie* 18 (1987): 405.
———. "Rights, Legal Reasoning, and Rational Discourse." *Ratio Juris* 5 (1992): 143.

———. *Theorie der Grundrechte.* Baden-Baden: Nomos, 1985.

———. *Theorie der juristischen Argumentation.* 2d enlarged ed. Frankfurt: Suhrkamp, 1991.

———. *A Theory of Legal Argumentation.* Translated by Ruth Adler and Neil MacCormick. Oxford: Clarendon Press, 1989. Original German edition: *Theorie der juristischen Argumentation* (1978).

Apel, Karl-Otto. *Diskurs und Verantwortung: Das Problem des Übergangs zur postkonventionellen Moral.* Frankfurt: Suhrkamp, 1988.

———. *Gemeinschaft und Gerechtigkeit.* Frankfurt: Fischer, 1993.

———. "Grenzen der Diskursethik: Versuch einer Zwischenbilanz." *Zeitschrift für philosophische Forschung* 40 (1986): 3.

———. "Is the Ethics of the Ideal Communication Community a Utopia?" In *The Communicative Ethics Controversy,* edited by Seyla Benhabib and Fred Dallmayr, 23. Cambridge, Mass.: MIT Press, 1990.

———. "Kann der postkantische Standpunkt der Moralität noch einmal in substantielle Sittlichkeit 'aufgehoben' werden?" In *Moralität und Sittlichkeit: Das Problem Hegels und die Diskursethik,* edited by Wolfgang Kuhlmann, 217. Frankfurt: Suhrkamp, 1986.

———. "Das Problem der Begründung einer Verantwortungsethik im Zeitalter der Wissenschaft." In *Wissenschaft und Ethik,* edited by Eberhard Braun, 11. Bern: Peter Lang, 1986.

———. "The Problems of Philosophical Foundations in Light of a Transcendental Pragmatics of Language." In *After Philosophy: End or Transformation,* edited by Thomas McCarthy, 250. Cambridge, Mass.: MIT Press, 1987.

———. *Towards a Transformation of Philosophy.* Translated by Glyn Adey and David Frisby. London: Routledge and Kegan Paul, 1980. Original German edition: *Transformation der Philosophie* (2 vols. 1973).

———. *Transzendental Pragmatik.* Frankfurt: Suhrkamp, 1993.

Benhabib, Seyla, and Fred Dallmayr, eds. *The Communicative Ethics Controversy.* Cambridge, Mass.: MIT Press, 1990.

Bolte, Gerhard, ed. *Unkritische Theorie: Gegen Habermas.* Luneburg: Klampen, 1989.

Cortina, Adela. "Diskursethik und Menschenrechte." *Archiv für Rechts- und Sozialphilosophie* 76 (1990): 37.

Dreier, Ralf. "Rechtsphilosophie und Diskurstheorie." *Zeitschrift für philosophische Forschung* 48 (1994): 90.

Dwars, Ingrid. "Application Discourse and the Special-Case Thesis." *Ratio Juris* 5 (1992): 67.

Eder, Klaus. "Die Autorität des Rechts: Eine soziale Kritik prozeduraler Rationalität." *Zeitschrift für Rechtssoziologie* 8 (1987): 1.

———. "Critique of Habermas' Contribution to the Sociology of Law." *Law and Society Review* 22 (1988): 931.

———. "Prozedurale Legitimität: Moderne Rechtsentwicklung jenseits von formaler Rationalisierung." *Zeitschrift für Rechtssoziologie* 7 (1986): 1.

Fusfield, William. "Can Jürgen Habermas' 'Begründungsprogram' Escape Hans Albert's *Münchhausen Trilemma*?" *Rhetorik* 8 (1989): 73.

Günther, Klaus. "Critical Remarks on Robert Alexy's 'Special Case' Thesis." *Ratio Juris* 6 (1993): 143.

———. "The Idea of Impartiality and the Functional Determinacy of the Law." *Northwestern Univ. Law Review* 83 (1989): 151.

———. "Ein normativer Begriff der Kohärenz für eine Theorie der juristischen Argumentation." *Rechtstheorie* 20 (1989): 163.

———. *The Sense of Appropriateness: Application Discourses in Morality and Law.* Translated by John Farrell. Albany: State Univ. of New York Press, 1993. Original German edition: *Der Sinn für Angemessenheit: Anwendungsdiskurs in Moral und Recht* (1988).

———. "Warum es Anwendungsdiskurs gibt." *Jahrbuch für Recht und Ethik* 1 (1993): 379.

Haarscher, Guy. "Perelman and Habermas." *Law and Philosophy* 5 (1986): 331.

Habermas, Jürgen. *Between Facts and Norms: Contributions to a Discourse Theory of Law and Democracy.* Translated by William Rehg. Cambridge, Mass.: MIT Press, 1995. Original German edition: *Faktizität und Geltung* (1992).

———. *Communication and the Evolution of Society.* Translated by Thomas McCarthy. Cambridge, Mass.: MIT Press, 1979. Original German edition: *Zur Rekonstruktion des historischenMaterialismus* (1976).

———. *Erläuterung zur Diskursethik.* Frankfurt: Suhrkamp, 1991.

———. "Human Rights and Popular Sovereignty." *Ratio Juris* 7 (1994): 1.

———. "Justice and Solidarity: On the Discussion Concerning State Six." In *The Moral Domain: Essays in the Ongoing Discussion Between Philosophy and the Social Sciences,* edited by Thomas Wren, 224. Cambridge, Mass.: MIT Press, 1990.

———. *Justification and Application: Remarks on Discourse Ethics.* Cambridge, Mass.: MIT Press, 1993. Original German essays in various collections.

———. "Law and Morality," *The Tanner Lectures on Human Values* 8 (1988): 217.

———. *Moral Consciousness and Communicative Action.* Translated by Christian Lenhardt and Shierry Weber Nicholsen. Cambridge, Mass.: MIT Press, 1990. Original German edition: *Moral Bewußtsein und kommunikatives Handeln* (1983).

———. "Moralität und Sittlichkeit." In *Moralität und Sittlichkeit: Das Problem Hegels und die Diskursethik,* edited by Wolfgang Kuhlmann, 16. Frankfurt: Suhrkamp, 1986.

———. *The Philosophical Discourse of Modernity: Twelve Lectures.* Translated by Frederick G. Lawrence. Cambridge, Mass.: MIT Press, 1988. Original German edition: *Philosophischer Diskurs der Moderne* (1985).

———. *The Structural Transformation of the Public Sphere: An Inquiry into a Category of Bourgeois Speech.* Translated by Thomas Burger. Cambridge, Mass.: MIT Press, 1991. Original German edition: *Strukturwandel der Öffentlichkeit* (1962).

———. *The Theory of Communicative Action.* Translated by Thomas McCarthy. Boston: Beacon Press, 2 vol. 1984 and 1987. Original German edition: *Theorie des kommunikativen Handeln* (2 vols. 1981).

———. *Vorstudien und Ergänzungen zur Theorie des kommunikativen Handelns.* Frankfurt: Suhrkamp, 1984.

———. "Wie ist Legitimität durch Legalität möglich?" *Kritische Justiz* 20 (1987): 1.

Höffe, Otfried. "Eine Konversion der kritischen Theorie?" *Rechtshistorisches Journal* 12 (1993): 70.

Kern, Lucian, and Hans-Peter Müller, eds. *Gerechtigkeit: Diskurs oder Markt?* Opladen: Westdeutscher, 1986.

Kettner, Matthias. "Scientific Knowledge, Discourse Ethics, and Consensus Formation on Public Policy Issues." In *Science, Politics and Morality: Scientific Uncertainty and Decisionmaking,* edited by Rene von Schomberg, 161. Dordrecht: Kluwer, 1992.

———. "Warum es Anwendungsfragen, aber keine 'Anwendungsdiskurse' gibt." *Jahrbuch für Recht und Ethik* 1 (1993): 376.

Keuth, Herbert. *Erkenntnis oder Entscheidung? Zur Kritik der kritischen Theorie.* Tübingen: Mohr, 1993.

———. "Fallibilismus versus transzendentalpragmatische Letzbegründung." *Zeitschrift für allgemeine Wissenschaftstheorie* 14 (1983): 320.

Krawietz, Werner, and Robert Alexy, eds. *Metatheorie juristischer Argumentation.* Berlin: Duncker and Humblot, 1983.

Kuhlmann, Wolfgang. "Reflexive Letzbegründung versus radikaler Fallibilismus." *Zeitschrift für allgemeine Wissenschaftstheorie* 16 (1985): 357.

———. *Sprachphilosophie, Hermeneutik, Ethik.* Wurzburg: Könighausen and Neumann, 1992.

———, ed. *Moralität und Sittlichkeit: Das Problem Hegels und die Diskursethik.* Frankfurt: Suhrkamp, 1986.

Leist, Anton. "Diesseits der Transzendentalpragmatik: Gibt es sprachpragmatische Argumente für Moral?" *Zeitschrift für philosophische Forschung* 43 (1989): 301.

Lübbe, Weyma. "Wie ist Legitimität durch Legalität möglich?" *Archiv für Rechts- und Sozialphilosophie* 79 (1993): 80.

Luhmann, Niklas. "Quod omnes tangit: Anmerkungen zur Rechtstheorie von Jürgen Habermas." *Rechtshistorisches Journal* 12 (1993): 36.

McCarthy, Thomas. *The Critical Theory of Jürgen Habermas.* Cambridge, Mass.: MIT Press, 1978.

Peczenik, Aleksander. *The Basis of Legal Justification.* Lund, Sweden: A. Peczenik, 1983.

———. *Grundlagen der juristischen Argumentation.* Vienna: Springer, 1983.

———. "Legal Reasoning as a Special Case of Moral Reasoning." *Ratio Juris* 1 (1988): 123.

Schlink, Bernhard. "Abenddämmerung oder Morgendämmerung: Zu Jürgen Habermas' Diskurstheorie des democratischen Rechtsstaats." *Rechtshistorisches Journal* 12 (1993): 57.

Weinberger, Ota. "Conflicting Views on Practical Reason: Against Pseudo Arguments in Practical Philosophy." *Ratio Juris* 5 (1992): 231.

———. "Logische Analyse als Basis der juristischen Argumentation." In *Metatheorie juristischer Argumentation,* edited by Werner Krawietz and Robert Alexy, 200. Berlin: Duncker and Humblot, 1983.

White, Stephen. *The Cambridge Companion to Habermas.* Cambridge: Cambridge Univ. Press, 1995.

———. *The Recent Work of Jürgen Habermas: Reason, Justice, and Modernity.* Cambridge: Cambridge Univ. Press, 1988.

Feminist Jurisprudence

Böttger, Barbara. *Das Recht auf Gleichheit und Differenz.* Münster: Westfälisches Dampfboot, 1990.

Frommel, Monika. "Männliche Gerechtigkeitsmathematik versus weiblicher Kontextualismus?" *Archiv für Rechts- und Sozialphilosophie* Special Edition #44 (1990) 82.

Gerhard, Uta, ed. *Differenz und Gleichheit.* Frankfurt: Helmer, 1990.

Thürmer-Rohr, Christina. *Vagabonding: Feminist Thinking Cut Loose.* Translated by Lisa Weil. Boston: Beacon Press, 1991. Original German edition: *Vagabundinnen: Feministische Essays* (1990).

———. *Verlorene Narrenfreiheit.* Berlin: Orlanda Frauenverlag, 1994.

Hegelian Theory

Henrich, Dieter, and Rolf-Peter Horstmann. *Hegels Philosophie des Rechts: Die Theorie der Rechtsformen und ihre Logik.* Stuttgart: Kett-Cotta, 1982.
Hösle, Vittorio, ed. *Die Rechtsphilosophie des deutschen Idealismus.* Hamburg: F. Meiner, 1989.
Jermann, Christof. *Anspruch und Leistung von Hegels Rechtsphilosophie.* Stuttgart: Fromman-Holzboog, 1987.
Kuhlmann, Wolfgang, ed. *Moralität und Sittlichkeit: Das Problem Hegels und die Diskursethik.* Frankfurt: Suhrkamp, 1986.
Lucas, Hans-Christian, and Otto Pöggeler, eds. *Hegels Rechtsphilosophie im Zusammenhang der europäischen Verfassungsgeschichte.* Stuttgart: Fromman-Holzboog, 1986.
Schild, Wolfgang. "Rechtswissenschaft oder Jurisprudenz: Bemerkungen zu den Schwierigkeiten der Juristen mit Hegels Rechtsphilosophie." *Archiv für Rechts- und Sozialphilosophie* Special Edition 44 (1991): 328.
Siep, Ludwig. "Verfassung, Grundrechte und soziales Wohl in Hegels Philosophie des Rechts." *Archiv für Rechts- und Sozialphilosophie* Special Edition 44 (1991): 361.

Hermeneutics

Albert, Hans. *Kritik der reinen Hermeneutik: Der Antirealismus und das Problem des Verstehens.* Tübingen: Mohr, 1994.
Frommel, Monika. *Die Rezeption der Hermeneutik bei Karl Larenz und Josef Esser.* Ebelsbach: R. Gremer, 1981.
Hassemer, Winfried. *Dimensionen der Hermeneutik.* Heidelberg: C. F. Müller, 1984.
Hegenbarth, Rainer. *Juristische Hermeneutik und linguistische Pragmatik.* Königstein: Athenäum, 1982.
Kaufmann, Arthur. *Beiträge zur juristischen Hermeneutik.* Köln: Heymann, 1984.
———. "Durch Naturrecht und Rechtspositivismus zur juristischen Hermeneutik." *Juristenzeitung* 30 (1975): 337.
———. *Über Gerechtigkeit.* Köln: Heymann, 1993.
Krawietz, Werner, et al., eds. *Argumentation und Hermeneutik in der Jurisprudenz.* Berlin: Duncker and Humblot, 1979.

Institutional Positivism

Bankowski, Zenon. "Institutional Legal Positivism?" *Rechtstheorie* 20 (1989): 289.
Koller, Peter et al., eds. *Institution und Recht: Grazer Internationales Symposion zu Ehren von Ota Weinberger.* Berlin: Duncker and Humblot, 1994.
Krawietz, Werner. "Ansätze zu einem Neuen Institutionalismus in der modernen Rechtstheorie der Gegenwart." *Juristenzeitung* 40 (1985): 706.
———. *Rechtsnorm und Rechtswirklichkeit.* Berlin: Duncker and Humblot, 1993.
Krawietz, Werner, and Ota Weinberger. *Helmut Schelsky als Soziologe und politischer Denker.* Stuttgart: Steiner, 1985.
Krawietz, Werner, and Robert Alexy, eds. *Metatheorie juristischer Argumentation.* Berlin: Duncker and Humblot, 1983.
Larenz, Karl. *Methodenlehre der Rechtswissenschaft.* 6th ed. Berlin: Springer, 1991.
MacCormick, Neil, and Ota Weinberger. *An Institutional Theory of Law: New Approaches to Legal Positivism.* Translated by Ruth Adler and Neil MacCormick.

Dordrecht: Reidel, 1986. Original German edition: *Grundlagen des Institutionalistischen Rechtspositivismus* (1985).
Schelsky, Helmut. *Person und Institution.* Wurzburg: Könighausen and Neumann, 1980.
Schelsky, Helmut et al., eds. *Theorie der Normen: Festgabe für Ota Weinberger.* Berlin: Duncker and Humblot, 1984.
Tammelo, Ilmar, and Aulis Aarnio, eds. *Zum Fortschritt von Theorie und Technik in Recht und Ethik.* Berlin: Duncker and Humblot, 1981.
Tammelo, Ilmar, and Helmut Schreiner, eds. *Strukturierungen und Entscheidungen im Rechtsdenken.* Vienna: Springer, 1978.
Weinberger, Christiane. *Evolution und Ethologie: Wissenschaftstheoretische Analysen.* Vienna: Springer, 1983.
Weinberger, Ota. "Conflicting Views on Practical Reason: Against Pseudo-Arguments in Practical Philosophy." *Ratio Juris* 5 (1992): 252.
———. "The Expressive Conception of Norms—An Impasse for the Logic of Norms." *Law and Philosophy* 5 (1985): 165.
———. *Moral und Vernunft: Beiträge zu Ethik, Gerechtigkeitstheorie und Normenlogik.* Vienna: Bohlau, 1992.
———. *Norm und Institution: Eine Einführung in die Theorie des Rechts.* Vienna: Manz, 1988.
———. "Der normenlogische Skeptizismus." *Rechtstheorie* 17 (1986): 13.
———. *Normentheorie als Grundlage der Jurisprudenz und Ethik: Eine Auseinandersetzung mit Hans Kelsens Theorie der Normen.* Berlin: Duncker and Humblot, 1981.
———. *Rechtsgeltung.* Stuttgart: Steiner, 1986.
———. *Rechtslogik.* 2d ed. Vienna: Springer, 1989.
———. *Studien zur formal-finalistischen Handlungstheorie.* Frankfurt: Peter Lang, 1983.
———. *Theoretische Grundlagen der Rechtspolitik.* Stuttgart: Steiner, 1992.
Weinberger, Ota, and Werner Krawietz, eds. *Reine Rechtslehre im Spiegel ihrer Fortsetzer und Kritiker.* Vienna: Springer, 1988.
Weinberger, Ota, and Vladimir Kubes, eds. *Die Brünner rechtstheoretische Schule (Normative Theorie).* Vienna: Manz, 1980.
Weinberger, Ota, and Christiane Weinberger. *Logik, Semantik, Hermeneutik.* Munich: Beck, 1979.
Winkler, Gunther, ed. *Rechtstheorie und Rechtsinformatik.* Vienna: Springer, 1979.

Integrative Jurisprudence

Brugger, Winfried. "Das anthropologische Kreuz der Entscheidung." In *Recht und Ideologie: Festschrift für Hermann Klenner,* edited by Gerhard Haney, Werner Maihofer, and Gerhard Sprenger, 13. Freiburg: Haufe, 1995.
———. "Konkretisierung des Rechts und Auslegung der Gesetze." *Archiv für öffentlichen Rechts* 119 (1994): 1.
———. "Legal Methods, Schools of Jurisprudence, and Anthropology: Some Remarks from a German Point of View." *American Jour. Comparative Law* 42 (1994): 395.

Kantian Theory

Bielefeldt, Heiner. *Neuzeitliches Freiheitsrecht und politische Gerechtigkeit: Perspektiven der Gesellschaftsvertragtheorie.* Wurzburg: Könighausen and Neumann, 1990.

Brugger, Winfried. "Grundlinien der kantischen Rechtsphilosophie." *Juristenzeitung* 19 (1990): 893.

Dreier, Ralf. *Rechtsbegriff und Rechtsidee: Kants Rechtsbegriff und seine Bedeutung für die gegenwärtige Diskussion.* Frankfurt: Metzner, 1986.

Höffe, Otfried. *Immanuel Kant.* Translated by Marshall Farrier. Albany: State Univ. of New York Press, 1994. Original German edition: *Immanuel Kant* (1983).

———. *Katagorische Rechtsprinzipien: Ein Kontrapunkt der Moderne.* Frankfurt: Suhrkamp, 1990.

———. *Moral als Preis der Moderne: Ein Versuch über Wissenschaft, Technik und Umwelt.* Frankfurt: Suhrkamp, 1993.

———. *Political Justice: Foundations for a Critical Philosophy of Law and the State.* Translated by Jeffrey C. Cohen. Cambridge: Polity Press, 1995. Original German edition: *Politische Gerechtigkeit: Grundlegung einer kritischen Philosophie von Recht und Staat* (1987).

———. *Den Staat braucht selbst ein Volk von Teufeln.* Stuttgart: Reclam, 1988.

———. "Universalist Ethics and the Faculty of Judgment: An Aristotelian Looks at Kant." *Philosophical Forum* 25 (1993): 55.

Kersting, Wolfgang. *Wohlgeordnete Freiheit: Immanuel Kants Recht- und Staatsphilosophie.* Berlin: de Gruyter, 1984.

Kühl, Kristian. "Die Bedeutung der Kantischen Unterscheidungen von Legalität und Moralität sowie von Rechtspflichten und Tugendpflichten für das Strafrecht." In *Recht und Moral,* edited by Helmut Jung, 139. Frankfurt: Peter Lang, 1991.

———. *Eigentumsordnung als Freiheitsordnung—Zur Aktualität der kantischen Rechts- und Eigentumslehre.* Freiburg: Alber, 1984.

———."Rehabilitierung und Aktualisierung des kantischen Vernunftrechts." *Archiv für Rechts- und Sozialphilosophie* Special Edition 44 (1991): 212.

Maus, Ingeborg. *Zur Aufklärung der Demokratietheorie: Rechts- und demokratietheoretische Überlegungen im Anschluß an Kant.* Frankfurt: Suhrkamp 1992.

Naucke, Wolfgang. *Rechtsphilosophische Grundbegriffe.* 2d ed. Frankfurt: Metzner, 1986.

Wellmer, Albrecht. *Ethik und Dialog: Elemente des moralischen Urteils bei Kant und in der Diskursethik.* Frankfurt: Suhrkamp, 1986.

Law and Economics

Adams, Michael. *Ökonomische Analyse der Gefährdungs- und Verschuldenshaftung.* Heidelberg: Decker, 1985.

Assmann, Heinz-Dieter et al., eds. *Ökonomische Analyse des Rechts.* New ed. Kronberg: Athenäum, 1993.

Fezer, Karl-Heinz. "Nochmals: Kritik und der ökonomischen analyse des Rechts." *Juristenzeitung* 43 (1988): 223.

Kirchner, Christian. "The Difficult Reception of Law and Economics in Germany." *Intern. Review of Law and Economics* 11 (1991): 277.

Lehmann, Michael. *Bürgerliches Recht und Handelsrecht—eine juristische und ökonomische Analyse.* Munich: Beck, 1983.

Nagel, Bernhard, and Thomas Eger. *Wirtschaftsrecht II: Eigentum, Delikt, Vertrag mit einer Einführung in die ökonomische Analyse des Rechts.* 2d ed. Munich: Oldenbourg, 1989.

Ott, Claus. "Die ökonomische Analyse des Rechts—Irrweg oder Chance wissenschaftlicher Rechtserkenntnis?" *Juristenzeitung* 43 (1988): 213.

———, ed. *Allokationseffizienz in der Rechtsordnung.* Berlin: Springer, 1989.

Ott, Claus, and Hans Schäfer. *Ökonomische Probleme des Zivilrechts.* Berlin: Springer, 1991.

Schäfer, Hans, and Claus Ott. *Lehrbuch der ökonomischen Analyse des Zivilrechts.* Berlin: Springer, 1986.

Schanze, Erich. "Rechtsnorm und ökonomisches Kalkül." *Jour. Inst. Theory of Economics* (1982): 297.

Marxist Theory

Haney, Gerhard. "Das Widerspruchsvolle des Rechtsbegriffs." *Archiv für Rechts- und Sozialphilosophie* Special Edition 44 (1991): 110.

Klenner, Hermann. "Rechtsphilosophisches zur ontologischen und zur gnoseologischen Dimension der Sein/Sollen-Problematik." *Archiv für Rechts- und Sozialphilosophie* Special Edition 44 (1991): 163.

Mollnau, Karl. "Die Babelsberger Konferenz oder: Vom Beginn der Niedergangsjurisprudenz in der DDR." *Archiv für Rechts- und Sozialphilosophie* Special Edition 44 (1991): 236.

Neo-Kelsenism

Gianformaggio, Letizia. "Hans Kelsen on the Deduction of Validity." *Rechtstheorie* 20 (1990): 181.

———, *Hans Kelsen's Legal Theory.* Torino: G. Giapichelli Editore, 1990.

Krawietz, Werner, and Helmut Schelsky, eds. *Rechtssystem und gesellschaftliche Basis bei Hans Kelsen.* Berlin: Duncker and Humblot, 1984.

Krawietz, Werner et al., eds. *Ideologiekritik und Demokratietheorie bei Hans Kelsen.* Berlin: Duncker and Humblot, 1982.

Ott, Walter. *Der Rechtspositivismus: Kritische Würdigung auf der Grundlage eines juristischen Pragmatismus.* 2d. ed. Berlin: Duncker and Humblot, 1992.

Paulson, Stanley. "Continental Normativism and Its British Counterpart: How Are They Different?" *Ratio Juris* 6 (1993): 227.

———. "Kelsen and the Marburg School: Reconstructive and Historical Perspectives." In *Prescriptive Formality and Normative Rationality in Modern Legal Systems,* edited by Werner Krawietz et al., 481. Berlin: Duncker and Humblot, 1994.

———. "Kelsen's Legal Theory: The Final Round." *Oxford Jour. Legal Studies* 12 (1992): 265.

———. "The Neo-Kantian Dimension of Kelsen's Pure Theory of Law." *Oxford Jour. Legal Studies* 12 (1992): 311.

———. "Die unterschiedlichen Formulierung der 'Grundnorm.'" In *Rechtsnorm und Rechtswirklichkeit,* edited by Aulis Aarnio et al., 53. Berlin: Duncker and Humblot, 1993.

———, ed. *Hans Kelsen und die Rechtssoziologie: Auseinandersetzung mit Hermann U. Kantorowicz, Eugen Ehrlich, und Max Weber.* Aalen: Scientia, 1992.

Pawlik, Michael. *Die Reine Rechtslehre und die Rechtstheorie H. L. A. Harts: Ein kritischer Vergleich.* Berlin: Duncker and Humblot, 1993.

Sieckmann, Jan-Reinard. *Regelmodelle und Prinzipienmodelle des Rechtssystems.* Baden-Baden: Nomos, 1990.

Thienel, Rudolf. *Kritischer Rationalismus und Jurisprudenz: Zugleich eine Kritik an*

Hans Alberts Konzept einer sozialtechnischen Jurisprudenz. Vienna: Österreichische Staatsdruckerei, 1991.
Walter, Robert, ed. *Schwerpunkte der reinen Rechtslehre.* Vienna: Manz, 1992.
Weinberger, Ota, and Werner Krawietz. *Reine Rechtslehre im Spiegel ihrer Fortsetzer und Kritiker.* Vienna: Springer, 1988.

Rhetorical Theory

Ballweg Ottmar. "Analytical Rhetoric, Semiotic, and Law." In *Law and Semiotics,* edited by Roberta Kevelson, 25. New York: Plenum Press, 1987.
———. "Analytische Rhetorik als juristische Grundlagenforschung." *Archiv für Rechts- und Sozialphilosophie* Special Edition 44 (1991): 45.
———. "Entwurf einer analytischen Rhetorik." In *Rhetorik und Philosophie,* edited by Helmut Schanze, 229. Munich: W. Fink, 1989.
———. "Phronetik, Semiotik, und Rhetorik." In *Rhetorische Rechtstheorie,* edited by Ottmar Ballweg and Thomas Seibert, 22. Freiburg: Alber, 1982.
———. "Rhetorik und Res humanae." In *Gedächtnisse für Peter Noll,* edited by Raimund Hauser et al., 13. Zürich: Schulthess, 1984.
———. "Rhetorik und Vertrauen." In *Kritik und Vertrauen,* edited by Erhard Denninger, 34. Frankfurt: A. Hain, 1990.
Breuer, Dieter, and Helmut Schanze, eds. *Topik: Beiträge zur interdisziplinären Diskussion.* Munich: W. Fink, 1981.
Bund, Elmar. *Juristische Logik und Argumentation.* Freiburg: Rombach, 1983.
Eberle, Norbert. *Zur Rhetorik des zivilprozessualen Beweises.* Frankfurt: Peter Lang, 1989.
Engisch, Karl. *Einführung in das juristische Denken.* 8th ed. Stuttgart: Kohlhammer, 1983.
Esser, Josef. *Juristisches Argumentieren im Wandel des Rechtsfindungskonzepts unseres Jahrhunderts.* Heidelberg: Winter, 1979.
Garrn, Heino. "Die 'Natur der Sache' als Grundlage der juristischen Argumentation." *Archiv für Rechts- und Sozialphilosophie* 68 (1982): 62.
———. *Zur Rationalität rechtlicher Entscheidung.* Stuttgart: Steiner, 1986.
———. "Zur rechtspraktischen Bedeutung einer Theorie der juristischen Rhetorik." *Archiv für Rechts- und Sozialphilosophie* Special Edition 44 (1991): 96.
Gast, Wolfgang. "Zur Einübung der Ungewißheit." *Archiv für Rechts- und Sozialphilosophie* 66 (1980): 147.
———. *Juristische Rhetorik: Auslegung, Begründung, Subsumption.* 2d ed. Heidelberg: Decker, 1992.
———. *Rechtserkenntnis und Gewaltsstrukturen.* Berlin: Duncker and Humblot, 1975.
Haft, Fritjof. *Juristische Rhetorik.* 4th ed. Freiburg: Alber, 1990.
Klug, Ulrich. *Juristische Logik.* 4th ed. Berlin: Springer, 1982.
Kopperschmidt, Josef. *Allgemeine Rhetorik: Einführung in der Theorie des persuasiven Kommunikation.* Stuttgart: Kohlhammer, 1985.
Müller, Friedrich. *Juristische Methodik.* 5th ed. Berlin: Duncker and Humblot, 1993.
Oppermann, Bernd. *Die Rezeption des nordamerikanischen Rechtsrealismus durch die Topikdiscussion.* Doctoral Dissertation: Frankfurt University, 1985.
Pawlowski, Hans-Martin. *Methodenlehre für Juristen.* 2d ed. Heidelberg: C. F. Müller, 1985.

Perelman, Chaim. *Juristische Logik als Argumentationslehre.* Munich: Alber, 1979.

———. *The Realm of Rhetoric.* Notre Dame, Ind.: Univ. of Notre Dame Press, 1982. German edition: *Das Reich der Rhetorik.* 1980.

Ptassek, Peter et al., eds. *Macht und Meinung: Die rhetorische Konstitution der politischen Welt.* Göttingen: Vanderhoeck and Ruprecht, 1992.

Rodingen, Hubert. *Pragmatik der Argumentation: Was Gesetze anrichten und was rechtens ist.* Freiburg: Alber, 1977.

———. "Von der Rationalität der Topik." In *Rhetorische Rechtslehre,* edited by Ottmar Ballweg and Thomas Seibert, 181. Freiburg: Alber, 1982.

———. "Rhetorik im Recht: Ortbestimmung und Überblick." *Rhetorik* (1981): 85.

Schneider, Peter. *". . . ein einzig Volk von Brüdern": Recht und Staat in der Literatur.* Frankfurt: Athenäum, 1987.

———. "Jurisprudenz, Utopie und Rhetorik." *Archiv für Rechts- und Sozial Philosophie* Special Edition 44 (1991): 337.

Schreckenberger, Waldemar. "Notizen über die rhetorische Semiotik: Unter besonderer Berücksichtigung der Geltungsproblematik in der Rechtstheorie." *Archiv für Rechts- und Sozialphilosophie* Special Edition 44 (1991): 348.

———. "Rhetorik, Politik, und Recht." *Der Staat* 4 (1994): 594.

———. *Rhetorische Semiotik: Analysen von Texten des Grundgesetzes und von rhetorischen Grundstrukturen der Argumentation des Bundesverfassungsgerichts.* Freiburg: Alber, 1978.

———. "Über den Zugang der modernen Logik zur Rechtsdogmatik." In *Rhetorische Rechtslehre,* edited by Ottmar Ballweg and Thomas Seibert, 155. Freiburg: Alber, 1982.

Seibert, Thomas-Michael. *Aktenanalysen: Zur Schriftform juristischer Deutung.* Tübingen: Narr, 1981.

———. "The Arguments of a Good Judge." In *Argumentation: Analysis and Practices,* edited by Frans H. van Eemeren et al., 119. Dordrecht: Faris, 1987.

———. "Der Durchschnittleser als Mittler gerichtlicher Kommunikationsvorstellungen." In *Rechtskultur als Sprachkultur,* edited by Georg Grewendorf, 332. Frankfurt: Suhrkamp, 1992.

———. "Erzählen als gesellschaftliche Kronstruktion von Kriminalität." In *Erzählte Kriminalität,* edited by Jorg Schönert, 73. Tübingen: Niemeyer, 1991.

———. "Mündlichkeit und Schriftform im Rechtsdiskurs" and "Linguistische Verhandlungsanalysen aus juristischer Sicht." Both in *Rechtsdiskurs: Untersuchungen zur Kommunikation in Gerichtsverfahren,* edited by Ludger Hofmann, Tübingen: Narr, 1989.

———. "Vom Nutzen und Nachteil des forensischen Modells für die Philosophie des Diskurs." In *Rhetorik und Philosophie,* edited by Helmut Schanze and Josef Kopperschmidt, 249. Munich: Fink, 1989.

———. "Orte der Wahrheit: Zur Semantik der Räume von Hauptverhandlung und Psychoanalyse." In *Psychiatrie, Psychotherapie und Recht,* edited by Franz Rotter, 157. Frankfurt: Peter Lang, 1993.

———. "Der Richter gilt als unparteilich: Fiktionen des Rechtsverfahrens." *Zeitschrift für Semiotik* 12 (1990): 187

———. "Zeichen und Gesetzesbindung." *Rechtstheorie* 22 (1991): 470.

Sobota, Katharina. "Don't Mention the Norm!" *Intern. Jour. Semiotics of Law* 4 (1991): 45.

———. *Sachlichkeit: Rhetorische Kunst der Juristen.* Frankfurt: Peter Lang, 1990.

———. "Stimmigkeit als Rechtsstruktur." *Archiv für Rechts- und Sozialphilosophie* 77 (1991): 243.

Struck, Gerhard. *Zur Theorie juristischer Argumentation.* Berlin: Duncker and Humblot, 1977.

Viehweg, Theodor. "Schritte zu einer rechtsrhetorischen Rechtstheorie." In *Kultur, Kriminalität, Strafrecht,* edited by Rüdiger Herren et al., 3. Berlin: Duncker and Humblot, 1977.

Systems Theory

Bankowski, Zenon. "How does it Feel to be on your Own?". *Ratio Juris* 7 (1994): 254.

Dahrendorf, Ralf. *Pfade aus Utopie: Arbeiten zur Theorie und Methode der Soziologie.* 2d ed. Munich: Piper, 1986.

Druwe, Ulrich. "Recht als autopoietisches System: Zur Kritik des reflexiven Rechtskonstrukts." *Jahreschrift für Rechtspolitologie* 4 (1990): 103.

Eigen, Manfred, and Peter Schuster. *The Hypercycle: A Principle of Natural Self-Organization.* Berlin: Springer, 1979.

Evan, William. *Social Structure and Law: Theoretical and Empirical Perspectives.* Newbury Park, Calif.: Sage, 1990.

Fischer, Hans, ed. *Autopoiesis: Eine Theorie im Brennpunkt der Kritik.* Heidelberg: Auer, 1991.

Foerster, Heinz von. *Observing Systems.* 2d ed. Seaside, Calif.: Intersystems, 1984.

———, ed. *Sicht und Einsicht: Versuche zu einer operativen Erkenntnistheorie.* Braunschweig: F. Viehweg, 1985.

Frey, Reiner. *Vom Subjekt zur Selbstreferenz: Rechtstheoretische Überlegungen zur Rekonstruktion der Rechtskategorie.* Berlin: Duncker and Humblot, 1989.

Fuchs, Peter. *Niklas Luhmann—beobachtet: Eine Einführung in die Systemtheorie.* Opladen: Westdeutscher, 1992.

Haferkampf, Hans, and Michael Schmid. *Sinn, Kommunikation, und sozialer Differenzierung: Beiträge zu Luhmanns Theorie sozialer Systeme.* Frankfurt: Suhrkamp, 1987.

Jacobsen, Arthur. "Autopoietic Law: The New Science of Niklas Luhmann." *Michigan Law Review* 87 (1989): 1647.

Kneer, Georg, and Armin Nassehi. *Niklas Luhmanns Theorie sozialer Systeme: Eine Einführung.* Munich: W. Fink, 1993.

———, and Armin Nassehi. "Verstehen des Verstehens: Eine systemtheoretische Revision der Hermeneutik." *Zeitschrift für Soziologie* 20 (1991): 341.

Luhmann, Niklas. *Ausdifferenzierung des Rechts: Beiträge zur Rechtssoziologie und Rechtstheorie.* Frankfurt: Suhrkamp, 1981.

———. "The Autopoiesis of Social Systems." In *Sociocybernetic Paradoxes: Observation, Control and Evolution of Self-Steering Systems,* edited by Felix Geyer and Jan van der Zouwen, 171. London: Sage 1986.

———. *Beobachtungen der Moderne.* Opladen: Westdeutscher, 1992.

———. "Closure and Openness: On Reality in the World of Law." In *Autopoietic Law: A New Approach to Law and Society,* edited by Gunther Teubner, 335. Berlin: de Gruyter, 1988.

———. *The Differentiation of Society.* Translated by Steven Holmes and Charles Larmore. New York: Columbia Univ. Press, 1982. Original German edition: *Soziologische Aufklärung* (1970).

———. *Erkenntnis als Konstruktion.* Bern: Benteli, 1988.

———. *Essays on Self-Reference.* New York: Columbia Univ. Press, 1990.

———. *Gesellschaftstruktur und Semantik.* 2 vols. Frankfurt: Suhrkamp, 1980–81.

———. *Gibt es in unserer Gesellschaft noch unverzichtbare Normen?*"Heidelberg: C. W. Müller, 1993.

———. *Legitimation durch Verfahren.* 3d ed. Frankfurt: Suhrkamp, 1993.

———. *Political Theory in the Welfare State.* Translated by John Bednarz, Jr. Berlin: de Gruyter, 1990. Original German edition: *Politische Theorie im Wohlfahrtsstaat* (1989).

———. *Das Recht der Gesellschaft.* Frankfurt: Suhrkamp, 1993.

———. "The Representation of Society Within Society." *Current Sociology* 35 (1987): 101.

———. *Risk: A Sociological Theory.* Translated by Rhodes Barrett. Berlin: de Gruyter, 1993. Original German edition: *Soziologie des Risikos* (1991).

———. "The Self-Description of Society: Crisis, Fashion and Sociological Theory." *Intern. Jour. Comparative Sociology* 25 (1984): 59.

———. *Social Systems.* Translated by John Bednarz, Jr. Stanford, Calif.: Stanford Univ. Press, 1995. Original German edition: *Soziale Systeme: Grundriss einer allgemeinen Theorie* (1984).

———. *A Sociological Theory of Law.* Translated by Elizabeth King and Martin Albrow. London: Routledge and Kegan Paul, 1985. Original German edition: *Rechtssoziologie* (2 vol. 1972).

———. "The Theory of Social Systems and Its Epistemology." *Philosophy of the Social Sciences* 16 (1986): 112.

———. "The Unity of the Legal System." In *Autopoietic Law: A New Approach to Law and Society,* edited by Gunther Teubner, 12. Berlin: de Gruyter, 1988.

———. *Die Wissenschaft der Gesellschaft.* 2d ed. Frankfurt: Suhrkamp, 1991.

———. *Zweckbegriff und Systemrationalität.* 5th ed. Frankfurt: Suhrkamp, 1991.

———, ed. *Beobachter.* 2d ed. Munich: Fink, 1992.

Münch, Richard. *Dialektik der Kommunikationsgesellschaft.* Frankfurt: Suhrkamp, 1991.

———. *Theory of Action: Towards a New Synthesis Going Beyond Parsons.* London: Routledge and Kegan Paul, 1987. Original German edition: *Theorie des Handelns: Zur Rekonstruktion der Beiträge von Talcott Parsons, Emile Durkheim und Max Weber* (1982).

Nassehi, Armin. *Die Zeit der Gesellschaft: Auf dem Weg zu einer soziologischen Theorie der Zeit.* Opladen: Westdeutscher, 1993.

Reese-Schäfer, Walter. *Luhmann zur Einführung.* Hamburg: Junius, 1992.

Rottleuthner, Hubert. "A Purified Theory of Law: Niklas Luhmann on the Autonomy of the Legal System." *Law and Society Review* 23 (1989): 779.

———. *Einführung in die Rechtssoziologie.* Darmstadt: Wissenschaftliche Buchgesellschaft, 1987.

Schelsky, Helmut. *Die Soziologen und das Recht.* Opladen: Westdeutscher, 1980.

Schmidt, Siegfried, ed. *Der Diskurs des Radikalen Konstruktivismus.* 2d ed. Frankfurt: Suhrkamp, 1988.

Schneider, Wolfgang. *Die Beobachtung von Kommunikation.* Opladen: Westdeutscher, 1994.

———. *Objektives Verstehen: Rekonstruktion eines Paradigmas—Gadamer, Popper, Toulmin, Luhmann.* Opladen: Westdeutscher, 1991.

Teubner, Gunther. "How the Law Thinks: Towards a Constructivist Epistemology of Law." *Law and Society Review* 28 (1989): 727.

———. *Law as an Autopoietic System.* Translated by Anne Bankowska and Ruth Adler. Oxford: Blackwell, 1993. Original German edition: *Recht al autopoietisches System* (1989).

———, ed., *Autopoietic Law: A New Approach to Law and Society.* Berlin: de Gruyter, 1988.

Wenzel, Harald. *Die Ordnung des Handelns: Talcott Parsons' Theorie des allgemeinen Handlungsystems.* Frankfurt: Suhrkamp, 1991.

Willke, Helmut. *Ironie des Staates: Grundlinien einer Staatstheorie polyzentrischer Gesellschaft.* Frankfurt: Suhrkamp, 1992.

———. *Systemtheorie: Eine Einführung in die Grundprobleme der Theorie sozialer Systeme.* 4th ed. Stuttgart: Fischer, 1993.

———. *Systemtheorie entwickelter Gesellschaften: Dynamik und Riskanz moderner gesellschaftlicher Selbstorganisation.* Weinheim: Juventa, 1989.

Index

Aarnio, Aulis, 111
Adorno, Theodor, 5–6
agreement as basis for decision, 107
Albert, Hans, 9, 30–43, 45–46, 74, 75, 106, 107, 119
Alexy, Robert, 11, 15, 44–60, 105, 107, 117, 119
analytical jurisprudence, 14–16. *See also* institutional positivism
Anscombe, Gertrude E. M., 8, 98
anthropological jurisprudence, 16–18
anthropological constants, 16
anthropological cross, 23
Apel, Karl-Otto, 10, 44, 48
application discourse, 58–59
Aquinas, Thomas, 2, 71
Aristotle, 18–19, 60, 65
Austin, John, 13, 71
Austin, John L., 8
autopoietic systems, 75–77, 79, 83–84, 86
Ayer, Alfred J., 8

Ballweg, Ottmar, 60
Baruzzi, Arno, 19
Begriffsjurisprudenz, 111
Bentham, Jeremy, 36, 71
Bertalanffy, Ludwig von, 74
binary code, 78–79
Bloch, Ernst, 6
Brown, George Spencer, 74
Brugger, Winfried, 23–24
Buchwald, Delf, 15, 105, 117

Chomsky, Noam, 60
Cicero, 60
Cohen, Felix S., 1
Coing, Helmut, 3 fn
Coke, Edward, 70, 113
common law, 70–72, 112–113
communitarianism, 28–29
consensus theory of truth, 46–47
consistent fallibilism, 34
construction of law, 66–67
core justification, 15
correspondence theory of truth, 32, 56, 96
cover justification, 15
critical rationalism, 30–43
critical theory, 5–6, 45

Davidson, Donald, 109
deontic logic, 97
Dewey, John, 109
differentiation of law, 16, 76, 83, 88–89
Dingler, Hugo, 30
discourse theory, 44–61
Dreier, Ralf, 15, 60
Durkheim, Emile, 73
Dworkin, Ronald, 23–24, 42, 60, 91, 100, 106, 111

Eisenberg, Melvin, 106
Engisch, Karl, 7
Esser, Josef, 21–22, 60
evolution of law, 16, 73, 83, 86, 109–111
existential philosophy, 6–7, 17–18

falsification of theory, 35
feminism, 29
final substantiation (*Letztbegründung*), 34, 45, 55, 59–60, 64, 101
Fish, Stanley, 106
Foerster, Heinz von, 74, 87
foreign influences, 111–112
Frankfurt School, 5–6, 43, 45

Freirechtler. See Free Law movement
Free Law movement, 88 fn, 111
Fuller, Lon, 3 fn
function of law, 75–77, 91

Gadamer, Hans-Georg, 7, 21
Garrn, Heino, 63 fn
Gast, Wolfgang, 60
Geiger, Theodore, 30
genetic legal theory, 16. *See also* differention of law
German Constitutional Court, 2, 5
Gilligan, Carol, 29
Grundnorm, 28, 40, 85, 101, 103
Günther, Klaus, 58–59

Habermas, Jürgen, 9–10, 31, 44–60, 74, 105, 107
Hart, H.L.A., 8, 28, 60, 100, 111
Hartmann, Nicolai, 2
Hauriou, Maurice, 94
Hayek, Friedrich, 7
Hegel, Georg Wilhelm Friedrich, 19–21
Heidegger, Martin, 7, 9, 17, 21, 45
hermeneutics, 21–23
historical jurisprudence. *See* evolution of law; anthropological jurisprudence
Hobbes, Thomas, 71 fn
Hoerster, Norbert, 61 fn
Höffe, Otfried, 27
horizon (hermeneutical), 22
Horkheimer, Max, 5–6, 45
Hume, David, 93
hypothetico-deductive model. *See* critical rationalism

ideal speech situation, 47
institutional facts, 94, 98
institutional positivism, 93–103
integrative jurisprudence, 23–24
interexistentials, 17–18
interpretation, 21–23, 101

James, William, 37, 109
Jaspers, Karl, 7

Kant, Immanuel, 24–27, 48, 57, 69, 107
Kaufmann, Arthur, 23
Kelsen, Hans, 27–28, 78, 91, 93, 100
Klug, Ulrich, 7
Koch, Hans-Joachim, 11–12, 105
Kohlberg, Lawrence, 10 fn
Kommers, Donald, 2 fn
Kraft, Victor, 30
Kühl, Kristian, 27 fn

Lampe, Ernst-Joachim, 16–17
language and law, 6–9, 12, 45, 48, 55, 107–108
Lasswell, Harold, 80, 87
law and economics, 29, 43
law as communication, 81–82, 87–89
law as professional opinion, 65–66
legal order, 117–118
legal antinomies, 3–4
Lempert, Richard, 32 fn
Locke, John, 71 fn
Luhmann, Niklas, 9, 19, 73–92, 101, 106, 107, 117, 119

MacCormick, Neil, 94
MacIntyre, Alasdair, 28, 29 fn
Maihofer, Werner, 7
Marxism, 5–6, 29, 54, 73, 105
material value philosophy, 2
Maturana, Humberto, 74, 87
McDougal, Myres, 80, 87
McKinnon, Catherine, 29
Mead, George Herbert, 10, 45
Mollnau, Karl, 6 fn
Morris, Charles William, 60
Münchhausen Trilemma, 32–34, 48. *See also* final substantiation

natural law, 1–5, 86–87
nature of the thing (*Natur der Sache*), 4
Naziism, 1, 3, 86, 111
Neo-Kelsenism, 27–28. *See also* Kelsen
Nietsche, Friedrich, 60
normative expectations, 76–77
Nozick, Robert, 105

observation of systems, 84–85, 90

Parsons, Talcott, 9, 74
Patzig, Günther, 15
Paulson, Stanley, 27
Peczenik, Aleksander, 111
Peirce, Charles Sanders, 44, 109
Perelman, Chaim, 47 fn, 60
performance characteristics, 37
Pollock, Friedrich, 5

Popper, Karl, 7–8, 30–31, 74, 75
positivism. *See* analytic jurisprudence; institutional positivism; Kelsen; *Grundnorm*
Pound, Roscoe, 29, 114
pragmatism 108. *See also* critical rationalism; rhetorical theory
primacy of praxis, 95
primary world, 17–18
pure theory of law, 27–28, 78, 91. *See also* Kelsen

Quine, Willard V., 109

Radbruch, Gustav, 3–5, 104
Radbruch Formula, 4
Rawls, John, 105, 111
real discourse, 48
Rentsch, Thomas, 16–18
rhetorical theory, 62–72
Romano, Santi, 94
Rorty, Richard, 109
rule of recognition. *See Grundnorm*
rules of discourse, 50–51
Rüßmann, Helmut, 11–12, 105
Russell, Bertrand, 8
Ryle, Gilbert, 8

Scheler, Max, 2
Schelsky, Helmut, 74, 93
Schneider, Peter, 60
Schreckenberger, Waldemar, 11
Schwerdtner, Peter, 30
Searle, John R., 94, 98, 107
self-referential systems. *See* autopoietic systems
semiotics, 62, 68
Shklar, Judith, 55 fn
skepticism, 63, 68
Smith, Adam, 73
Sobota, Katherina, 66 fn
social technology, 36, 38
sociology of law, 30–43, 73–92
Spaemann, Robert, 19
speech act, 10, 94
Story, Joseph, 73
structural coupling, 82

Teubner, Gunther, 74 fn, 81 fn
topics, 7, 62–72
transcendental anthropology, 17
transcendental basis of law. *See* final substantiation
transcendental pragmatics, 48
Tugendhat, Ernst, 57 fn

ultimate justification. *See* final substantiation
universal pragmatics, 48
universalizability, 25, 48, 56
univocality of law, 116–117

value-Platonism, 39–40, 47, 97
Varela, Francisco, 74, 87
Vico, Giambattista, 60
Viehweg, Theodor, 60
Vienna Circle, 7
Vining, Rutledge, 37

Walter, Robert, 40, 105, 119
Weber, Max, 30, 32, 73, 75, 95
Weinberger, Ota, 93–103, 105, 106, 108, 117, 119
Welzel, Hans, 3 fn
Weyr, Frantisek, 93
White, James Boyd, 106
Wieacker, Franz, 60
Wiener, Norbert, 74
Willke, Helmut, 74 fn
Wittgenstein, Ludwig 7, 10, 17, 45, 109, 111
Wright, Georg Hendryk von, 97 fn, 111

Zippelius, Reinhold, 30